The Poetry of Li Shang-yin

The Poetry of
Li Shang-yin
Ninth-Century Baroque
Chinese Poet

❖

BY JAMES J. Y. LIU

THE UNIVERSITY OF CHICAGO PRESS · CHICAGO & LONDON

Library of Congress Catalog Card Number: 68–30695

THE UNIVERSITY OF CHICAGO PRESS, CHICAGO 60637
THE UNIVERSITY OF CHICAGO PRESS, LTD., LONDON W.C.1

To Joan and Edward Kracke

Preface

The primary purpose of this book is to make a contribution to the critical study of Li Shang-yin, one of the most fascinating of Chinese poets. Logically, I suppose, a Chinese critic on Chinese poetry should write in his own language, as I have had occasion to do in the past, but the fact that I am living in an English-speaking country and teaching Chinese literature to Western students makes me feel a desire to bring Chinese poetry a little closer to them, as well as to other readers interested in Chinese literature but not conversant with the language. It seems to me I can best fulfill this desire, without denying myself the opportunity of practicing criticism of Chinese poetry, by combining critical discussion with translation and exegesis, for it would be eminently impracticable to quote Li's poems in the original (which few can read) while discussing them in English. Moreover, Li's poetry being notoriously difficult, even students of Chinese literature, I venture to think, may find the translations and notes helpful. As for the reader without knowledge of Chinese, I hope he will gain some idea of the richness, subtlety, and complexity of Li Shang-yin's poetry, inadequate as my translations inevitably are. How far I have succeeded in attempting to combine the role of a critic with that of an interpreter of Chinese poetry to Western readers, and to reconcile the rival claims of scholarship and exposition (or *vulgarisation* in the French sense), I can only let the reader judge; but I wish to say that I have tried to keep the main body of the book free from over-technical discussions so that it should remain comprehensible to the reader who does not know Chinese, while the additional notes, the bibliography, and the list of references are chiefly intended for the specialist. On the whole, I have relegated details concerning sources and references to the bibliography and the list of references, especially with regard to works in Chinese, but some references to works in English which the reader may wish to consult are given in footnotes.

Since critical discussions of Li Shang-yin's poetry would be meaningless to someone who has not read it, such discussions naturally have to follow the translations. Similarly, since a number of the poems cannot be understood without some knowledge of the historical background and the poet's life, I have found it necessary to provide such knowledge first. Thus, the book falls into three parts. In Part I, the introduction, I have supplied such historical and biographical information as seemed desirable for an adequate understanding of Li's poetry, without attempting a comprehensive survey of the history of the period or a full-length biography. In addition, I have discussed various schools of interpretations of Li's poetry and described my own approach to it; I have also dealt with the problems of translating Chinese poetry, particularly Li's, into English, and stated the principles and methods which I followed.

Part II consists of translations of a hundred of Li Shang-yin's poems, about one sixth of his extant poetical works, each accompanied by notes and a commentary, unless the poem is so simple as to require no such exegesis. The notes on each poem are meant to explain particular expressions, allusions, and so forth, and the commentary is concerned with the total meaning of the poem. Most of the notes are based on those contained in annotated editions of Li Shang-yin, but I have omitted some which merely give the sources of the poet's expressions without shedding any light on the context, and added others on facts which Chinese readers may be presumed to know but Western ones cannot. I have not indicated the literary sources of Li Shang-yin's allusions, although I have checked them, for these would mean nothing to the general reader, and to explain what they were would involve too many digressions and distractions. Specialists who wish to identify the sources of allusions can find them in the editions to which I refer in the list of references. In the commentaries, I have been mainly concerned with offering my own interpretations of the poems, and although I have occasionally referred to previous commentators, I have not thought it necessary or desirable to mention every interpretation that has been suggested for every poem. In some cases, when the poem is so allusive that even with the notes and the commentary it may still seem puzzling, I have added a prose paraphrase as well. Since no arbitrary line of demarcation can be drawn between interpretation and analysis, some of the commentaries in fact contain critical analyses, especially in regard to longer poems, which are analyzed structurally in the commentaries immediately following the translations rather than in later discussions in Part III. It is hoped that the reader, after reading the notes and commentary, will return to the translated poem and read it with greater understanding and enjoyment. At first reading, some of the poems may seem baffling or "leave one cold," but if the reader will be patient enough to go on until the end of the book (not at one sitting!) he may find the effort worthwhile, and his initial impression may be modified. In the case of relatively simple and straightforward poems, I have not added commentaries to labor the obvious, but have left some of the interpretation to the reader's imagination.

Not all the poems translated here are among Li Shang-yin's best or most difficult, because I wished to make the selection representative of his poetry as a whole. For the same reason, I have not confined the selection to poems which lend themselves easily to translation. Thus, although most of his best-known poems are included, I have also included some less well-known and less interesting ones, to avoid creating a one-sided impression of Li's poetry. About two thirds of the poems presented have not previously been translated into English, to the best of my knowledge. The translated poems are arranged roughly in three groups. The first group (Poems 1–44) consists of more or less ambiguous poems, which cannot be dated with certainty; the second group (Poems 45–88), of personal and social poems of a more explicit and conventional nature, placed as far as possible in chronological order; the third group (Poems 89–100), of poems on historical or contemporary events. I hope this arrangement may help to show the range of Li Shang-yin's themes and the variety of his styles.

I have given some thought to, but decided against, providing the Chinese texts of the poems, transliterations in the Roman alphabet, or word-for-word translations. Apart from considerations of space and cost, the usefulness of any of these may be questioned. Anyone with a modicum of Chinese should be able to locate the original poems from the list of references and to find out the literal meanings of individual words from dictionaries, while to someone who does not read Chinese, transliterated and literally translated poems may seem merely baffling. Speaking of translations of Russian poetry, Edmund Wilson remarked, "Transliterated Russian means as little to anyone who does not read Russian as if it were printed in Russian characters, and for anyone who does read Russian it is an unnecessary nuisance to have to transpose it back into the Cyrillic alphabet before one can recognize it."[1] How much more so in the case of Chinese!

Part III is devoted to a critical study of Li Shang-yin's poetry. Since criticism without criteria would amount to a contradiction in terms, and since criteria for poetry can hardly be formulated without some theoretical basis, I have thought it desirable to explain first the theoretical grounds of my criticism of Li Shang-yin's poetry and the critical standards applied. In attempting to adumbrate a theory of poetry, I have elaborated and clarified a view of poetry evolved in my earlier work *The Art of Chinese Poetry*, and the critical discussions of Li Shang-yin's poetry may be regarded as practical applications of this view.

With regard to methodology and terminology, I would like to make clear that I have not tried to impose the "New Criticisms" or any other school of modern Western criticism on Chinese poetry, nor have I followed strictly any traditional Chinese school, but simply used whatever terms, concepts, and methods that promised to be fruitful in interpreting, analysing and evaluating Li's poetry. For example, when there exist both traditional Chinese terms and corresponding English ones for certain poetic devices, I have used the existing English terms (for example, "rhyme" for *yün*, "alliteration" for *shuang-sheng*, "antithesis" for *tui*). When Chinese terms have no English counterparts, I have translated them (for example, "Ancient Verse" for *Ku-shih*, "Regulated

[1] *New York Review of Books*, 4, no. 12 (July 15, 1965).

Verse" for *Lü-shih*). When, in trying to draw attention to certain modes of poetic expression, I found traditional Chinese terminology inadequate, I have borrowed Western terms such as "imagery" and "symbolism". However, in view of the Tower of Babel that exists in contemporary Western literary criticism,[2] I have had, at times, to redefine the terms used and to draw new distinctions (for example, those between "simple imagery" and "compound imagery" and among different types of compound imagery). The use of Western critical and even rhetorical and grammatical terms does not imply that the poet himself thought in such terms. Of course, Li Shang-yin did not think in terms of "verbs" and "nouns" or "images" and "symbols" (any more than Shakespeare did, for that matter), but this should not prevent us from using these terms to describe what he did, just as in describing ancient Chinese bronze vessels we are entitled to use modern geometrical, physical, and chemical terms of which the ancient Chinese craftsmen had no knowledge. It is one thing to attribute to an ancient writer conscious ideas, beliefs, and attitudes which he could not have entertained, but quite another to describe in modern terms what he wrote. To use modern Western terms in discussing Li's poetry is therefore not to falsify it; on the contrary, this may illuminate aspects of his poetry which previous commentators have not noticed, or have perceived but not bothered to discuss in concrete terms.

It should also be pointed out that the critical discussions are based on the original poems rather than the translations, for it would be patently absurd if I were to criticize my own translations instead of Li Shang-yin's poems. Nor would it be fair to the poet to leave out of the discussions everything that I have not been able to preserve in the translations. If anyone should ask, "What is the point of talking about qualities of Li's poetry not found in the translations?" I would reply by asking a similar question: "What is the point of writing a book on art and discussing qualities not perceptible in the reproductions used as illustrations?" Nevertheless, I have tried to keep the translations as close to the originals as possible so that the reader will not feel that the translations he has read and the poems discussed are totally different things.

In the final chapter, I have briefly indicated Li Shang-yin's position among Chinese poets, and suggested reasons why he should have a special appeal to contemporary Western readers and why he may be called a "baroque" poet.

Chinese words and names are romanized according to a modified form of the Wade-Giles system: the circumflex above the *e* is omitted in all cases, and so is the breve above the *u* in *ssu*, *tzu*, and *tz'u*. I have consistently written *yi* instead of *i* to avoid possible confusion with the Roman numeral. Well-known place names are given in the form most commonly used in English. In transcribing lines of poetry, I have

[2] See R. S. Crane, *The Languages of Criticism and the Structure of Poetry*, pp. 3–38, 80–115; René Wellek, *Concepts of Criticism*, pp. 334–64.

followed the modern Pekinese pronunciation, which is used by a majority of Chinese readers, though it obviously differs from the poet's own. However, in discussing alliterative and rhyming syllables I have added the reconstructed T'ang pronunciation (known as Ancient Chinese in sinological circles), using the symbols devised by Professor Bernhard Karlgren.

Chinese characters for words and names mentioned in the text are to be found in the glossary-index, apart from those given in the additional notes and the bibliography.

Acknowledgments

Some of the material in this book has appeared in articles in the following publications: *East-West Center Review* (Honolulu, Hawaii, 1964), *Journal of the American Oriental Society* (1965), *Yearbook of Comparative and General Literature* (Bloomington, Indiana, 1966), and *Wen-lin: Studies in the Chinese Humanities* (Madison, Wisconsin, 1968). I am indebted to the editors concerned for permission to reprint these articles in revised form.

I also wish to thank H. G. Creel, E. A. Kracke, and T. H. Tsien for having kindly read parts of the manuscript and made helpful comments.

Contents

PART I

Introduction

I

Historical Background

The first half of the ninth century, which roughly coincided with Li Shang-yin's life span, saw the gradual disintegration of the T'ang dynasty, first founded in 618. The deep-rooted causes of this disintegration can be traced back at least a century. As a matter of fact, although the T'ang is culturally one of the most glorious periods of Chinese history, even in its earlier years it was seldom free from rebellions, palace coups, and political intrigues. But these were counter-balanced by military expansions abroad and efficient administration at home during the reigns of the first three emperors, Kao-tsu (618–26), T'ai-tsung (626–49), and Kao-tsung (649–83).[1] Later, however, the usurpation of Empress Wu, who, not content with ruling as Empress Dowager, styled herself "Emperor" and changed the dynastic name from T'ang to Chou in 690, shook the very foundations of the dynasty. Although she was forced to abdicate in 705, and the dynasty was restored, irreparable harm had been done. After two feeble emperors, Hsüan-tsung came to the throne. The early part of his reign (713–41) was marked by some improvements in the government and by cultural brilliance, but in his later years (742–56) his control of the government slackened, and his reign ended with the disastrous rebellion of An Lu-shan and Shih Ssu-ming, which lasted from 755 to 763.[2] The dynasty survived, but it never regained its former strength. The empire continued to decline, despite the efforts of a few conscientious rulers and ministers, who effected temporary relief but no lasting renovation, so that by the beginning of the ninth century the central government had lost control over parts of the empire. Among the more immediate causes of the disintegration of the T'ang dynasty, three may be mentioned: the domination of the Court by eunuchs, the struggle between two rival political factions, and the disturbances created by provincial warlords. A thorough discussion of any of these factors could fill a volume. Here I can only give a concise account of each. Further details about events which had special bearings on Li Shang-yin's life and works will be given later, in the Biographical Sketch or as notes accompanying particular poems.

[1] These are not their names but posthumous titles, by which Chinese emperors are customarily known. Dates refer to their reigns.
[2] See E. G. Pulleyblank, *Background of the Rebellion of An Lu-shan.*

THE COURT AND THE EUNUCHS

No less than six emperors reigned during Li Shang-yin's lifetime. The first of these, Hsien-tsung (reigned 805–20), was reasonably conscientious, and with the help of able ministers managed to suppress several rebellions, including the major rebellion of Wu Yüan-chi.[3] But he entrusted eunuchs with political and military power, and he indulged in superstitions, vainly and foolishly wishing for eternal life. He sent envoys to fetch a Buddhist relic, and believed a Taoist magician who provided him with "immortality pills." When he died suddenly at the age of forty-two, his death was officially blamed on the pills, although he was probably murdered by the eunuchs.

Hsien-tsung had twenty sons, by various wives. At the time of his death, his third son, known in history as Mu-tsung (reigned 821–24) succeeded him with the support of a group of eunuchs. These eunuchs killed another eunuch, T'u-t'u Ch'eng-ts'ui, and Hsien-tsung's second son, Prince Yün, because T'u-t'u had suggested to Hsien-tsung that Prince Yün should be made Heir Apparent. This, as we shall see, was but the first of a series of killings carried out by the eunuchs in connection with successions to the throne.

Mu-tsung was a typical "bad emperor." He was fond of luxury and amused himself with banquets, variety-shows, boat-races, hunting, polo, and the like, and died of "immortality drugs" at the age of twenty-nine. He was succeeded by his eldest son, Ching-tsung, who was then a boy of fourteen.

Ching-tsung (reigned 824–27), whose accession was supported by the eunuchs, emulated his father in extravagance and pleasure-seeking. He was killed by the eunuchs after a drinking bout and a game of polo, aged only seventeen, but already the father of five sons by different concubines. The eunuchs who killed Ching-tsung tried to set Hsien-tsung's sixth son, Prince Wu, on the throne, but another group of eunuchs, with the concurrence of the chief minister[4] P'ei Tu, succeeded in proclaiming as emperor Mu-tsung's second son, after killing the rival claimant and the eunuchs who supported him.

The new emperor, Wen-tsung (reigned 827–40), proved a much better ruler than his two predecessors. He was a sensitive and cultured young man, and a passable poet. Although he too owed his succession to the throne to the eunuchs, he wished to eliminate them. With the help of two able but unscrupulous officials, Li Hsün and Cheng Chu, he succeeded in killing several powerful eunuchs, including those believed responsible for the death of Hsien-tsung in 820. However, a palace coup, designed to destroy the remaining eunuchs in 835, backfired, and the eunuchs, led by Ch'iu Shih-liang, retaliated by slaughtering the clans of eleven high officials, including all the chief ministers. This outrage, known in Chinese history as the "Sweet Dew Incident,"[5]

---

[3] See Poem 100 and notes.

[4] For an explanation of this term, see Additional Note 1.

[5] This incident will be described in connection with Poems 89 and 90.

fully demonstrated the power and ruthlessness of the eunuchs. After this, Emperor Wen-tsung led an unhappy life. About four years later he died at the age of thirty-two.

At the death of Wen-tsung, the eunuchs put on the throne Mu-tsung's fifth son, to be known historically as Wu-tsung (reigned 840–46). At the same time they killed two princes—Ching-tsung's fifth son, Prince Ch'eng-mei, who had been proclaimed Heir Apparent by Wen-tsung before his own death, and Prince Jung, Emperor Mu-tsung's eighth son.[6] Wu-tsung is chiefly remembered for his persecution of Buddhists. He destroyed thousands of Buddhist temples and confiscated their land, forcing some 260,000 monks and nuns to return to secular life. On the other hand, he believed in popular Taoism and took "elixirs of life," as a result of which he died aged thirty-two.

The new emperor set up by the eunuchs to succeed Wu-tsung was Hsüan-tsung (reigned 846–59),[7] thirteenth son of Hsien-tsung. In his youth he had appeared (probably by intention) dull-witted and very taciturn. However, after assuming the throne at the age of thirty-seven, he displayed considerable shrewdness. He made a point of remembering the names of palace attendants down to the lowest ones, as well as those of junior officials and even jailors mentioned in official reports. He secretly ordered a member of the Academy of Letters (Han-lin Yüan) to compile a reference book containing information about the various provinces, then astonished the provincial officials with his apparently intimate knowledge of every part of the empire. At Court audiences he maintained a solemn air while the ministers made their reports, but as soon as official business was over he would say, "Now we can chatter," and, with a sudden change of expression, talk about trivial matters. In this way he kept the officials in awe. Even his most trusted minister, Ling-hu T'ao,[8] who served him as chief minister for ten years, told others that he always perspired in fear when reporting to the emperor. But with all his shrewdness and his ability to cower the officials, Hsüan-tsung was unable to get rid of the eunuchs. For this, the officials must share the blame. For example, when Ling-hu T'ao was asked by the emperor how to eliminate the eunuchs, he replied, "Just do not let them go free if they commit any crimes, and do not fill any vacancies, then they will naturally be reduced to nothing." This sounds like an evasive answer and shows how much the officials feared the eunuchs. Hsüan-tsung was yet another emperor who took "elixirs of life" and died as a result, aged forty-nine.

Such, then, were the emperors who theoretically ruled as absolute monarchs: almost all of them owed their accession to the eunuchs, and two were killed by them, not to mention the various princes killed. I have gone into some detail about the complicated relations among the

---

[6] See Additional Note 2.

[7] Not to be confused with Hsüan-tsung (713–56), written differently in Chinese.

[8] Ling-hu T'ao is one of the important figures in Li Shang-yin's life and will be mentioned again later.

successive emperors, so as to show the tangled problems of succession created by polygamy and made worse by the power and pitilessness of the eunuchs. The following table may help to make the picture clearer (vertical lines indicate descent; lines with arrows indicate succession to the throne; a dagger means "murdered by eunuchs"):

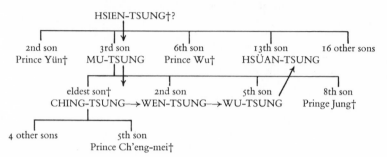

HSIEN-TSUNG†?

| 2nd son Prince Yün† | 3rd son MU-TSUNG | 6th son Prince Wu† | 13th son HSÜAN-TSUNG | 16 other sons |

| eldest son† CHING-TSUNG → | 2nd son WEN-TSUNG → | 5th son WU-TSUNG | 8th son Prince Jung† |

| 4 other sons | 5th son Prince Ch'eng-mei† |

How did the eunuchs come to possess such power? The answer lies chiefly in the fact that they were in control of the palace armies. Emperor Su-tsung (reigned 756–62) first started the pernicious practice of attaching eunuchs to armies as "army observers" (*kuan-chün-jung-shih*) or "army superintendents" (*chien-chün*), who were comparable to modern political commissars. Under later emperors the eunuchs not only gained control of the palace armies known as the Left and Right Divine Strategy Armies[9] but also extended their power over some provincial troops.

One may further wonder why the emperors entrusted the eunuchs with power in the first place. There seem to be several reasons. First, an emperor might feel that a eunuch, who could not aspire to the throne, would be more trustworthy than a high official, who might become powerful enough to form a threat to the throne. Second, whereas at the beginning of the T'ang dynasty, the imperial family and the high officials and generals all came from the same social class (the aristocracy of North China, who had been the ruling class under the Northern Dynasties for several centuries), after the reign of Empress Wu, who did not belong to this class herself and introduced new men into the government, a gap grew between the emperors and some of the high officials who were men of modest origins, so that the eunuchs had a chance to gain power by taking advantage of the emperor's lack of confidence in the officials. Third, the officials, as Confucian scholars, often thought it their duty to lecture the emperor, while the eunuchs, being mostly ill-educated, tended to encourage the emperor to indulge in sensual pleasures. Anyone who has read the long-winded sermonizing memorials by Chinese officials must feel a secret sympathy for an emperor who might wish to let his hair down occasionally. And if such an emperor should turn to the eunuchs for company and advice, is it to be wondered at? Finally, the strife between political factions made it

---

[9] See Additional Note 3

difficult for an emperor to know which officials could be trusted, so that the eunuchs had one more chance to obtain power by default.

In short, the eunuchs first gained influence because, being personal servants of the crown, they were thought to be more loyal than the officials. Then they became so powerful that they could no longer be removed, even when an emperor wished to be rid of them. At the same time, some officials, instead of closing their ranks to fight against the eunuchs as their common enemy, allied themselves with the eunuchs in their struggles against each other, or contented themselves with a modus vivendi with the eunuchs. For instance, the poet Yüan Chen (779–831), who at first came into open conflict with the eunuchs, later changed his attitude and obtained the position of chief minister with the help of the eunuch Ts'ui T'an-chün. Li Shang-yin's denunciation of the eunuchs in some of his poems is therefore the more remarkable.[10]

Another outstanding opponent of the eunuchs was Liu Fen. In 828, when he took the Imperial Examination,[11] known as the examination of "virtuous and upright men capable of outspoken advice," he wrote a bitter indictment against the eunuchs. At such examinations the candidates were supposed to answer questions set in the name of the emperor concerning state policy, but usually the successful ones were chosen on the basis of literary skill rather than political views. Liu Fen, however, took the expression "outspoken advice" literally, and expressed his views in no uncertain terms. His examination paper, which runs to some five thousand characters and is the only one of its kind known to have survived, contains the words:

> Why should Your Majesty let a few intimate and ignoble servants control the great administration of the empire, issuing orders in Your Majesty's name without, and stealing Your Majesty's authority within, so that their power intimidates the Court and their influence overwhelms the country? The officials dare not accuse them of their crimes, and the Son of Heaven cannot control their hearts. Disaster will rise inside the screens and treachery occur within the curtains ... Now the loyal and virtuous officials have not received confidence and trust, while eunuchs have the power to dethrone an emperor, so that His Late Majesty could not end his reign in propriety and Your Majesty could not begin yours with propriety ... this is why the country will be in danger ... Now the country is poor and refugees are seen everywhere. Those who are hungry cannot get food; those who are cold cannot get clothing; widowers, widows, orphans, and childless ones cannot survive; old people, young children, and sick ones cannot find means of support. Moreover, the power of the state

---

[10] See Poems 52, 53, 89, and 90.
[11] The term will be explained later.

is solely in the hands of a few close attendants. Greedy officials extort money from the people so as to accumulate wealth with which to secure their own favored positions; wicked clerks take advantage of the situation and abuse the law. Bitter complaints of grievances reach the Nine Heavens above and the Nine Springs beneath. The spirits and gods are angry, and the *yin* and *yang* forces of Nature are out of order as a result. The Emperor's gates are thousands of miles away from the people so that they cannot appeal to him. Scholars have nowhere to turn for civilizing influence; commoners have nowhere to turn for the protection of their lives. Officials are lawless and people are poor; bandits and thieves rise side by side. The situation is such that at any moment the empire may collapse.

These are strong words indeed. They created such a sensation at the time that, though the examiners did not dare to pass him, his paper was circulated among scholars and it moved many to tears. Li Ho,[12] who passed the examination at the top of the list and was given a post, remarked, "Liu Fen failed but I passed: how can I be so thick-skinned?" Thereupon he sent a memorial to the throne, saying, "If by any unfortunate chance Fen should die, then all the world would say Your Majesty killed an upright and outspoken man," and offered to hand over his own post to Liu. His request was refused, but his warning against public resentment possibly saved Liu's life. Nevertheless, a few years later Liu was exiled to distant Liu-chou (in modern Kwangsi province) and died. Li Shang-yin was a friend of Liu's and wrote several poems to mourn his death.[13]

Since all opposition to the eunuchs failed, they stayed in power during the remaining years of the T'ang dynasty. After they were finally eliminated by Chu Ch'üan-chung in 903, he himself usurped the throne four years later. Thus the domination of the Court by the eunuchs ended only with the dynasty itself, which they helped to ruin.

POLITICAL FACTIONS

While the eunuchs dominated the Court, the officials were divided by a strife between two factions, which lasted forty years. The two factions are known as the "Li faction" and the "Niu faction", named after Li Te-yü (787–850) and Niu Seng-ju (779–848) respectively. Although some historians think these are misnomers,[14] the fact remains that there were two rival groups of politicians, and it is convenient to refer to them by these traditional labels. Of course these were not organized political parties in the modern sense, but groups of individuals with shifting alliances.

The rivalry between the two factions started as a personal feud. In

[12] Not to be confused with the famous poet Li Ho (790–816).
[13] See Poems 52 and 53.
[14] See Additional Note 4.

809, Niu Seng-ju and his friend Li Tsung-min[15] both took the Imperial Examination, and in their papers criticized the government strongly. They passed the examination, but later the examiners were transferred to provincial posts, and Niu and Li Tsung-min themselves were kept in junior positions. For this they blamed the chief minister Li Chi-fu (758–812), Li Te-yü's father, although it could well have been due to the eunuchs' influence rather than Li Chi-fu's. After Li Chi-fu's death, Niu Seng-ju and Li Tsung-min became prominent. Then, in 821, occurred a scandal which involved Li Tsung-min and deepened his enmity to Li Te-yü. In that year, Li Tsung-min's son-in-law Su Ch'ao passed the Literary Examination.[16] Li Te-yü, who was then an Academician of the Academy of Letters, together with other Academicians, accused the chief examiner Ch'ien Hui of favoritism. Consequently, the Emperor ordered Po Chü-yi and another official to reexamine the candidates. This time Su Cha'o failed. The original chief examiner Ch'ien Hui was banished for favoritism and Li Tsung-min was also banished for influencing the examiner.

During the next two decades, all three leading figures of the two factions—Li Te-yü on the one hand, Niu Seng-ju and Li Tsung-min on the other—held power at various times. It would be pointless to follow in detail the ups and downs of their respective political fortunes. Suffice it to say that when one faction gained more power, members of the opposite faction would be banished or at least relegated to nominally high but actually powerless positions. Then, during the reign of Wu-tsung (reigned 840–46), Li Te-yü was triumphant. In 844, when he was ennobled as Duke of Wei, his enemies Niu Seng-ju and Li Tsung-min were banished to Hsün-chou (in modern Kwangtung province) and Feng-chou (also in Kwangtung) respectively. The situation was reversed when Wu-tsung was succeeded by Hsüan-tsung in 846 and two members of the Niu faction, Po Min-chung (Po Chü-yi's cousin) and Ling-hu T'ao, came to power. Li Te-yü was repeatedly demoted and finally banished to Ya-chou (on Hainan island, off the south coast of China) in 848. He arrived there early the following year and died at the beginning of 850. Meanwhile, Niu had died in 848 as the Crown Prince's Junior Tutor (*t'ai-tzu-shao-shih*, an honorary title) in Lo-yang, and Li Tsung-min had died in 846 as prefectural assistant (*ssu-ma*) of Ch'en-chou (in modern Hunan). Thus ended the strife which involved most of the important political figures of the day and even influenced the lives of junior officials like Li Shang-yin, as we shall see.

According to one modern authority, Professor Ch'en Yin-k'e, the strife between the two factions was due not only to personal animosity but also to different social backgrounds. The Li faction represented the traditional ruling class of North China, whereas the Niu faction represented the "new men" who had risen through the Literary Examina-

---

[15] Not related to Li Te-yü.
[16] The term will be explained below.

tion.[17] The former advocated Classical Confucian scholarship and emphasized strict observance of ritual; the latter esteemed literary talent above scholarship and often adopted a more free and easy way of life. Li Te-yü's dislike of "Presented Scholars" (those who had passed the Literary Examination) was well-known, and on one occasion he said to Emperor Wu-tsung:

> I have not taken the examinations and should not speak against the Literary Examination, but my grandfather, at the end of the T'ien-pao period, because he had no other way of entering official service, forced himself to take it and passed. However, after that he did not keep a copy of the *Literary Anthology*[18] at home because he disliked its emphasis on superficial elegance and its lack of substance. In fact, prominent officials at Court should be chosen from among the sons or younger brothers of ministers. Why? Because they are used to official business since youth, and are naturally familiar with Court affairs. They will know the proper etiquette and procedures without being taught. Scholars from poor families, though they may have outstanding talents, can only learn step by step after passing the examinations, and cannot be familiar with Court procedures.

Li Te-yü's friend Cheng T'an likewise tried several times to abolish the Literary Examination during the reign of Wen-tsung, but the emperor refused to comply. The contrast between the two groups may be further illustrated by the following incident. Once Wen-tsung showed one of his poems to Cheng T'an, then chief minister, and the latter's reaction was: "I beg Your Majesty to reserve your wise thoughts for the affairs of state so as to fulfill the hopes of the world." After Cheng left, the emperor showed the poem to Li Tsung-min, who sighed with admiration and bowed low after reading each line. Thus it is perhaps truer to say that the two factions represented two different attitudes toward life rather than two different social classes. The Li faction consisted of men who were conservatives and sticklers for convention, while the Niu faction showed a more liberal mentality.

There also seem to have been some genuine differences in policy between the two factions. On the whole, the Li faction may be called the "war party" and the Niu faction the "peace party." When Li Te-yü's father, Li Chi-fu, was chief minister, he was in favor of using force to subjugate insubordinate provincial generals, but he died before he could carry out his plans. Te-yü himself continued his father's policy toward the warlords. He also advocated a strong policy toward the

---

[17] Although Niu himself came from a distinguished family and Li Tsung-min was an Imperial clansman, many of their followers such as Po Min-chung were of humbler origins.

[18] A famous anthology edited by Prince Hsiao T'ung (501–31) of the Liang dynasty.

Tibetans, which Niu Seng-ju opposed. In 831, a Tibetan general defected with the prefecture of Wei-chou (in modern Szechwan), which had been under Tibetan occupation since 763. Li Te-yü, as military governor of Hsi-ch'uan (western Szechwan), sent Chinese troops to take over the garrison of the prefecture. However, Niu Seng-ju, who was then in power, persuaded the emperor that this would break a peace treaty with the Tibetans and might bring military disaster. Li Te-yü was forced to hand back Wei-chou as well as the Tibetans who had defected. These were then killed by their king. Later, Li argued that the Tibetans had never taken peace treaties very seriously anyway, and that Niu had greatly exaggerated the dangers of a Tibetan invasion, but it was too late. Some historians think that Niu frustrated Li's efforts out of sheer personal malice. A more charitable view would be that Niu was genuinely afraid that to offend the Tibetans might lead to serious consequences for China. However that may be, the disagreement between the two certainly did not work for the best interests of the government.

It is difficult at this late date to form a completely impartial judgement on the two factions, since historical records, based on contemporary accounts, are vitiated by bias in favor of either faction, depending on the writer's own sympathies. Even modern historians are not free from partiality. We can only say that both sides engaged in mutual recriminations and retaliations, although as individuals neither Li Te-yü nor Niu Seng-ju seems to have been without principles. Also, as I have said before, both factions sometimes allied themselves with the eunuchs, thus encouraging the eunuchs' abuse of power and unwittingly weakening the position of officialdom to which they themselves belonged.

PROVINCIAL WARLORDS

In order to understand the rise of provincial warlords, we have to have some idea of the structures of T'ang civil and military administrations in the provinces. In civil administration, the empire was divided into prefectures (chou),[19] each with a prefect (tz'u-shih).[20] Under each prefecture were a number of districts (hsien), governed by magistrates (ling).

In addition, there were commissioners holding various titles, sent out to inspect and report on the local officials. These were intended to act in a supervisory capacity, but as time went on they tended to encroach upon the authority of local officials and to form an authority at the superprefectural level.

For military purposes the empire was divided, from the beginning

---

[19] These were called chün from 742 to 757.

[20] The prefectures in which the three capitals—Ch'ang-an, the western capital, Lo-yang, the eastern capital, and T'ai-yüan, the northern capital—were located were governed by senior prefects (yin), each of whom held the concurrent title of Lord Constable (liu-shou). A few other important prefectures also had senior prefects.

of the dynasty, into provinces or circuits (*tao*), also known as military regions (*chün*),[21] each covering several prefectures. The commanding general of each province was called commander-in-chief (*ta-tsung-kuan*, later changed to *ta-tu-tu*), under whom there were a number of garrisons (*fu*), varying in size from 800 to 1,200 men. The soldiers were conscripted and took turns to do service. In times of war they would be sent to fight; in times of peace they would return to the fields. This is the so-called militia system (*fu-ping chih*) as it functioned in early T'ang times.

During the reign of Kao-tsung (649–83), when Empress Wu was in actual control of the government, the militia system was allowed to fall into disuse, and many soldiers deserted. Instead, hired soldiers were used. With standing armies of mercenaries, the provincial generals grew in power. Sometimes, a commander-in-chief who was given imperial insignia (*chieh*) as a sign of delegated authority was called *chieh-tu-shih*, literally "commissioner with insignia," a term often translated as "military governor." From 711 onward, this came to be used as a normal official title.

The military governors became even more powerful under Hsüan-tsung (713–56), and several of them were of foreign descent. Traditional Chinese historians believe that it was Li Lin-fu, chief minister from 734 to 752, who recommended the appointment of foreign generals to provincial governorships, to avoid possible competition, since a Chinese scholar-official who held a governorship might become a candidate for the position of chief minister while an unlettered "barbarian" general could not. Whether this was true or not, it was the view held by many, including Li Shang-yin.[22] Nevertheless, it was one of these foreign generals, An Lu-shan, who started the rebellion that nearly overthrew the dynasty. Although the rebellion was finally suppressed, the power of other military governors could no longer be curbed. And since they usually held concurrent posts as prefects and commissioners, they became virtual rulers of large areas, each comprising several prefectures, and the division of power among administrative, supervisory, and military officials ceased to exist.

In late T'ang times, some provincial governors were practically independent warlords, who owed only nominal allegiance to the crown and sometimes openly defied the central government. Moreover, they often engaged in fighting and intriguing against each other and brought untold miseries to the common people. The Court either tried to appease them by bestowing official honors on them, or attempted to subdue them by force. In the former case, the Court was merely accepting a fait accompli with a face-saving device; in the latter case, it met with various degrees of success, but even when successful it had to strain its financial resources. To make matters worse,

---

[21] Not to be confused with the *chün* translated as "prefecture" above. The two words are written differently in Chinese.

[22] See Poem 91.

the imperial troops sometimes behaved little better than bandits, and it was not always easy to tell the difference between "rebels" and "loyal troops," for a "rebel" could become a high official overnight if he accepted imperial insignia as a sign of "recognition," whereas a "loyal" general might turn against the central government and be branded a "rebel." The whole situation was similar to that which existed during the early years of the Chinese Republic (*cir.* 1912–27). Of course there were exceptions. When a high official with vested political interests at Court was sent to a provincial post, he would naturally remain loyal. But in general the military governors were more of a threat than a support to the Court, and in the end it was a military governor, Chu Ch'üan-chung, who usurped the throne.

The three factors mentioned above—usurpation of power by the eunuchs, political factions, and provincial warlords—all contributed to the fall of the T'ang dynasty in 907. Naturally there were other factors —social and economic—which I have not discussed. But quite apart from my incompetence to deal with such questions, they are not particularly relevant to Li Shang-yin's poetry. Also, we should remember that, against the unhappy picture of the political situation sketched above, we should juxtapose one of a society with a high level of cultural sophistication. To realize that there is no contradiction between political instability and cultural sophistication one need only think of the England of the first Elizabeth or the Italy of the Renaissance. Both aspects of late T'ang society are reflected in Li Shang-yin's poetry.

2

Biographical Sketch

Li Shang-yin, whose courtesy name is Yi-shan, also styled himself Yü-hsi-sheng, or "Scholar of the Jade Stream" (after the name of a river by the Wang-wu Mountain near his ancestral home), and Fan-nan-sheng, or "Scholar of Fan-nan" (referring to the southern suburbs of Ch'ang-an, where he spent part of his life). His ancestral home was in Ho-nei district, Huai-chou prefecture (modern Ch'in-yang district in Honan province), and according to Chinese custom he was regarded as a native of this place, although from the time of his grandfather the family had lived in Cheng-chou, about seventy miles away. The Lis claimed to be descended from Li Hao (351–417), founder of the Kingdom of Western Liang, from whom the T'ang imperial house and the poet Li Po also claimed descent, but all three claims are questionable. In any case, Li Shang-yin's family was far from being wealthy or influential: his great-great-grandfather, great-grandfather, grandfather, and father all held junior provincial posts. At the time of the poet's birth, his father Li Ssu was serving as magistrate of Huo-chia district (in modern Honan).

The date of Li Shang-yin's birth is a matter of controversy. Various years have been suggested, the most likely being 812 or 813. It would be tedious and unprofitable to enter here into the intricate arguments in favor of either date, since these arguments are all based on internal evidence and depend to a large extent on tortuous readings of Li's own writings. Personally I am inclined to accept 813, and in the following account of his life I shall mention his age on the assumption that he was born in this year.

When Shang-yin was about a year old, his father left Huo-chia and joined the staff of Meng Chien, prefect of Yüeh-chou (present-day Shao-hsing in Chekiang province) and commissioner (*kuan-ch'a-shih*) for Che-tung. Three years later, the senior Li left Yüeh-chou and went to Jun-chou (now Chen-chiang in Kiangsu province) to be a staff member of Li Hsiao, commissioner for Che-hsi. Thus the poet spent his early childhood in southeast China, a part of the country famous for its natural beauty. In 821 Shang-yin's father died, and his mother took the family back to Cheng-chou. It was probably then that he studied the Confucian Classics with an uncle, who was a "gentleman in retire-ment" (*ch'u-shih*, a scholar who refused to enter public service). This uncle, who lived from 787 to 829, was apparently a man of high principles, and when he died Shang-yin wrote admiringly of his moral integrity and his literary and calligraphic talents.

After the mourning period for his father was over in 823, Shang-yin moved to Lo-yang with his family. Like most famous Chinese poets, he showed precocious literary gifts. Although his claim in a letter addressed to one of his patrons that he studied the Classics in his fifth year and toyed with the writing brush and ink-slab in his seventh need not be taken literally, it is probably true, as he says in the preface to the first collection of his prose works, that he wrote two essays entitled "On Talents" and "On Sages" in his sixteenth year (fifteen years old by Western reckoning).[1] In any case, when he was sixteen his literary talents attracted the attention of Ling-hu Ch'u (766–837), then military governor of T'ien-p'ing Region (in modern Shantung province). Ling-hu, who had been chief minister ten years previously, was now an elder statesman and an influential figure in the Niu faction. He appointed Li Shang-yin to his staff as an inspector (hsün-kuan, a junior post of no fixed rank), took care of the latter's material needs, and told his own sons to befriend the young poet. Moreover, Ling-hu Ch'u was an expert in writing official documents in the ornate euphuistic style known as "parallel prose" (p'ien-wen) and gave Li the benefit of his experience in this difficult art. When, about two years later, Ling-hu was transferred to T'ai-yüan to be the senior prefect there, Li Shang-yin in all probability went with him.

In the following year, 833, Li Shang-yin went to Ch'ang-an and took the Literary Examination as a private candidate, but failed. Since examinations played an important part in his life, as indeed they did in the lives of most Chinese literary men, and since references to various kinds of examinations are made in these pages, it may be worthwhile explaining the examination system in some detail.

Of the numerous kinds of examinations that existed in T'ang times, the most important ones are the following: first, the hsiu-ts'ai or "Budding Talent" examination, which consisted of writing five essays on state policy. At the beginning of the dynasty, this was the highest examination, but later, due to its difficulty and the small number of candidates who passed, it was no longer held regularly. The second was the ming-ching or "Elucidating the Classics" and the third the chin-shih or "Presenting Scholars." These two have been called by the late Dr. Arthur Waley the Classical Examination and the Literary Examination respectively. I have adopted Waley's nomenclature for these, but I use the term "Presented Scholar" when referring to someone who passed the latter examination. The Classical Examination emphasized identification of passages from the Confucian Classics; the

---

[1] The Chinese way of counting age is to call a child "1 sui" after birth and add a year to his age after each Chinese New Year. Thus there is a discrepancy of about a year between the Chinese age and that given by Western reckoning. When I write "so many years old," I mean by Western reckoning; when I write "in his xth year," I mean the Chinese sui.

Literary Examination included writing poems in Regulated Verse, rhymed prose (*fu*), as well as essays on current affairs. Since the former examination was mainly a test of memory, whereas the latter afforded some scope for originality, those who passed the former were often despised by those who passed the latter.

Candidates for these examinations were of two kinds: graduates of government colleges, called "Students" (*sheng-t'u*), and private candidates, called "Local Tributes" (*hsiang-kung*, since human talents were considered tribute to the Emperor in the same way as local products). The "Students" came from the Imperial University (*Kuo-tzu-chien*, which had seven colleges) and the Literary Institutes in the capital, as well as the provincial, prefectural, and district colleges supported by the government. The private candidates had to present themselves to the local authorities for a preliminary examination. After passing this they were allowed to join the government students in the capital for the examinations.

The examinations were held in Ch'ang-an in the First Month every year. The list of successful candidates, having been prepared by the Ministry of Rites, was submitted to the Central Secretariat (*Chung-shu-sheng*) and the Chancellery (*Men-hsia-sheng*), two of the three main branches of the central government, for confirmation.

In addition to the annual examinations, there were special ones held at irregular intervals by imperial decree known as *chih-chü*; these are the ones to which I have referred as "Imperial Examinations." They were theoretically held under the Emperor's personal supervision and carried a variety of fancy names, such as "virtuous and upright men capable of outspoken advice" and "widely learned in the Classics." They could be taken by those who had already passed the regular examinations, and they were supposed to be an expression of the Emperor's eager desire to seek men of outstanding talents and elicit their advice, although, as we have seen, when candidates took this seriously and expressed their true opinions, they were more likely to get into trouble than to get quick promotion.

Success at the regular examinations (like getting a degree in modern days) only meant that one was qualified, not that one could expect an immediate appointment. The selection of men to fill official posts was called *ch'üan* and was a quite separate procedure from the examinations, although it did involve a further examination (which Waley called the Placing Examination). In order to obtain a post, one had to appear before a selection board composed of senior officials of the Ministry of Civil Office. Every year, in the Fifth Month, announcements of posts available and qualifications required were made in the prefectures and districts. Then, in the Tenth Month, candidates were assembled in the capital for selection. Four criteria were used for selection: "Appearance: tall and imposing; Speech: eloquent and decent; Calligraphy: powerful and beautiful formal hand; Judgments: superior literary style and reasoning." Candidates were first tested in calligraphy and writing "judgments"[2] on hypothetical cases, then interviewed for "Speech" and "Appearance." Those who could pass an examination consisting of three essays (called the *hung-tz'u* or "Grand Rhetoric" examination) or one consisting of three "judgments" (called the *pa-ts'ui* or "Outstanding Talent") could be given posts even if they did not meet all the other requirements. After the successful candidates had been tentatively assigned posts, the list was submitted to the Grand Secretariat (*Shang-shu-sheng*), one of the three branches of the central administration and the one directly above the ministries. It was then passed on to the Chancellery, where it was read by a policy reviewer (*chi-shih-chung*), checked by a vice-chancellor (*men-hsia shih-lang*), and finally examined by the chancellor (*shih-chung*),[3] before being presented to the throne. Appointments were then made in the name of the Emperor.

The T'ang examinations, like all examinations, were not always sure guides to one's true abilities. Moreover, although favoritism was occasionally exposed and punished, it was quite common, and candidates often presented their writings to high officials in the hope of influencing the examiners. If it is true that, as Li Shang-yin boasted, he never did this, then his failure to pass the Literary Examination in 833 would have come as no surprise, though still, no doubt, a disappointment.

After his failure he apparently went home to Cheng-chou for a while, but he soon returned to the capital, Ch'ang-an, where he carried on his studies. Early next year, when the examinations were held again, he was unable to take part owing to illness. Having missed his chance, he went to Yen-chou (present-day Tzu-yang in Shantung province) as a secretary to Ts'ui Jung, who had just been appointed commissioner for Yen-chou and Hai-chou. Ts'ui, however, died on the 22d day of the Sixth Month (July 31, 834 in the Julian calendar), only a few months after his arrival in Yen-chou. Thus Li Shang-yin found himself without a patron or a job, and probably went home.

In 835 Li Shang-yin again sat for the Literary Examination as a private candidate and again failed. He subsequently returned to Cheng-chou. It was about this time that he studied Taoism, possibly as a reaction to his failures at the examinations. In his poetry he refers to his "having studied immortality east of the Yü-yang Mountain" (a mountain situated about ten miles to the west of his ancestral home, Ho-nei) and addresses several Taoist priests as "fellow-students." But he was far from being indifferent to contemporary political affairs, as can be witnessed by the two highly indignant poems he wrote after the notorious "Sweet Dew Incident."[4]

Early in 837 Li at last passed the Literary Examination and became a Presented Scholar. It is interesting to note that the examination that year included a piece in rhymed prose (*fu*) on the subject "*Ch'in* and *se*

---

[2] See Arthur Waley, *The Life and Times of Po Chü-i*, p. 28.

[3] In theory there were two chancellors, but the posts were not always filled.

[4] See Poems 89 and 90.

(two kinds of zither) Playing in Concord" and a poem on the famous "Rainbow Skirts and Feather Jackets" dance music.[5] These topics must have appealed to Li Shang-yin, in whose poetry there are numerous references to music and dancing, particularly to the zither. Unfortunately his compositions on this occasion are no longer extant, although the poem by his friend Li Hung, who came first in the examination, has survived and is included in the *Complete T'ang Poetry*.

Li Shang-yin's success was in no small measure due to the influence of Ling-hu Ch'u's son Ling hu T'ao, who was then a Senior Advisor (*tso pu-ch'üeh*) in the Chancellery and a friend of the chief examiner Kao Chieh. But, as I said before, passing the examination did not mean an immediate appointment, and Li Shang-yin was still without an official post. Meanwhile, after a visit to his mother at Cheng-chou, he rushed to Hsing-yüan (present-day Nan-cheng in Shensi province, over 200 miles to the southwest of Ch'ang-an), in answer to the summons of Ling-hu Ch'u, now senior prefect of Hsing-yüan, who was dying and required Li's services for the last time: to draft on Ling-hu's behalf his deathbed memorial to the throne. In this memorial Ling-hu Ch'u begs the Emperor to take a lenient attitude to his subjects after the recent deaths of so many, caused by the "Sweet Dew Incident," and one sees the hand of Li Shang-yin at work. Ling-hu Ch'u died on the 12th day of the Eleventh Month (December 13), and Li escorted his remains back to Ch'ang-an in the Twelfth Month (January, 838). It was during the return journey that he wrote the moving long poem "Written While Traveling Through the Western Suburbs,"[6] which again shows his concern for contemporary affairs.

In 838, when Li Shang-yin was twenty-five years old, he joined the staff of Wang Mao-yüan, military governor of Ching and Yüan with headquarters at Ching-chou (in modern Kansu province), and soon afterwards married a daughter of Wang's. This marriage is regarded by some scholars as a crucial event in Li's life; let us, therefore, pause for a moment to consider its significance. Wang Mao-yüan came from a rich and influential family, his father having been a military governor of several prefectures and held the title of minister of rites. In his youth Wang Mao-yüan was fond of studying, and he sent a memorial to Emperor Te-tsung to recommend himself. As a result, he was appointed a collator in the Imperial Library (*Mi-shu-sheng chiao-shu-lang*). Later, Wang distinguished himself in military service by killing a rebel leader. Subsequently he held a number of high military posts, and was regarded as an important member of the Li Te-yü faction. Now, since Li Shang-yin's first patron, Ling-hu Ch'u, belonged to the Niu faction, while his father-in-law belonged to the opposite faction, some writers, including the historiographers responsible for the two official histories of the T'ang dynasty (the *Old T'ang History* and the *New T'ang History*),

---

[5] See Waley, *The Life and Times of Po Chü-i*, pp. 154–5.
[6] See Poem 91.

believe that Ling-hu Ch'u's son Ling-hu T'ao resented the marriage, and they consider Li's subsequent lack of success in his official career to be due to Ling-hu T'ao's refusal to promote the poet's interests. This view is questionable on several counts. In the first place Li Shang-yin was not important enough to be considered a member of either faction; to Ling-hu Ch'u's patronage he owed personal gratitude rather than political allegiance, and his marriage to Wang Mao-yüan's daughter would not necessarily make him a member of the Li Te-yü faction. Second, Li Shang-yin was poor and needed a job to support his mother as well as three younger brothers and a younger sister.[7] Since Ling-hu Ch'u had died and his son T'ao was in mourning, the latter (who was not yet a powerful official in any case) could hardly blame Li for seeking patronage elsewhere. What is more, years later, when the younger Ling-hu had become chief minister, he did help Li obtain a post, as we shall see later. As for marrying into an influential family, this would not have been condemned, for it was quite common for a man to try to promote his own interests by means of an advantageous marriage, and young Presented Scholars who had just passed the Literary Examination were regarded as highly eligible by rich and noble families. In short, although Li may have been prompted to marry Wang's daughter by a desire for advancement, this is not the same thing as being a political turncoat. Also, judging by the poems he wrote to mourn his wife's death years later, he seems to have had a genuine affection for her. We need not, therefore, think of his marriage as a purely "political" one.

To resume the story of Li's life: After his marriage, he presented himself at the Ministry of Civil Office for selection and took the "Grand Rhetoric" examination,[8] but failed. According to a letter he wrote two years later to a certain Presented Scholar T'ao, the two examiners, Academicians Chou and Li (identified as Chou Ch'ih and Li Hui), had already passed him, but when the list was submitted to the Central Secretariat,[9] someone there remarked, "This man is intolerable; remove him." This incident has again been interpreted by some scholars as a consequence of Li's marriage: it is assumed that the official who removed Li's name must have been a friend of the Ling-hus who resented Li's marriage. But there is no evidence at all that this was so. It seems more likely that the poet had earned some notoriety by his outspoken political poems. Whatever the reason, he failed to obtain an official position and remained on his father-in-law's staff until the next year, 839, when he finally "took off serge" (*shih-he*, that is, ceased to be a commoner, or, as one might say, "took silk"). He was appointed a collator in the Imperial Library, a post that his father-in-law once held,

---

[7] For Li Shang-yin's brothers and sisters, see Additional Note 5.
[8] See Additional Note 6.
[9] See Additional Note 6.

and one which carried with it the "full ninth rank, upper division."[10] However, he was soon transferred to Hung-nung (in modern Honan) to be the sheriff (*wei*) of the district. This must have been a great disappointment to him, for not only did the new post carry a lower rank (associate ninth rank, upper division), but its duties were much less congenial—instead of working on literary texts as he had done in the Imperial Library, he now had to assist in local administration and deal with criminal cases and collection of taxes. Moreover, a post in the Imperial Library was much envied, since it offered possibilities of entering the Academy of Letters, which in turn could lead to quick promotion to the highest offices.[11] To imagine how Li Shang-yin must have felt, we might think of someone suddenly finding himself "transferred" from the Library of Congress to a position as county sheriff, were such a thing possible.

While serving as sheriff of Hung-nung, Li offended a superior official, Commissioner Sun Chien, by having changed the sentence of a prisoner condemned to die. We do not know the details of the case, but the incident seems to show Li's sense of justice and his courage in incurring the displeasure of a senior official. As a result, he was suspended from his duties. But Sun Chien was replaced by Yao Ho, a well-known poet, who ordered Li Shang-yin to resume his post. Li's movements during the next two years are not clear. Some scholars believe that he took a trip to what is now Hunan province, but this is largely based on references to that region in some of his poems, which are hard to date. Judging from the fact that he drafted documents on behalf of two officials near Hung-nung, it is safer to assume that Li stayed in Hung-nung until 842, when he joined his father-in-law's staff once more. Wang Mao-yüan had now become military governor of Chung-wu Region and commissioner for Ch'en-chou and Hsü-chou, with his headquarters at Hsü-chou (modern Hsü-ch'ang in Honan province).

In the Tenth Month of the same year (November, 842), Li Shang-yin passed the "Outstanding Talent" examination, and was appointed a sub-editor (*cheng-tzu*) in the Imperial Library, a post similar to the one he had held before in the same department but with a slightly lower rank (full ninth rank, lower division). Things seemed to be turning for the better, but soon his mother died, which meant that he had to leave his post and go into mourning. Meanwhile a rebellion broke out, which had some effect on his life, and will be described below.

In the Fourth Month (May) of 843 occurred the death of Liu Ts'ung-chien, military governor of Chao-yi Region (which covered several

---

[10] Civil officials were classified in nine ranks, each divided into two categories, "full" (*cheng*) and "associate" (*tsung*). From the fourth rank down, each "full" or "associate" rank was subdivided into "upper" (*shang*) and "lower" (*hsia*) divisions. Thus, there were altogether thirty rungs in the bureaucratic ladder. However, high rank does not necessarily indicate real power. Chief ministers only held the third rank, while purely honorary titles like "Grand Tutor" and "Grand Marshal" carried the first rank.

[11] The Academicians were concerned with much more than literary matters and acted as personal advisers to the Emperor.

prefectures corresponding to parts of modern Honan and Shansi). At the time of the "Sweet Dew Incident" he had been the only high official to protest the outrage by sending three successive memorials to the throne to ask for what crimes the chief ministers had been killed and to denounce the eunuchs. Now, after his death, his nephew and adopted heir Liu Chen succeeded him, with the support of the troops. The Court refused to recognize Liu Chen as the legitimate successor and ordered him to escort his uncle's remains to Lo-yang (in other words, to leave his troops). Liu Chen, not surprisingly, refused. The Court summoned a meeting of high officials to discuss whether Liu should be punished or pardoned. Most officials were in favor of appeasement, but Li Te-yü (who, it may be recalled, was generally in favor of warlike measures) insisted on a punitive expedition, and he won. Consequently, Wang Mao-yüan was tranferred from Chung-wu Region to Ho-yang Region and ordered to prepare for the campaign, together with a few other generals. Wang stationed his troops at Wan-shan, a small town near Li Shang-yin's ancestral home in Huai-chou, but before taking any military action sent a letter to Liu Chen, urging him to submit to the Court. This letter was written by Li Shang-yin, who may have joined his father-in-law at the latter's headquarters, though he could have sent the draft by a courier. In writing the letter, Li Shang-yin, who had shown strong indignation against the eunuchs when the "Sweet Dew Incident" took place, must have felt the irony of the situation and the ambiguous moral standards of the times: Liu Chen, whose uncle had raised a lone voice of protest against the eunuchs, was now a rebel, while Wang Mao-yüan, who had spent his whole fortune to bribe the palace armies under the eunuchs' control so as to save his skin at that time, was now one of those ordered to suppress Liu. The letter produced no effect. One of Wang's subordinate officers, sent to attack Liu, suffered setbacks, and soon Wang himself became ill. He was replaced by another general, and died about the end of the Ninth Month (October). Eventually the rebellion was suppressed, in the Eighth Month of the following year (September/October, 844). Liu Chen was killed by one of his own subordinates, who surrendered to the government. Liu's whole family, as well as surviving relatives of the victims of the "Sweet Dew Incident," who had been hiding under the protection of the Lius, were all executed.

After the rebellion was over, Li Shang-yin went back to Cheng-chou to bury his mother. He also reburied an elder sister who had died when the poet was in his infancy, the uncle with whom he had studied the Confucian Classics, a little niece who had died five years previously,[12] and his great-grandmother—the first three in Cheng-chou and the last-named in the ancestral home, Huai-chou. It should be explained that until recently it was a Chinese cutsom for a person to be buried with his forefathers, and if circumstances did not allow this at the time of

[12] See Additional Note 7.

death, the remains should be temporarily buried, but eventually re-buried in the family burial ground. In particular, married couples should be buried together, no matter how long one spouse had outlived the other. That was why Li Shang-yin had to send his great-grand-mother's remains back to Huai-chou to be reburied in the same tomb as his great-grandfather, while the others had to be buried in Cheng-chou, where the family tombs, from his grandfather's down, were situated. To the spirits of the deceased relatives Li Shang-yin wrote moving addresses, although one of them he had barely seen, and anoth-er had died long before he was born.

His melancholy duty done, Li Shang-yin moved to Yung-lo district (in modern Shensi), where he led a quiet life. During the spring of the ensuing year, 845, he returned to Cheng-chou at the invitation of the prefect Li Pao, who was his father's first cousin. But a month after Shang-yin's arrival, Li Pao relinquished his post, and the former went with him to Lo-yang. It was there that the poet met the girl named Liu-chih ("Willow Branch"), who fell in love with him and for whom he wrote a set of poems (Poems 60–64 in this volume). In the Tenth Month (November), his mourning for his mother was over, and he resumed his post in the Imperial Library.

In 846 the famous poet Po Chü-yi died, and there is a story that he was reborn as Li Shang-yin's son. The story goes that Po, in his last years, was very fond of Li's poetry, and told the latter, "If, after my death, I should be reborn as your son, I would be content." Therefore, when Li had a son, he gave the child the pet name Po-lao ("Old Po"). When the boy grew up, he showed no great literary talent and was teased by his father's friend and fellow-poet Wen T'ing-yün: "Are you worthy to be Lo-t'ien's [Po Chü-yi's] reincarnation?" Of course we cannot take this story seriously, but it is not impossible that Po might have expressed such a wish to Li. In fact, Li did write Po's tomb inscrip-tion at the request of the latter's adopted heir. Considering that Li Shang-yin was far from being a high official, the honor of being asked to write the inscription suggests how highly Po thought of Li's literary gifts. And since, as far as we know, the only other man for whom Li Shang-yin ever wrote a tomb inscription was his first patron Ling-hu Ch'u, Li on his part presumably admired Po. It is pleasant to think of two of the most celebrated poets of China, the one full of years and honor, the other young and struggling, being bound by ties of friend-ship and mutual admiration, in spite of the wide differences between their writings.

During the next few years, and indeed for the rest of his life, Li Shang-yin traveled extensively as he moved from one post to another, partly as a result of political maneuvers and partly out of sheer bad luck. In 847 he followed Cheng Ya, who had just been appointed commis-sioner for Kuei-kuan and prefect of Kuei-chou (modern Kweilin in Kwangsi province, some 1,600 miles away from Ch'ang-an), as a clerk (*shu-chi*) with the honorary title of secretary (*yüan-wai-lang*) in the

Department of Waterways, Ministry of Works (associate sixth rank, upper division). He probably arrived in Kweilin about the Fifth Month (June), and in the winter he went on a mission to Nan-chün (modern Chiang-ling in Hupeh). Meanwhile, he had found time, in the Tenth Month (November/December), to edit the first collection of his prose works, entitled *Fan-nan chia-chi*, which consisted of official documents he had written on behalf of various patrons and friends as well as his own letters, mostly in the parallel style. He accomplished his mission and returned to Kweilin in the First Month of the following year (February, 848), and was temporarily in charge of the administration of Chao-p'ing prefecture. In the following month, Cheng Ya was demoted to the position of prefect of Hsün-chou (in Kwangtung), and Li Shang-yin once more lost his post. Cheng's demotion represented one of a series of victories of the Niu faction over the Li faction. Ever since Hsüan-tsung came to the throne in 846, the Niu faction had been in ascendency. The once powerful Li Te-yü, leader of the opposite faction, was exiled to distant Ya-chou and died there, as we have seen. Among prominent men of the Niu faction now in power were Ling-hu T'ao, at this time Academician in charge of drafting imperial edicts, and Po Min-chung, chief minister and minister of justice. These two were mainly responsible for Cheng's demotion, and Li Shang-yin became an unwitting victim of their political maneuvering.

After journeying through Hunan, Li returned to Ch'ang-an in the autumn of 848. In the Tenth Month he was appointed sheriff of Chou-chih, within the metropolitan area. Thus he had retrogressed in his career—having previously reached the sixth rank, he was now back to the ninth. However, before taking up his post and on presenting himself to the metropolitan prefect, he was kept by the latter on his own staff as a temporary military counselor (*ts'an-chün-shih*, which normally carried the full seventh rank, lower division). In spite of the title, Li's actual duties were to draft memorials to the throne. In this capacity he wrote several memorials congratulating the Emperor on recent military successes, as well as a funeral eulogy for the burial of Niu Seng-ju, who had died recently and been posthumously given the honorary title of Grand Marshal. This last-mentioned piece caused the metropolitan prefect (whose surname seems to have been Niu but whose full name we do not know) to say, "The tomb inscription of our Grand Marshal by Secretary Tu [Tu Mu] and the funeral eulogy by you will both live for ever!" Alas, this prophecy is only half fulfilled: the text of Tu Mu's inscription has survived but Li Shang-yin's piece has not.

In less than a year's time, Li again left the capital. This time he joined the staff of Lu Hung-chih,[13] military governor of Wu-ning Region, with headquarters in Hsü-chou (in modern Kiangsu).[14] Li was given the post of supervisor (*p'an-kuan*) with the nominal title of imperial

[13] See Additional Note 8.
[14] Not to be confused with the Hsü-chou in Honan mentioned earlier. The two names are written differently in Chinese.

censor (*shih-yü-shih*, associate sixth rank, lower division), and stayed in Hsü-chou for two years, until the death of Lu in 851. Having again lost his patron and his post, Li returned to Ch'ang-an and presented his writings to Ling-hu T'ao, who had now risen to be chief minister with the concurrent titles of under-secretary of the Central Secretariat (*Chung-shu shih-lang*) and minister of rites. Consequently, Li was appointed a professor at University College[15] (*T'ai-hsüeh po-shih*, full sixth rank, upper division). In this new post he lectured on the Confucian Classics and taught the students to write essays.

In the same year, his wife died. Leaving his children, one boy and one girl, in the capital, Li himself went to Szechwan on the staff of Liu Chung-ying, military governor of Tung-ch'uan (eastern Szechwan) and prefect of Tzu-chou. Li served as clerk with the honorary title of principal secretary in the Ministry of Works (*Kung-pu lang-chung*, associate fifth rank, upper division, the highest rank he ever attained), but his duties sometimes involved participating in military affairs. Apart from a visit to Hsi-ch'uan (western Szechwan) to try a legal case, and another visit to Yü-chou (present-day Pa-hsien in Szechwan) to greet a senior official passing through, Li remained in Tzu-chou for five years. According to the preface he wrote to the second collection of his prose works, dated Tenth Day, Eleventh Month, Seventh Year of the Ta-chung period (December 13, 853), he had embraced Buddhism since the death of his wife. We also learn that he paid out of his own salary the cost of having the *Lotus Sutra* engraved in gold characters on five stone walls in a Buddhist monastery. It may also be mentioned here that his patron Liu Chung-ying wished to present him with a singing girl named Chang Yi-hsien as a concubine, but Li declined. In his letter to Liu Chung-ying declining the "gift," Li Shang-yin also seems to disclaim the reputation of being a romantic character: "As for seductive ladies of the south and skillful entertainers of the houses of pleasure, though I have touched on them in my writings, I have not really associated with them in romance." How far he is telling the truth we cannot know, but the incident, together with his interest in Buddhism, does suggest that, during this period of his life at least, he was not engrossed in romantic love affairs.

Late in 855, Liu Chung-ying was summoned to the Court, and Li Shang-yin followed him back to Ch'ang-an. The following year, when Liu was appointed vice-minister of war and concurrently chief censor (*yü-shih tai-fu*) and commissioner for the transportation of salt and iron, he secured a post for Li as salt and iron assessor (*yen-t'ieh t'ui-kuan*). When Liu was promoted to be minister of justice and ceased to be commissioner for salt and iron in 858, Li Shang-yin lost his position for the last time. He returned to Cheng-chou and died soon afterwards, aged only about forty-five. Before his death, he became an even more devout Buddhist and served the famous monk Chih-hsüan as his

---

[15] One of the seven colleges of the Imperial University (*Kuo-tzu-chien*).

spiritual master. On his deathbed, Li sent a letter and a *gatha* to Chih-hsüan to say farewell. After a lifetime of disappointments and frustrations, then, Li Shang-yin seems finally to have found some solace in Buddhism.

In the above account of Li Shang-yin's life, I have kept to known facts and refrained from speculations, to avoid falling into the vicious circle of deducing biographical data from his poems and then reading his poems in the light of the supposed biography. Nor have I attempted amateur psychoanalysis, as one recent writer on Li Shang-yin has done. Furthermore, when we read someone's poetry, we can hardly avoid forming some sort of impression of the man, and, at the same time, our understanding of his poems can easily be influenced by our impression of him as a man. We must, therefore, make a conscious effort to correct any oversubjective impression we may have formed of the poet with knowledge derived from external sources. With respect to Li Shang-yin, his letters and other prose writings, a few poems addressed to him and written in his memory by friends, as well as his biographies in the two official histories of the T'ang period (brief and full of factual errors as they are), all provide clues to his personality. Based on such sources, then, my impression of him is that of a brilliant, proud, highly emotional, and somewhat impulsive man, who took life seriously. He had a strong sense of justice and felt profound indignation about the conditions that prevailed in the country and about his own lot. By the standards of his time he was a failure, for he did not rise to high official rank, and, of course, in those days in China an official career was the only possible one for a literary man. Other professions either did not exist or were despised, and there was no such thing as a professional writer, although literary talents were highly esteemed. For a man descended from officials, it was both a privilege and an obligation to enter public service. The variety of posts Li Shang-yin held—from sheriff to salt and iron assessor—may seem incongruous with his being a poet, but most Chinese poets (and some Western ones too) have had to take incongruous and uncongenial jobs. By modern Western standards, too, Li's fate can hardly be called a happy one, for it must be frustrating for a brilliant and ambitious man to spend years as a ghost writer working for politicians and generals, which was what happened to him. I have given details of the titles and ranks he held at various times, for, tedious as these may seem to the reader, they represent the ups and downs of his life and reflect his changing hopes and disappointments. Similarly, I have described the precise titles of other officials and the workings of the bureaucratic machine to some extent, in the hope of re-creating something of the atmosphere of the bureaucratic world in which he lived. His failure in official life was somewhat compensated for by his literary reputation, although his contemporaries seem to have admired him more for his official documents and letters in "parallel prose" than for his poetry.

In private life Li Shang-yin was affectionate and sensitive. He wrote fondly of his wife and children and movingly of his deceased relatives, some of whom he had never seen. A cynic might say then that he was being either hypocritical or merely conventional when expressing deep grief over his dead relatives, but neither need be the case, for an imaginative and sensitive person can be genuinely moved by meditation on death itself and by the plight of the survivors. I have deliberately said nothing about his possible love affairs, for these cannot be discussed apart from various interpretations of his poems, which form the subject of the next chapter.

3

Interpretations of Li's Poetry

Li Shang-yin is one of the most ambiguous, if not *the* most ambiguous, of Chinese poets. In a later chapter (Part III, 4) I shall discuss what kinds of ambiguities are found in his poetry and whether they are justified. For the present, I wish to draw attention to the fact that these ambiguities have given rise to widely divergent interpretations of Li's poetry. Since it is obviously neither possible nor desirable to mention all who have written on Li Shang-yin, I shall refer only to a few scholars who have made fairly comprehensive studies of his poetry. These may be said to fall into three schools.

To the first school belong those who see, in many of Li's ambiguous poems, veiled references to his patrons or his would-be patrons, especially to Ling-hu T'ao, son of Ling-hu Ch'u, the poet's first patron. This school is represented by Feng Hao (1719–1801), whose edition of Li Shang-yin's poetry remains the standard one, and Chang Ts'ai-t'ien (1862–1945), who wrote the most authoritative work on the poet's life.[1] Both are inclined to interpret Li's ambiguous poems as personal allegory involving the poet's relation with the younger Ling-hu. For instance, the poems without titles, which apparently express a hopeless passion for a woman (see Poems, 4, 5, 6) are said to reveal the poet's ardent desire for Ling-hu T'ao's patronage, and those poems which describe a deserted woman (for example, Poems 17 and 18) are supposed to reflect the poet's own frustrations in his official career. Both Feng and Chang resort to possible puns and other word-plays as hidden clues to the true meaning of Li's poems, and in most cases the hypothetical clues lead to Ling-hu T'ao. Thus, according to this school, Li Shang-yin's whole life was dominated by his desire for official advancement and his remorse over having lost the patronage of the Ling-hu family by his marriage with Wang Mao-yüan's daughter, and his most celebrated poems are reiterations of such feelings.

The second school of Li Shang-yin's interpreters believe that most of his ambiguous poems allude to various clandestine love affairs with certain Taoist nuns and Court ladies. The best-known exponent of this view is Miss Su Hsüeh-lin, whose book *Researches on the love affairs of Li Shang-yin*,[2] has exerted considerable influence on modern literary

[1] *Yü-hsi-sheng nien-p'u hui-chien* ("A comprehensive commentary on the biographical chronology of Li Shang-yin,"), 1917.

[2] *Li Yi-shan lüan-ai shih-chi k'ao*, 1927.

historians and readers. If we can believe Miss Su, Li Shang-yin had a love affair with one of the sisters named Sung who were Taoist nuns in the Hua-yang Temple in Ch'ang-an, but she deserted him for a Taoist priest called Yung, thus causing the poet to feel great sorrow and jealousy. Many of Li's poems containing allusions to Taoist goddesses (for example, Poems 21–26, 28–33) are supposed to refer to this nun. Further, according to Miss Su, the poet later fell in love with two sisters called Fei-luan ("Flying Phoenix") and Ch'ing-feng ("Agile Phoenix") who had been presented to Emperor Ching-tsung as Court entertainers. Their surname, Miss Su says, was Lu, and they carried on a secret intrigue with Li Shang-yin. Later, continues Miss Su, when Emperor Wen-tsung executed several Court entertainers in 839, the Lu sisters, for fear of implicating themselves and the poet, committed suicide by leaping into a well. Many of Li's ambiguous poems are seen by Miss Su to contain references, couched in obscure terms, to this tragic love story. Another scholar who appears to belong to this school is Chu Hsieh, who published an article entitled "A New Interpretation of Li Shang-yin's Poetry."[3] Though he makes no mention of Miss Su, his conclusions on many of the poems are similar to hers, except that he says only that Li had love affairs with Court ladies and Taoist nuns, but does not attempt to identify them by name.

Scholars of the third school are those who advocate the view that Li Shang-yin's ambiguous poems are mostly satires upon the Court and political factions. This view has been expressed by Mr. Ku Yi-ch'ün in his book *A critical discussion on Li Shang-yin,*[4] and by Mr. Sun Chen-t'ao in his article "Hidden Meanings in Li Shang-yin's Poetry."[5] These writers maintain that Li's poems that involve Taoist nuns are not auto-biographical love poems but satirical poems about imperial princesses who had taken Taoist vows, and that many of his other ambiguous poems are also political in nature, alluding to imperial concubines, courtiers, and eunuchs. At the same time, they tend to regard undeniable love poems as written for the poet's wife.

All the three views mentioned above have some justification in the light of Li Shang-yin's life and of Chinese literary history, but none of them is entirely convincing. The first view, that Li's poems contain hidden references to Ling-hu T'ao, may be true in a few cases, but can hardly be true in all. Although it is a well-established convention (one that goes back to the poet Ch'ü Yüan of the fourth century B.C.) for a Chinese poet to compare himself to a woman and his sovereign or patron to the husband or lover, can we really believe that it was Li's longing for Ling-hu's favor and the latter's coolness that reduced the poet to such constant heart-rending sorrow and abject despair as are shown in some of his poems? Further, in Li Shang-yin's collected poems there are several addressed to Ling-hu T'ao. They are largely conven-

[3] "Li Shang-yin shih hsin-ch'üan," 1937.

[4] *Li Shang-yin p'ing-lun,* 1958.

[5] "Li Shang-yin shih t'an-wei" 1960.

tional poems of friendship, occasionally with a hint of an appeal for help, but with nothing in them suggesting intense emotions. It is hard to reconcile these conventional poems with the passionate love poems which are supposedly intended for, or at least inspired by, the same person. In their eagerness to find the sinister shadow of Ling-hu T'ao in the most unlikely places, both Feng Hao and Chang Ts'ai-t'ien rely on far-fetched interpretations, which do more credit to their imagination than to their erudition. Consequently, in spite of their immensely painstaking scholarship, they manage to obscure rather than to elucidate Li Shang-yin's poems.

The view held by the second school, that most of Li Shang-yin's ambiguous poems deal with clandestine love affairs, is the one that appeals most readily to modern readers, but we would do well to pause before following Miss Su Hsüeh-lin all the way. In the first place, although many of Li's poems are undoubtedly concerned with love, we cannot say for certain how far they are autobiographical. After all, love poetry does not have to be based on personal experience. For example, Emily Brontë's passionate poem, "Cold in the earth, and the deep snow piled above thee," was based not on real experience but on childhood fantasy.[6] Second, Miss Su's whole reconstruction of Li Shang-yin's love life depends on ingenious reading between the lines of his poetry rather than independent external evidence, and has been questioned by Mr. Ku Yi-ch'ün and others. Specifically, Miss Su says that Li had a love affair with one of the Sung sisters of Hua-yang Temple, but neither of the two poems addressed to them in Li's collected poems (one of which is given in this volume as Poem 35) can be called an unequivocal love poem. Miss Su's theory that the nun shifted her affection to the Taoist priest Yung is likewise based on flimsy grounds and doubtful interpretation of some of Li's poems. As for the two Court entertainers Fei-luan and Ch'ing-feng, there is no external evidence that they were acquainted with Li Shang-yin, and circumstances would not have allowed them to carry on a secret intrigue with him easily. Miss Su suggests that these two girls gave the poet a zither (*se*) as a present, and that he gave them a jade plate in return, but, as Mr. Ku pointed out, the zither measured some seven or eight feet long, and it would have been extremely difficult to smuggle this cumbersome instrument out of the palace! What Miss Su calls the "palace purge," during which the two girls are supposed to have committed suicide, is also largely a product of her imagination. Official history merely mentions that Emperor Wen-tsung executed a number of Court entertainers who had spoken against the former Crown Prince; there is no evidence that these two girls were involved, or that the "purge" had anything to do with secret love affairs. Even if it were true that Li Shang-yin had love affairs with the various ladies suggested by Miss Su, it still would not

[6] The poem is addressed by "R. Alcona" to "J. Brenzaida," two of the characters who inhabit Gondal, the imaginary island invented by Emily and Anne Brontë in their childhood. See *The Complete Poems of Emily Jane Brontë* ed. C. W. Hatfield, pp. 222–2

mean that each of his ambiguous poems must refer to one of them. In truth, we can only say that some of Li's poems appear to concern Court ladies and Taoist nuns, but we cannot prove which poem is for which lady.

The third view, that Li's ambiguous poems are for the most part political satires, also seems exaggerated. True, Li wrote some political poems denouncing the eunuchs and politicians. It is possible, also, that some of his poems about Taoist nuns allude to princesses, since it was notorious that many T'ang princesses lived in Taoist temples, ostensibly to devote themselves to religion but actually to lead licentious lives free from the restrictions of the palace. But it is surely going too far to say that Li Shang-yin had no extramarital love affairs, and to read all his poems as political allegory or as love poems for his wife.

To be fair to the adherents of the three views, it should be pointed out that they do not always hold these views exclusively. Those who advocate the first and the third views sometimes would allow a poem to be a love poem, and those who hold the second view occasionally admit that what looks like a love poem may have political implications. But the tendency of each school to interpret Li's poetry in a particular way remains. It seems to me that each school is biased in its interpretation of his poetry by its own preconceived notions of his character. Those who accept the official historians' portrait of Li Shang-yin as a political opportunist have no difficulty in believing that his most intense and personal poems are expressions of frustrated ambition; those who would like to see him as a Chinese Don Juan can easily find support for their view in his numerous poems which, at least ostensibly, deal with love; and those who wish to paint him as an upright Confucian moralist or a rebel against "feudal society" see hidden references to contemporary political events or expressions of his "social awareness" everywhere in his poetry. Indeed, one can find "internal evidence" in a poet's works to support almost any theory one has formed, and in Li Shang-yin's poems this is all too easy to do. I do not mean to imply that all three portraits of Li Shang-yin are totally false; on the contrary, there may well be some truth in each, but each seems to err by emphasizing only one aspect of his character. As a brilliant man, he naturally had his ambitions, but his writings afford ample proof that he did not spend his whole life bemoaning his lack of success and regretting one possible miscalculation in the political game, but found time for the "better things of life," such as wine, women, and song. At the same time, his works show that he was interested in many things other than love: he dabbled in Taoism in his early life and Buddhism in his later years, and his erudition is exceptional even among Chinese poets. Some of his poems reveal a deep concern for contemporary affairs, but this does not mean he was so devoted to public issues that he found no time for personal feelings. We need not join those scholars, both ancient and modern, who condemn Li Shang-yin either as an unscrupulous careerist, who betrayed his first patron for self-advancement, or as a decadent philanderer, who squandered his life in amorous adventures. On the other hand, there is no need to try to whitewash his character and deny, as Mr. Ku has done,[7] that Li ever had romantic love affairs with Court ladies or Taoist nuns. Most literary men in T'ang times openly associated with courtesans (who were often highly cultured), and some Taoist nuns were courtesans in everything but name. For instance, the poetess Yü Hsüan-chi, who was at first a scholar's concubine, became a Taoist nun of doubtful morals and wrote love poems to several men, including the poet Wen T'ing-yün. Nor need we regard Li Shang-yin as a great Confucian statesman manqué, or a social rebel. As far as I can see, his consciously held beliefs were the usual mixture of Confucianism, Taoism, and Buddhism. His protests against social and political abuses were Confucian in inspiration; Taoism provided him with a means of momentary escape from the harsh realities of life and also with material for his imagination to work on; Buddhism gave him some comfort in later life, although it does not seem to have penetrated his mind deeply, as it did, for instance, the poet Wang Wei's. But in the final analysis, it is not a poet's conscious beliefs and ideas that interest us, but how they may have affected his poetry. Similarly, the kind of man he was is only of interest to us in so far as this affected the kind of poetry he wrote.

Another objection which may be raised against all the three schools of Li Shang-yin's interpreters mentioned above is that they all seem to have fallen under the "intentional fallacy,"[8] in that they are all bent on discovering the poet's intentions in writing his poems. Did he write such and such a poem to plead for Ling-hu's favor? Or to express his passion for Fei-luan and Ch'ing-feng? Or to denounce a certain Court lady or official? Now, short of resurrecting Li Shang-yin, we can never be sure. But does it matter in any case? The poet's *external* intention or motive is not necessarily the same as the *artistic* intention of the poem: the former is what caused him to write, the latter is the guiding principle which has shaped the poem. As critics, we are concerned with the latter, not the former.

In addition to the adherents of the three schools, there are some who feel that one can appreciate the beauty of Li Shang-yin's poetry without understanding what it means. For example, Feng Pan (1602–71) remarked, "Such poetry is good even though it is not understood, just as when one sees Hsi Shih, one does not have to know her name to realize she is a beauty." Similarly, Liang Ch'i-ch'ao (1873–1929) said of Li Shang-yin's ambiguous poems, "What they are about I cannot determine. I cannot even explain the literal meaning line by line. Yet I feel they are beautiful, and when I read them, they give me a new kind of pleasure in my mind. We must realize that Beauty is many-sided, that Beauty is mysterious by nature. If we still acknowledge the value

---

[7] Strangely enough, although Mr. Ku refutes Miss Su's theories about Li Shang-yin's love affairs, he invents another one for the poet with the girl Willow Branch, with whom Li says explicitly he did not have a love affair. See Poems 60–64.

[8] See W. K. Wimsatt, Jr. with Monroe C. Beardsley, *The Verbal Icon*, pp. 3–18.

of Beauty, we cannot lightly brush aside this kind of writing." These sentiments have been echoed by some contemporary scholars, who apply the word "aestheticism" to Li Shang-yin's poetry, and think it is enough to feel the beauty of his imagery without trying to understand what it means. I confess I find it hard to feel wholehearted sympathy with this attitude. For one thing, I believe that poetry consists of words —and words have meanings—and that an adequate understanding of poetry will enhance and not detract from one's enjoyment of it. Furthermore, to regard Li Shang-yin as an aesthete who dedicated himself to the pursuit of Beauty and who wrote poetry in the spirit of "art for art's sake" is as inappropriate as to think of him as a Romanticist who devoted his life to the search for perfect Love.

My own approach to Li Shang-yin's poetry, then, is as follows. As far as his ambiguous poems are concerned, I think it is possible to make sense of them without committing ourselves to a definite theory about the person or occasion they were written for. Second, I believe that a poem can mean more than one thing at the same time, on different levels. I prefer, therefore, a symbolic reading of these poems to an allegorical one: the former allows room for different interpretations of the same poem, the latter involves definite identification of elements in a poem with actual persons and events. Further, instead of taking each poem as an autobiographical revelation, it would be better to take each one dramatically. In other words, we should try to reconstruct, from hints in a poem itself, a dramatic situation in the context of which the poem can make sense in one way or another, or in more than one way, but not to identify the prototypes of the dramatis personae. To draw an analogy with Western poetry, those interminable attempts to identify the Dark Lady and "Mr. W. H." are no doubt fascinating in themselves, but they are hardly relevant to our understanding and evaluation of Shakespeare's sonnets. All we need is the dramatic situation implicit in the sonnets themselves.

Naturally not all Li Shang-yin's poems are ambiguous. Some of them contain explicit references to his friends and relatives, or to historical and contemporary events. These poems of course cannot be treated in the same way as the ambiguous ones, and can be understood only in the light of what we know of the poet's life and times, just as, say, Milton's *Lycidas* or Marvell's *Horatian Ode upon Cromwell's Return from Ireland* can be understood only in the context of the relevant biographical and historical facts. We should not forget, however, that biographical and historical data, valuable as they are in helping us to understand poetry, provide no ground for critical judgment. That Li Shang-yin wrote angry protests against the eunuchs and fond recollections of his wife and children does not necessarily make these good poems. It is only the extent to which he has succeeded in enabling us to enter into the worlds of moral indignation, conjugal affection, and paternal love that can afford us some guide to the value of these poems as poetry.

In brief, it is not my intention to discredit previous commentators on Li Shang-yin's poetry, but rather to bring out the full range of possible meanings of his poems and then to examine them critically and objectively, avoiding as far as possible any distorted interpretation or biased judgment due to impressions of him as a man.

4

Problems of Translation

Robert Frost's well-known quip that poetry is what disappears in translation is true if we take it to mean that no translation of poetry can ever be a perfect re-creation of the original: even if a translation succeeds in being a perfect poem, it is bound to be a different poem from the original. The remark is not true, however, if it is understood to imply a concept of "poetry" as a mysterious entity or substance distinct from the actual "poem." In fact, if the Coleridgean distinction between "poetry" and "poem" were true,[1] presumably one would be able to extract this substance called "poetry" and inject it into a new "poem" in another language. This, unfortunately, one cannot do. "Poetry" is simply a collective name for "poems," and each poem is a unique verbal symbol with its own polyphonic structure of sound, meaning, and imagery.[2] When a reader follows and responds to the development of this verbal structure, he re-creates the poem. In other words, a poem has no separate existence apart from the poet's experience of creating it in his mind, and the reader's of re-creating it in *his* mind. Of course, no two readers will respond to the same poem in exactly the same way, just as no two spectators of a painting will see exactly the same picture, and no two pianists will play the same piece of music in exactly the same manner. Nevertheless, among readers of similar linguistic and cultural backgrounds and comparable experience and sensibility, there should be sufficient common ground for them to talk about the same "poem." Similarly, the poem in the poet's own mind and that re-created by a reader immersed in the same cultural tradition and endowed with the requisite knowledge and sensibility should have sufficient in common to justify calling the latter the same poem. Therefore, to translate a poem is to try to reproduce the verbal structure of the original, so that the reader of the translation will respond to it, as far as possible, in the same way that the translator responded to the original poem, thereby re-creating, to some extent, what the poet originally created. Such, I believe, is the aim of translating poetry.

In attempting to achieve this aim, every translator is faced with the

---

[1] Cf. Coleridge, *Biographia Literaria* (ed. J. Shawcross), vol. 2, pp. 11, 268; W. K. Wimsatt, Jr., *The Verbal Icon*, p. 61, footnote.

[2] This point will be developed later in Part III, 1.

eternal dilemma between "literal" and "literary" translations, and has
to steer a dangerous course between the Scylla of dull pedantry and the
Charybdis of irresponsible dilettantism. Absolute literalness in translation is not only undesirable but at times impossible, as I shall endeavor
to show below. On the other hand, excessive freedom will result in a
new poem, good or bad as the case may be, which will bear little or no
relation to the original and will have ceased to be a translation. In translating Chinese poetry, particularly Li Shang-yin's poetry, into English,
one is faced with this dilemma at every turn—with regard to individual
words, imagery, allusions, syntax, rhythm, and the like. Even if all
would-be translators agreed in theory that one should aim at the
"golden mean" between extreme literalness and free rendering, in
practice probably no two translators would agree where precisely the
golden mean lies in each given case, and every translator would have to
decide for himself. I shall now discuss some of the problems involved in
translating Li Shang-yin's poems, and explain how I tried to meet them.

To begin with individual words: one cannot draw easy equations
between Chinese and English words even on the literal level, since the
referents of Chinese words may not have precise counterparts in the
West. That is to say, a Chinese word may refer to an object which does
not exist in the West and for which there is therefore no English word.
Flora and *fauna* provide obvious examples. Many Chinese flowers and
trees have no English names, only Latin names, which, as Professor
David Hawkes remarked, "no translator of any literary pretentions
whatever could for a moment consider using."[3] One might add that
even if one threw all aesthetic considerations to the winds, it is doubtful
whether a Western reader would be familiar with such botanical terms.
One might as well transliterate the Chinese word, and write *wu-t'ung*,
for instance, instead of *Sterculia platanifolia* for this particular tree.
However, transliteration should only be used as a last resort: if used too
often, it will defeat the very purpose of translation. Another method
(one of several used by Hawkes) is to translate the Chinese name
literally. This can be applied only to a Chinese name with an obvious
meaning but cannot be used for a word like *wu-t'ung*, which is simply
the name of a tree with no other meaning. Moreover, in using this
method one runs the risk of attracting undue attention to the literal
meaning of what, to the Chinese, is no more than a name. For example,
if we were to translate *mu-tan* as "male vermilion" instead of "peony,"
the reader would be intrigued by this fanciful name and distracted from
the image of the flower. On the whole, when an approximate English
equivalent exists, it is better to use it than to transliterate or to translate
the literal meaning of the Chinese. This applies to fabulous animals and
birds as well as to actual flora and fauna. It is true that *lung* and *feng* are
not the same creatures as "dragon" and "phoenix" in Western mythology, but most Western readers are probably by now familiar with

[3] *Ch'u Tz'u, Songs of the South*, p. vii.

these words as translations from Chinese and may have seen pictorial representations of these fabulous creatures, so that there seems to be little danger that anyone would think of the kind of dragon killed by St. George or of the Egyptian phoenix when encountering these words in a translation of Chinese poetry.

Sometimes a Chinese word has more than one referent and therefore requires different translations in different contexts. A constant problem is the word *lou*, which is used for any building of two or more stories and can refer to various objects, such as a turret on the city wall, a tower, an elaborate pleasure pavilion, or even the staircase in a building. In poetry it is not always clear which object is meant, and how one should translate the word depends on what seems to be uppermost in the poet's mind. If he seems to be suggesting the height of the building, one might use "tower;" if he seems to be emphasizing its splendor, one might use "mansion." And when Li Shang-yin writes, "moon slants over *lou*" (in Poem 4), since he is concerned with the effect of the moonlight on the roof of the *lou* rather than the shape of the *lou* itself, I think one is justified in translating this as "the moonlight slants over the roof."

Of course, the "meaning" of a word includes not only its referent but also its implications and associations.[4] The apparent English equivalent of a Chinese word may in fact carry quite different implications. For example, as I once pointed out, the word *tsui*, commonly translated as "drunk" or "intoxicated," generally implies, when used in poetry, not sensual enjoyment or gay conviviality but an escape from the sorrows of the world into a state of self-oblivion.[5] In my eagerness to correct any wrong impression that Western readers might have formed, I went too far in avoiding the words "drunk" and "intoxicated" altogether and translating *tsui* as "rapt with wine." I now realize that to translate the word this way in all contexts would be absurd, and have fallen back on "drunk" and "intoxicated" in my translations of Li Shang-yin, though I still feel that the reader should be warned that "drunkenness" in Chinese poetry is not quite the same thing as drunkenness in real life, in China or anywhere else.

Then, an English word which has the same referent as a Chinese one may not have the relevant associations, or may even have undesirable ones. The word *liu* refers to the willow tree, but it is often associated with parting, while the word "willow" is not. Faced with such a word, the translator has no choice, to my way of thinking, but to mention in a note that such an association exists. Ideally, of course, the reader should automatically associate the willow with parting, but how could a Western reader do so without being told of the connection between the two—that it was an ancient Chinese custom to break a willow twig when seeing a friend off? Take another example: The word *tu-chüan*, which refers to a bird identified as the cuckoo, has associations, due to

[4] See Liu, *The Art of Chinese Poetry*, pp. 9–13.
[5] *Ibid.*, pp. 58–60.

a legend, with unhappy illicit love. One may hesitate to translate it as "cuckoo" because of the unfortunate associations of this word in English (although on the other hand the cuckoo features prominently in the first known English poem, "sumer is icumen in," not to mention Wordsworth's "To the Cuckoo"), but should one substitute a more "poetic" bird such as the nightingale, which has associations with the illicit love of Tereus for Philomela? In general, I think that when a translator has to choose between an English word which has the same referent as a Chinese word but lacks the relevant associations, and one which does have similar associations but refers to a different object, he should choose the former, while informing the reader of the associations that the original word evokes. After all, no object is intrinsically more "poetic" than another, and words acquire poetic associations only by usage. Is it too much to hope that the Western reader, having learnt that the willow is associated with parting and the cuckoo with unhappy love, and having encountered these words repeatedly in translations of Chinese poetry, will eventually respond to them as a Chinese reader does to the original words?

The above discussion on the referents, implications, and associations of words also applies to the imagery evoked by the words. It is generally recognized that imagery is one of the most vital elements of poetry (some even call it the "soul of poetry") and the one that best survives the process of translation and should be kept at all costs. However, a translator has to guard against the danger of adding new imagery to the poem or reviving "dead metaphors" (which I prefer to call "fossilized imagery") in an attempt to improve upon the original. For instance, the expression *yün-pin*, literally "cloud [-like] hair-over-the-temples," is a cliché in Chinese. Originally it was meant to compare a woman's piled-up dark hair falling over the temples to clusters of clouds, but it has long become a fossilized image, as hackneyed as "raven locks" in English. When this expression occurs in one of Li Shang-yin's poems (Poem 6), one might simply translate it as "dark hair" and suppress the fossilized image, since to most readers and presumably to the poet himself it means little more than that. I realize that, in the original poem in question, "cloud-hair" forms a contrast to "moonlight" in the next line, so that not to translate the former literally is to miss this contrast, but perhaps this loss is sufficiently compensated for by the new contrast between "*dark* hair" and "moon*light*." In any case, to translate *yün-pin* as "cloudy temples" would hardly convey the original image: would the Western reader realize that "cloudy" is meant to suggest dark color and thick clusters rather than murkiness?

In deciding whether an image is fossilized or not, one has to consider the date of the poem in relation to the earliest known usage of the image, as well as how it is used in the present context. This involves several further considerations, such as whether the image is given a new twist, and whether it is combined with another image. I have suggested elsewhere the criteria for judging imagery and the ways in which a hackneyed image can be given new life;[6] suffice it to give just one example here. In Li Shang-yin's poem *Chamber Music* (Poem 79), he uses the well-worn image "autumn waves" for a woman's eyes, but it is given a new lease of life by being fused with another water image suggested by the preceding line. In such cases, fossilized imagery is at least partially revived and may be preserved in translation.

Problems of translation also arise from allusions, the use of which is a common poetic device in Chinese and forms an essential part of Li Shang-yin's art as a poet. I have attempted previously to describe the various poetic functions of allusions[7] and will not repeat myself here. But, I wish to emphasize two points concerned with translating allusive poems. First, allusions in poetry, if properly used, are not merely substitutes for common nouns or abstract epithets but add something to the total meaning and effect of the poem. For instance, Li Shang-yin alludes many times to Ch'ang-o, who, according to legend, stole her husband King Yi's elixir of life and fled to the moon. Her name is not merely a synonym for "a goddess" or "an immortal" but suggests that the poet is comparing a Taoist nun to this goddess, since a nun's taking vows of chastity may be compared to the goddess's renunciation of the human world, and Taoists were concerned with the search for the elixir of life. Such allusions, therefore, should be kept in the translation; otherwise many lines or even whole poems may become pointless. Generally speaking, all allusions should be retained, unless they are so hackneyed that they become idiomatic expressions without any particular significance, comparable to the use of "Romeo" as a vulgar substitute for "lover" in English. They are then no more effective, poetically, than fossilized images, and need not be translated.

The second point about allusions that I wish to stress is that once they are recognized as poetically effective, one should explain them as fully as it is practical to do, since the more a reader knows about the person or story alluded to, the more fully he will understand its significance in the poetic context, and the more definite his response to it will be. The name Ch'ang-o means nothing to a Western reader; when he learns that this is the Chinese goddess of the moon, it means something; and when he is further told the story about her theft of the elixir of life from her husband and her flight to the moon, it becomes even more meaningful. Therefore, I believe it is worthwhile to give the reader as much information as is relevant. After all, reading poetry in one's own language also requires considerable extrapoetic knowledge—of history, cultural environment, previous literature, and so forth—except that this knowledge is assumed to have been assimilated beforehand. In reading translations of poetry which is the product of a different culture, one simply has to absorb such knowledge on an *ad hoc* basis. I do not see how a conscientious translator can avoid the task of providing such information or how a serious reader can avoid the trouble of

---

[6] *Ibid.*, 114–23.
[7] *Ibid.*, pp. 132–36.

reading it. It seems to me that to offer a translation of an allusive Chinese poem to the Western reader without any explanation is like showing a pietà to a Chinese who has never heard of Christianity and expecting him to respond to it, without telling him what it is all about. Nor need one feel undue misgivings that detailed explanations may kill the reader's enjoyment of Chinese poetry. Such explanations, like critical analyses, are meant to help the reader develop a deeper under-standing of and a fuller response to poetry. No one whose response to poetry is more than a vague impression of "beauty", mixed with com-placency at his own aesthetic sensibility and a sentimental identification with the poet, need fear that his enjoyment of poetry will be ruined by elaborate exegeses and detailed analyses.

Next, we may consider problems arising from grammatical differ-ences between Chinese and English. First of all, the absence of inflec-tions in Chinese often leaves the translator in doubt about what number, gender, case, etc., he should adopt in English. Unless he is content with pidgin English, he has to be more explicit than the original and to choose one of several possible meanings, and his choice has to be guided by the context.

Second, in Classical Chinese, there is great flexibility with regard to "parts of speech," and the same word can often function as noun, adjective, verb, and adverb. The greater rigidity of English often makes it necessary to paraphrase and thus lose some of the conciseness and concreteness of the original. In the following couplet (from Poem 71)

> *ling   yün   ch'un   chü-ju*
> mountain-range   cloud   spring   marshy
> *chiang   yüeh   yeh   ch'ing   ming*
> river   moon   night   clear   bright

the words for "spring" (*ch'un*) and "night" (*yeh*) are used adverbially. Unfortunately one cannot do so in English ("nightly" as an adverb would give the wrong meaning—"every night" instead of "at night") and one has to write something like:

> Dank clouds hang over the mountain range in spring;
> The river moon shines clear and bright at night.

The same couplet also illustrates how one may have to add verbs which are not in the original, since, in Chinese, words corresponding to English adjectives are used verbally (known as "stative verbs"), and to translate these always by the weak copula is not satisfactory ("the clouds *are* dank," "the moon *is* clear and bright," and so forth.)

Another grammatical feature of the language of Chinese poetry which differs strikingly from English grammatical usage is the frequent omission of the subject of a verb and of connective particles (the correlatives of "and," "but," "when," "if," etc.) The result is a kind of ambiguity which is taken for granted in Chinese but attracts attention if kept in English. I am inclined to think that a translator should supply the missing subject even though this may involve committing himself to one of several possible interpretations of a line, for to leave it out may send the reader on a wild goose chase after who the subject is and distract his attention from the immediate impact of the line. To a Chinese reader, the absence of the subject is a familiar phenomenon and causes no surprise: he responds to the situation and mood of the poem immediately, without asking who the subject is. Such a question will arise, if at all, only after the initial response, when the reader begins to analyze his response intellectually. This is not so with a Western reader. Moreover, to use the first person pronoun is not necessarily to identify the speaker with the poet himself, for the "I" of the poem can be taken to represent a dramatis persona;[8] the second person pronoun can be used impersonally; and sometimes the use of the noncommittal "one" or the passive voice may provide further ways of dealing with the problem. On the other hand, to omit the subject in English may give a misleading impression. For instance, a line without a subject may be taken as imperative, when it is not intended to be.

Furthermore, in following too closely the grammatical structure of the original, a translator runs the risk of making a poem more ambiguous than it really is. Now, ambiguity in poetry does not mean confusion but multiplicity of meaning; an ambiguous line is one that can make sense in more than one way, but usually (even in Li Shang-yin's most ambiguous poems) it makes some kind of immediate sense. To keep all the grammatical ambiguities of Chinese in an English translation might turn a line that makes sense in more than one way into one that makes no sense at all. It seems to me better to choose one of several possible meanings, at the cost of losing the ambiguity, than to render the line meaningless or more enigmatic than it is in the original.

Even if a translation that leaves out all the subjects and conjunctions is not too obscure and is technically English, it may give a wrong impression of the style of the original, since lines in English without subjects or conjunctions may sound like telegrams or newspaper headlines. If it should be asked: Since all Classical Chinese is written in a terse telegraphic style, why not reproduce it? The answer would be: Chinese poems do *not* sound like Chinese telegrams, not only because the former possess qualities (for example, rhythm, tone-pattern, rhyme) which the latter do not, but also because features common to both (such as omission of subject) are common to other kinds of writing as well and thus do not attract attention in Chinese the way they would in English. Granted that some readers may like this novel style in English, it would still be true that the translator had turned a common linguistic feature into a rhetorical device—asyndeton—thus giving a false idea of the original style. Incidentally, the use of asyndeton also tends to break up a line into segments and produce a staccato effect.

[8] Cf. René Wellek and Austin Warren, *Theory of Literature*, p. 70.

True, all Chinese poetry sounds rather staccato compared with English, as Chinese consists mainly of monosyllabic words and disyllabic compounds, but would anyone recommend that translations of Chinese poetry should be confined to English words of one or two syllables?

Let us now consider the ambiguous nature of Chinese syntax more closely. A line can usually be construed in various ways, but some ways of construing it, though grammatically possible, are automatically ruled out on the ground of sense. In the line

> *la   chao   pan   lung   chin   fei-ts'ui*
> candle   light   half   encircle   gold   kingfisher

we may take the word *chao*, commonly used as a verb ("to shine"), to be a noun ("light") in this instance, and the word *lung*, which usually means "cage," to be a verb, meaning "to encircle."[9] Thus the whole line is seen to mean

> The candle's light half encircles the golden kingfishers.

That it is no arbitrary decision to take *chao* as a noun and *lung* as a verb and not vice versa can be shown by comparing this line with the next, with which it forms an antithetical couplet:

> *she   hsün   wei   tu   hsiu   fu-jung*
> musk   perfume   subtly   pass-through   embroidered   lotus
> (The musk perfume subtly permeates the embroidered lotus flowers.)

Since, in an antithetical couplet, the corresponding syllables normally match each other syntactically, it is clear that "candle's light" contrasts with "musk perfume," "half encircles" with "subtly permeates," and "golden kingfishers" with "embroidered lotus flowers."

It may be worthwhile to add that, although Chinese word-order is generally similar to English, this is not always so. An obvious case is the use of postpositions in Chinese, where English would require prepositions. Thus *shan shang mu*, if translated word for word, would be "mountain above tree," which is precisely the opposite of what the phrase means.

In short, if we pushed to the extreme the attempt to follow the grammatical structure of Chinese in English translations—to omit all subjects and conjunctions, and to do away with all inflections—the result would of course be a sort of pidgin English, which would not only be aesthetically unsatisfactory but even unintelligible or misleading. After all, translation is not just turning individual words into words of another language (and even this is not always possible, as we have seen). A succession of English words is not necessarily English, and one cannot write English with Chinese grammar, which is what it amounts to if one tries to preserve the grammatical features of Chinese and totally disregard the demands of English grammar and idiom. Nor should one

---

[9] It is possible to take *lung* as passive, "encircled by."

exaggerate the ambiguity of Chinese. The fact is, one automatically rejects irrelevant meanings which are grammatically possible; otherwise all language would be intolerably ambiguous. This happens in English too. For instance, the sentence "I saw a man with a telescope" could mean either "I saw a man who was carrying a telescope," or "Using a telescope, I saw a man," but no one in his right mind would take it to mean "I habitually use a telescope to *saw* a man," although I am told that a computer actually produced all three possible meanings. In translating Chinese, one would do well to avoid emulating the computer!

There remains one more aspect of poetry to be considered in connection with the difficulties of translation—the sound-pattern. It goes without saying that the tone-patterns of Chinese cannot be reproduced in English. As for rhyme, I formerly advocated reproducing the original rhyme schemes in translations of Chinese poetry and tried to put this into practice, with unfortunate results, for which I have been criticized by several reviewers. I now realize the virtual impossibility of keeping the rhymes without damage to the meaning, and no longer wish to insist on the use of rhymes. Thus, two of the most important elements of Chinese versification, tone-pattern and rhyme, have to go. However, something of the rhythmic pattern of the whole poem may be salvaged, based on the number of lines and of syllables in each line. Although English requires more syllables than does Classical Chinese to say the same thing, so that one cannot keep the number of syllables unchanged, it is possible to have a corresponding number of stresses, which after all form the basis of rhythm in English verse. The practice of translating a poem line for line, giving as many stresses in each line as there are syllables in the original Chinese, was initiated by Arthur Waley and has been adopted by several other translators, including myself. This seems to me the best if not the only way of approaching the original rhythm. But even this is not always possible, especially when one is translating some of Li Shang-yin's highly complex and condensed lines, which require considerable expansion to make sense in English. In such cases I have sacrificed regularity of rhythm, rather than distorted or simplified the sense.

In brief, I believe that one should try to make the sound-pattern of the translation bear some resemblance to that of the original, rather than cast the translation into a conventional English meter or use free verse with complete disregard for the original verse form. To turn a Chinese antithetical couplet into a Heroic Couplet or into several lines of free verse in English is to produce a totally different effect and to change drastically the sound-pattern, which is part of the complex verbal structure of the poem; and to change the order of the lines is to alter the sequence of thought and pattern of imagery as well.

Apart from the total sound-pattern of a poem, there are specific auditory devices, such as alliteration, onomatopoeia, repetition, and reduplication, of which a translator should not remain unaware. But any effort to reproduce such devices must be subject to considerations of meaning. An example of onomatopoeia may be given from Poem 5:

sa-sa[10] tung feng hsi yü lai
sa-sa east wind fine rain come

where the first two syllables imitate the sound of the wind. I have endeavored to preserve this effect by rendering the line as:

The east wind *soughs* and *sighs* as a fine drizzle falls.

Repetition occurs in the opening line of Poem 6:

hsiang chien shih nan★ pieh yi nan★
mutual see time hard part also hard.

Leaving aside the tone-pattern, which cannot be reproduced, we may note that the line consists of seven syllables with a caesura after the fourth, and that the syllable *nan* ("hard") occurs at the end of each half of the line:

— — — —★/— — —★

Previously I translated this line as follows:

Hard it is for us to meet/and hard to go away.[11]

This version contains seven stresses with a caesura after the fourth, but the word *pieh* ("to part") was rendered as "go away" for the sake of rhyme. I have tried to remove this inaccuracy in the revised version, which now stands:

It is hard for us to meet/and also hard to part.

This still has seven stresses with a caesura after the fourth, and the repeated syllable "hard" occurs in the same position in both halves of the line. As for the meaning, the only addition is "for us," which is implied by "mutual" in the original. This is the nearest I can get to the original both in meaning and in sound; whether it is the most satisfactory version as a line of English verse is, of course, a different question.

Reduplication of monosyllabic words (as distinct from repetition of words at intervals) in Chinese poetry may be a conscious device, but sometimes it is only idiomatic usage.[12] Hence, one should exercise caution, to avoid distorting the sense for the sake of the sound. For instance, the word for "day," *jih*, when reduplicated as *jih-jih*, means "every day," and to translate it as "day after day" may be closer to the original in sound but is less accurate in meaning.

All the problems discussed above are closely interrelated, because the various linguistic elements from which such problems arise are integrated into an organic whole in each poem. Since many of these problems are involved in the translating of the very first poem given in this

---

[10] In Ancient Chinese, *sâp-sâp*.
[11] Liu, *Chinese Poetry*, p. 28.
[12] *Ibid.*, pp. 36–37.

volume, and since this is Li Shang-yin's most famous poem, I would like to use it as an illustration of the problems of translation. This will necessitate a lengthy discussion, for which I must ask the reader's forbearance.

The first two words of the poem are used as its title: *Chin se*. *Chin* is generally translated as "brocade," although, according to Professor E. H. Schafer, it really refers to "polychrome damask."[13] However, the word is here used adjectivally and may be translated as "ornamented."[14] The *se* is an ancient twenty-five-stringed instrument, placed horizontally on the table or across the knees. The nearest equivalent in English is "zither," and the instrument is described as such in Western works on Chinese music.[15] The word has been variously translated as "harp", "psaltery," and "lute," no doubt because of the poetic associations of these words, but it seems to me doubtful whether we have the right to change the key symbol of the poem. As we shall see later, the poet is using this musical instrument as a symbol of bygone years: the strings lying in a row, as if in an extending vista, remind him of the years of his life. I think the effect of this symbolic image is altered if we try to visualize, instead of a many-stringed instrument lying horizontally, one that is standing or being held upright. I have therefore translated the title as *The Ornamented Zither*. The opening line runs:

> chin   se   wu   tuan   wu-shih   hsüan[γien][16]
> ornamented   zither   no   reason   fifty   strings

This may be rendered quite literally as:

> The ornamented zither, for no reason, has fifty strings.

Why the poet wrote "fifty strings" instead of "twenty-five strings" will be discussed later, in the commentary on the poem, but does not concern us here, since it does not cause any problem of translation. The second line reads:

> yi   hsüan   yi   chu   ssu   hua   nien[nien]
> one   string   one   bridge   think   flower   year

The word *chu* has been translated as "peg" or "fret," though in fact it refers to a movable bridge attached to each string, as illustrated in Chinese books on music. The verb *ssu*, "think," is to be taken in the sense of "make one think." The phrase *hua nien*, literally "flowery years," is a conventional expression for "youthful years," and the metaphor had better be left out. The whole line, then, may be rendered:

> Each string, each bridge, recalls a youthful year.

---

[13] Schafer, *The Golden Peaches of Samarkand*, p. 196.

[14] The word has previously been translated as "inlaid", which is not accurate, since we know from Chinese works on music that an inlaid *se* was called *pao se* ("precious zither"), while the *chin se* was a zither painted with ornamental designs.

[15] See *New Oxford History of Music*, 1: 89–90; *Grove's Dictionary of Music and Musicians*, 2: 237–8; Joseph Needham, *Science and Civilization in China*, vol. 4, part 1, p. 130.

[16] The Ancient Chinese pronunciations of the rhyming syllables are given in square brackets.

The third line,

> Chuang   Sheng   hsiao   meng   mi   hu-tieh
> Chuang   master   morning   dream   confuse   butterfly,

alludes to the famous allegory in the *Chuang Tzu*, in which the philosopher Master Chuang (Chuang Tzu or Chuang Sheng) says that he dreamed of being a butterfly and then poses the question: was it really he who dreamed of being a butterfly or was it the butterfly that dreamed of being Master Chuang? The syntax of the line is ambiguous. The first four syllables could be intrepreted variously as: "Master Chuang's morning dream," "Master Chuang in his morning dream," "Master Chuang, while dreaming in the morning," and so forth. The remaining syllables could mean, "confused a (or 'the') butterfly," "was confused by (or 'with') a (or 'the') butterfly." I have chosen to interpret the line as:

> Master Chuang was confused by his morning dream of the
> butterfly.

The next line goes:

> Wang Ti   ch'un   hsin   t'o   tu-chüan [kiwen]
> Wang Emperor   spring   heart   entrust   cuckoo

This alludes to the story that a legendary ruler of Shu, named Tu Yü and also styled Emperor Wang, had a love affair with his prime minister's wife and died of shame, and that after his death his soul was metamorphosed into the cuckoo, called in Chinese *tu-yü*, or *tu-chüan*, or *tzu-kuei*, which is said to cry and shed blood in late spring. The "spring heart," apart from its literal meaning of "heart in spring," could also mean "amorous heart," since in Chinese literature "spring" often means "amorous" or "erotic." Hence, the line may be translated as:

> Emperor Wang's amorous heart in spring is entrusted to
> the cuckoo.

The next two lines are highly allusive:

> ts'ang   hai   yüeh   ming   chu   yu   lei
> vast   sea   moon   bright   pearl   have   tear
>
> Lan-   t'ien   jih   nuan   yü   sheng   yen [·ien]
> Indigo-field   sun   warm   jade   produce   smoke

Among the numerous possible allusions involved in these two lines, we may mention four here. First, it was believed that when the moon was full, pearls would appear, but when the moon waned, the oysters would become empty. Second, there is a story about a mermaid who, on leaving her human host, asked for a jade plate. On this she shed tears, which turned into pearls. Third, Lan-t'ien ("Indigo-field") is the name of a mountain famous for producing jade. Lastly, a daughter of the King of Wu (fifth century B.C.), named Jade (*Yü*), died of a broken heart when her father refused to let her marry the youth she loved. Afterward, her spirit appeared and disappeared like smoke. Literally, the two lines mean:

> In the vast sea, under a bright moon, pearls have tears;
> On Indigo Mountain, in the warm sun, jade engenders smoke.

The last two lines run:

> *tz'u   ch'ing   k'e   tai   ch'eng   chui-yi*
> this   feeling   may   await   become   memory
>
> *chih   shih   tang   shih   yi   wang-jan* [*ńžiän*]
> only   is   that   time   already   bewildered

The word *k'e* can be taken to mean "may" or "might", or as an interrogative particle, so that line 7 could be rendered as

> This feeling might have become a thing to be remembered

or as

> How could this feeling wait to become a memory?

I have chosen the first alternative. The last line presents no particular problem:

> Only, at the time you were already bewildered and lost.

So far, I have translated the poem fairly literally, to show what the original is like. I have also made a freer version, which I venture to give below for comparison:

The Ornamented Zither

> Why should the ornamented zither have fifty strings,
> Each reverberating with echoes of a bygone year?
> How can you tell the dreamer from the dream, the man
>   from the butterfly,
> Or the Emperor's amorous heart in spring from the
>   cuckoo's cry?
> Go and seek the moonlit mermaid shedding tears of pearls,
> Then burn with the jade in the sun till you vanish in smoke.
> All this could have become a memory to be cherished
> But for the bewilderment you felt even at the time.

While this freer version might create a more immediate impression on the Western reader, it unfortunately cannot be used as a basis for critical analysis and evaluation, since it departs considerably from the original poem. I have therefore used the more literal version in the main text. However, the two versions will, I hope, give some idea of the dilemma between literal and free translations. Since my primary concern is with critical discussions, I have often had to choose the more literal version even when fully aware of its inadequacy as poetry.

When all is said and done, translations of poetry are only compromises, between two different ways of thinking and feeling, and between the verbal structure of a poem in one language and what is poetic or at least tolerable in another. Ideally, a translator of poetry should be perfectly bilingual and bicultural, as sensitive to the subtleties and nuances of one language as he is able to convey them in the other. In other words, he would have to be as good a critic in one language as he is a poet in the other. Since such a paragon does not seem to exist anywhere, we have to be content with translations which primarily aim at showing what the original poems are like, and those which primarily attempt to be English poems in their own right. As long as the majority of Western readers cannot be expected to read Chinese, there will be need for translations of both kinds; and as long as there are people who can both read Chinese and write English, there will be new translations of Chinese poetry, just as there will always be new English versions of Homer and Dante.

Enough has been said to show that I have no illusions about translations of Chinese poetry, least of all my own, which naturally fall into the first category, since English is only my step-mother tongue, if I may coin a phrase. With all their imperfections, the translations in this volume may give some idea of the works of a great Chinese poet. Someone who has reason to believe that he is unlikely ever to visit the Louvre or the Uffizii may be glad to receive illustrated catalogues of their rich collections. As such, I offer my translations.

PART II

*Translations with Notes
and Commentaries*

POEM I

The Ornamented Zither

The ornamented zither, for no reason, has fifty strings.

Each string, each bridge, recalls a youthful year.

Master Chuang was confused by his morning dream of the butterfly;

Emperor Wang's amorous heart in spring is entrusted to the cuckoo.

In the vast sea, under a bright moon, pearls have tears;

On Indigo Mountain, in the warm sun, jade engenders smoke.

This feeling might have become a thing to be remembered,

Only, at the time you were already bewildered and lost.

NOTES

Title   See above, p. 44.

Line 1   The twenty-five-stringed zither is said to have had fifty strings originally, and the number was reduced in the following manner, according to legend. The god T'ai-ti told the goddess Su-nü ("The White Maid") to play the zither. She cried bitterly and could not be stopped. Thereupon the god ordered the zither broken into two halves, so that each half had only twenty-five strings.

Lines 3–4   See above, p.45.

Line 5   See above p. 45. The line may also allude to the expression "a pearl left in the vast sea" (*ts'ang-hai yi-chu*), first applied to Ti Jen-chieh (607–700), meaning someone whose talent is not appreciated.

Line 6   See above, p. 45. Two other allusions may be involved. First, the line may have been derived from a remark attributed to the poet Tai Shu-lun (732–89): "In poetry, there is a world which resembles Indigo Mountain in warm sunshine, when fine jade engenders smoke—one can look at it from a distance but cannot bring it close to one's eyes." Second, there is a story about Yang Yung-po, a dutiful son and upright man who lived on a mountain, where he provided free water for travelers on their arduous journey. One day a stranger came and, after taking a drink, gave Yang a bushel of pebbles and told him to plant them in the earth, saying that this would bring him a wife. The stranger then disappeared. Yang did as he was told, and the pebbles grew into jade. Later he acquired a good wife by offering her father the jade.

COMMENTARY

I have discussed various interpretations of this poem in an article (see Bibliography, section C), and shall summarize them here, adding a few details.

Theory I: That this is a love poem. This may be subdivided into three theories:

A. That it was written for a woman called Chin-se ("Ornamented Zither"), who was a maid or concubine in the household of Ling-hu Ch'u, or of his son Ling-hu T'ao. This was mentioned by Liu Pin (1023–89) and Chi Yu-kung (*fl.* 1126–33), and refuted by Hu Chen-heng (*fl.* 1573–1620) and others.

B. That it was written in recollection of a frustrated love affair with an unnamed woman. This is the view of Chi Yün (1724–1805).

C. That it was written for the death of Fei-luan and Ch'ing-feng, the two Court entertainers who allegedly carried on an intrigue with Li Shang-yin and gave him a zither. This is the theory of Miss Su Hsüeh-lin.[1]

Theory II: That the poem describes four kinds of music played on the zither. This theory was attributed by Huang Ch'ao-ying (*fl.* 1101–26) to the great poet Su Tung-p'o (1037–1101), but the attribution seems unfounded.

Theory III: That the poem was written in memory of Li Shang-yin's deceased wife. This was first suggested by Chu Ho-ling (1606–83) in his edition of Li's poetry. Chu pointed out that in the poem *Chamber Music* (Poem 79 in this volume), which was obviously written to mourn his wife, Li also mentioned an ornamented zither. Several scholars followed this lead and developed the theory further. Chu Yi-tsun (1629–1709) wrote,

> The zither has twenty-five strings, and when they are broken, they become fifty. Therefore the poet says, "for no reason," meaning the zither strings are broken for no reason. ["Broken strings" is a common Chinese expression for the death of one's wife.] Since each string reminds him of one year, this means she died at twenty-five. The butterfly and the cuckoo suggest that she has been transformed into other forms of life; the line about tears shed by pearls means that he weeps for her; the line about the jade means she is buried, as if one were to say "burying jade and entombing fragrance." ["Jade" and "fragrance" are conventional metaphors for beautiful ladies.]

Feng Hao, in his edition of Li Shang-yin's poetry, elaborated the theory further. According to him, fifty strings and fifty bridges make a hundred, therefore the second line means that the poet had wished that he and his wife could live together until old age. (It is a common

[1] Cf. above, pt. I, 3.

expression in Chinese to wish a couple to live happily together till they are a hundred years old.) The third line, Feng suggests, by referring to Chuang Tzu's dream of the butterfly, indirectly alludes to another story about this philosopher—the one about his beating an earthen pot and singing at the death of his wife; and line 4 refers to the poet's living in Shu (Szechwan), where Emperor Wang ruled. The next couplet he takes to refer to the poet's wife's beauty: the pearls describe her eyes, and the jade describes her complexion. Feng then quotes the story about Jade, the daughter of the King of Wu, without explaining how this fits the present context, and dismisses as irrelevant the remark about poetry attributed to Tai Shu-lun. On the last couplet, Feng comments that this means the poet already felt bewildered, as if in a dream, at the time of his marriage, since he had not expected to marry such a beauty. In modern times, Meng Sen published an article in 1926 to prove that the poem was written to lament Li's wife and that both the poet and his wife were in their twenty-fifth year when they married; hence the first line. Liu P'an-sui wrote an article in 1937, in which he reaffirmed this theory and took up Chu Ho-ling's suggestion that in the first line, for "fifty," we should read "fifteen," since there was once a fifteen-stringed zither, and since the poet and his wife had been married fifteen years when she died. He further argued that the allusions to pearls and jade should be regarded as references to the poet's children who had died.

Theory IV: That the poem laments the poet's misfortunes in life. Ho Cho (1661–1722) remarked that this poem expressed self-pity allegorically, although later he seems to have changed his mind and adopted the third theory. However, his remark has been taken up and developed by modern scholars. Chang Ts'ai-t'ien analyzed the poem as follows. The first couplet means that the poet realizes he is approaching fifty; the allusion to Chuang Tzu's dream of the butterfly in line 3 refers to changes in the contemporary world; line 4 shows the futility of writing; line 5 alludes to Li Te-yü, who was banished to Ya-chou, also called Chu-ya ("Pearl Cliff"), and died there; line 6 refers to Ling-hu T'ao, whose career is flourishing like jade in the sun, and who can be watched from a distance but cannot be approached; the final couplet means that the poet's fate is lamentable, and he realizes now that he was misled by others, as if lost in a fog.

Theory V: That the poem is an introduction to Li Shang-yin's collected poems. This was suggested by Ho Cho's friend Ch'eng Hsiang-heng, according to whom the second couplet expresses the poet's intention in writing and the third describes his poetic skill. Ho says that he was at first attracted by the originality of this theory but discarded it for lack of evidence.

Some scholars appear to combine two or three of the theories mentioned above. For instance, Hsü Yi (*fl.* 1111–23) combined Theories I and II when he said that a maid of Ling-hu Ch'u's could play the four

kinds of music mentioned in Theory II. Chang Chen-p'ei, in an article
published in 1933, interprets the poem mainly as a lament over the
poet's past but also refers to Li's mourning for his wife, thus combining
Theories III and IV. Similarly, Chu Hsieh, in his article published in
1937, states that the poem is "partly self-lament, partly lament for the
dead, and partly sighing over the past;" and Mr. Hsü Fu-kuan, in his
booklet *Huan-jao Li Yi-shan chin-se-shih ti chu wen-t'i* ("Problems
around Li Shang-yin's *chin-se* poem," 1963), sees the poem as a recollection of the poet's wife as well as an expression of his disappointments in
life. Mr. Ku Yi-ch'ün also seems to combine Theories III and IV: he
takes it to be not only an expression of the poet's sadness over his past
but also a dirge for the deaths of his wife (in the line about the jade), his
former patrons (whom the poet cries over like the tearful mermaid in
the story), his little niece, who Mr. Ku suspects is the poet's illegitimate
daughter,[2] and the girl named Willow Branch, with whom the poet
said he did not have a love affair, although Mr. Ku believes the contrary.[3] It may further be mentioned that Wang P'i-chiang, in an
article written in 1943 and published in 1962, combines Theories IV
and V by saying that the poem reviews the poet's past life and also
describes his own poetic excellence. Finally, Sung Hsiang-feng (1776–
1860) regarded the poem as a preface to the poet's works as well as a
self-lament and a dirge for his wife, thus combining Theories III, IV,
and V.

It seems to me that none of the above-mentioned theories is completely satisfactory. Theory IA, that "Ornamented Zither" was a
woman's name, is groundless gossip. Assuming for a moment that this
was indeed the case, what are we to make of the first two lines? Would
it not mean that the woman was fifty, if not a hundred? Theory IB,
that the poem is about an unidentified woman, is too vague and does
not explain the details of the poem. IC, that the poem mourns the death
of the two court entertainers Fei-luan and Ch'ing-feng, is not supported by indubitable proof. Besides, it would be strange for the poet
to compare the two girls to Emperor Wang, who died of shame and
not of fear, and who was a man. It also seems strange that the poet does
not allude to phoenixes, since the names of both girls contain the word
"phoenix" (*luan* and *feng* are two different species of the "phoenix").

Theory II, that the poem describes four kinds of music, does not fit
the actual words. How can we take the four middle lines as descriptions of music? And what has the last couplet to do with music?

Theory III, that the poem laments the death of Li's wife, has a
formidable list of learned supporters, but it is not free from loopholes.
First of all, although the two kinds of zither, *ch'in* and *se*, symbolize
conjugal concord, the poet does not mention them both, only the
latter, so that we cannot be sure he has conjugal love in mind. As for
the number of strings, since, in the story about the goddess, The White

[2] See Additional Note 7.
[3] *Ibid.* and Poems 60–64.

Maid, the fifty-stringed zither was broken into two halves of twenty-five strings each (presumably by splitting it lengthwise and not cross-wise), we cannot accept Chu Yi-tsun's theory that the fifty strings are formed by breaking the twenty-five, which is the exact reverse of what happened in the original story. The same commentator's suggestion that Li's wife died at twenty-five is absurd, for this would make her ten years old at the time of their marriage. The suggestion that we should emend "fifty" to read "fifteen" is no more acceptable, since in another poem Li Shang-yin mentions fifty strings on the zither (Poem 42), and there is no reason to think that he means fifteen here. As for Meng Sen's theory that the poet and his wife were both in their twenty-fifth year (25 *sui*) at the time of marriage, this does not agree with the chronology of Li's life, whether we accept Feng Hao's dating of Li's birth (813) or Chang Ts'ai-t'ien's (812); according to the former, Li would be twenty-five by Western reckoning but twenty-six *sui* by Chinese reckoning when he married in 838, and according to the latter, he would be twenty-seven *sui*. Even if we accept, for the sake of argument, the theory that Li was twenty-five then, it is unlikely that his wife was of the same age, for traditionally in China the bride is younger than the bridegroom. Finally, it is an interesting idea that, because fifty strings and fifty bridges make a hundred, the first couplet alludes to the common expression "to live in concord until a hundred years old," but it is equally plausible to take this as an allusion to the saying that "human life is at most a hundred years," in other words, as a reference to life in general rather than to married life in particular. With regard to the suggestion that line 2 alludes to Chuang Tzu's beating of the earthen pot at the time of his wife's death, one may point out that Chuang Tzu's beating the pot is not at all the same thing as Chuang Tzu's dreaming of being a butterfly! The whole point of the former story is that the philosopher did *not* mourn his wife's death, thereby indicating that he was above human emotions; surely it would be a strange way to mourn one's wife to allude to this story? And to take the butterfly and the cuckoo as symbols of transmigration seems inappropriate for a woman, let along the fact that they evoke irrelevant associations, which a careful poet like Li Shang-yin would have avoided had he in-tended the poem to be a lament for his wife. Next, if line 5 refers to her eyes, why should they be in tears? The line suggests a tearful parting in life rather than separation by death. Similarly, if line 6 refers to her complexion, why should the jade be in smoke? To me, the line suggests someone unattainable, vaguely seen from a distance—which is not the way one would describe one's own wife. If the story about the daughter of the King of Wu is relevant, it again suggests an un-fulfilled love, not marriage. As for the theory that pearls and jade allude to the poet's children who died, this is doubtful. We know that in 853, five years before the poet's death, his children were still alive, and there is no evidence that they died in his lifetime. Assuming this was so, it is not they who should be shedding tears, but the surviving father. Finally, if the poem mourns the poet's wife, why should he say, "this feeling *might have become* a thing to be remembered"?

Regarding Theory IV, that the poem laments the poet's own misfortunes, I think it is true that the poem contains a note of disappointment and sadness, but it is going too far to see hidden references to actual persons. Can we seriously believe that the word "pearls" refers to Li Te-yü because he died at Pearl Cliff, or that "jade" alludes to Ling-hu T'ao, who was inaccessible?

Theory V, that the poem is an introduction to Li's collected works, I find the most interesting. The zither may indeed be a fitting symbol of the poet's works, but there is no evidence that he placed this poem at the beginning of his collected poems. In fact, although Li Shang-yin edited two collections of his prose, we do not know whether he ever edited his poetry. Besides, this theory is somewhat too narrow in conception and cannot fully explain the whole poem.

Rather than accepting any of the above theories, I feel that it would be better to interpret the poem in more general terms. I am glad that I am not alone in this feeling. Professors Ch'en Shih-hsiang and Lao Kan also rejected the various attempts to pin the poem down to a particular person or event, although their interpretations naturally differ from each other and from mine in emphasis. Professor Ch'en sees the poem as an expression of "cosmic sorrow", whereas Professor Lao stresses the use of the zither as a symbol of the poet's works, thus showing some affinity with Theory V. My own reading, which might be regarded as complementary and supplementary to Professor Ch'en's and Professor Lao's without invalidating either, is as follows:

I propose to take the poem as a variation on the common theme that life is a dream. The poet meditates on the apparently unreal nature of life in general and of love in particular. Why, he asks, should the zither have fifty strings and fifty bridges, and why should a man have a number of years, say at most a hundred, to live? Just as the zither, for no reason, is given fifty strings, on which all kinds of music can be played, so is the poet, for no reason, given a number of years to live, to which Fate has attached a variety of experiences and from which it has elicited various kinds of poetry in response. When one recalls the past, who can tell what is real and what is unreal? Which is real: Chuang Tzu or the butterfly? Emperor Wang or the cuckoo? What has been or what might have been? This life or life after death? And the women one has loved, or imagines to have loved, whether they have parted from one in tears, or died and vanished like smoke, or remained out of reach like jade lying in a warm haze—are they real or unreal? Did one really love them or only dream of doing so? (Alternatively, when the poet realizes that his talents are unappreciated, he feels like an undetected pearl, which might be imagined to shed tears; and in vain has he achieved in his verse a poetic world as mysterious and inaccessible as jade in the misty air.) All these experiences of the past might have become memories to be cherished; only, even at the time they occurred, one was already bewildered and could not be sure they were real.

Taken in this way, the poem seems to gain in significance. This reading does not exclude remembrance of the poet's wife or anyone else, nor does it rule out meditation on his past life and his poetry. Written probably toward the end of Li Shang-yin's life, the poem shows him looking back on his whole life. As he sees the past years extending in a row like the strings of the zither, he feels they are all like a dream. All his loves and sufferings, his hopes and disappointments, are gone like music played on the zither, and only the strings remain— these are his poems. We share his meditation, his wistful recollection of the past, and his puzzlement, and we ask with him at the end of the poem, as we do with Keats at the end of the *Ode to a Nightingale:*

> Was it a vision or a waking dream?
> Fled is that music: do I wake or sleep?

Such, in outline, is my interpretation of this poem. I shall return to it and analyze its structure more fully in Part III, 2.

POEMS **2-3**

Peonies Damaged by Rain at Hui-chung

2   The bygone years at the Lower Park cannot be retrieved.

Today, in the western county, we suddenly meet again.

In the pavilion by the water, amidst evening rain, the chill remains;

On the silk mat, full of spring fragrance, warmth is unknown.

The dancing butterflies busily gather the scattered pollen;

A beautiful lady lies sadly behind a distant curtain.

"Let me ask my sweet companions in the streets by the Chang Terrace:

"How many branches, like Court ladies' waists, have been damaged?"

NOTES

Title   Hui-chung was the site of an ancient palace near Ching-chou, where the poet stayed in 838 and where his father-in-law was military governor.

Line 1   Lower Park. Hsia-yüan, former name of that part of the capital where the Meandering Stream (Ch'ü-chiang) was located.

Line 2   Western county. Ching-chou, in northwestern China.

Lines 5–6   For variant readings, see Additional Note 9.

Line 7   Chang Terrace. In Ch'ang-an, associated with willows and a singing girl named Willow. (See Liu, *The Art of Chinese Poetry*, pp. 111–12.)

COMMENTARY

This poem, as well as the next one, can be interpreted on several different levels. In the opening couplet, the poet regrets that the past years in the capital cannot be retrieved, but is glad to see the peonies here, as if meeting an old friend in a strange land. Lines 3 and 4 emphasize the cold weather (which may also symbolize uncongenial environment), and hint that the flowers are ravaged by such harsh climate. The silk mat (*chien*) in line 4 probably describes the grass metaphorically, and since the word *chien* refers to a sleeping mat, this metaphor (perhaps by unconscious association on the part of the poet) foreshadows the sleeping beauty mentioned in line 6. The butterflies gathering the scattered pollen in line 5 may be said to be "making hay while the sun shines": apprehensive of impending doom, they are determined to enjoy the peonies' fragrance to the last minute and to imbibe the last drop of beauty. The lady in line 6 may be taken metaphorically to represent the flowers or literally as a real person filled with sadness at the sight of the damaged flowers.[1] In the last couplet, the peonies ask their distant companions, the willows in the streets of Ch'ang-an: "How many of your branches, as slender as Court ladies' waists, have been ravaged by wind and rain?" Since the peonies here have been damaged by rain, they imagine the willows in the capital to have suffered a similar fate.

So far we have considered the poem on the literal level, as a poem about peonies. On another level, the poem may be regarded as a lament for a beautiful lady or ladies, and what is said of the flowers may also apply to a beauty whose youth is passing and whose charms are not appreciated. On yet another level, we may take the poem as an expression of the poet's regret that time is passing and his talents are being wasted in a region far from the Court, although we need not go so far as Chang Ts'ai-t'ien, who thinks that these poems show Li's disappointment at having failed the Grand Rhetoric examination and his regret at having incurred Ling-hu T'ao's displeasure by his marriage.

---

[1] For a different interpretation of lines 5–6 based on variant readings, see Additional Note 9.

3   *Laugh as you may at the pomegranate that blooms too late for
       spring;*

      To fade and fall before your time is even greater cause for grief.

      Tears sprinkled on jade plates repeatedly hurt one's heart;

      *Startled strings on the ornamented zither frequently break one's
       dreams.*

      Ten thousand miles of gloom—unlike the old garden;

      A whole year's life—gone with the drifting dust!

      After the Dance of the Front Brook, when you look back,

      You will feel the powdery beauty of today to be fresh still.

NOTES

Line 7   Dance of the Front Brook. An ancient dance tune, the words of
            which run to the effect that a flower by the brook will fall and float
            away and that even if it could ever come back it would no longer be
            fresh. Also, the Front Brook Village (Ch'ien-hsi Ts'un) was famous
            as a place for training dancing girls.

COMMENTARY

        The first line is grammatically ambiguous: the words that I
have translated as "laugh as you may," in the original literally read,
"recklessly laugh" (*lang hsiao*), and the subject is not identified. We
may take the line to be addressed to the peonies, or to the poet himself,
or to the reader, and paraphrase the first two lines together thus: "You
may laugh [or, one may laugh] at the pomegranate that blooms after
spring is over and misses the best part of the year, but you, the peony,
who blossom early and wither early, and what is more, are so damaged
by the rain that you will fall before your time, are even more to be
pitied." Further, the first line may contain an allusion to the following
episode. When the founder of the T'ang dynasty, Kao-tsu, ascended
the throne, K'ung Shao-an, an official who had served the previous Sui
dynasty, came to offer his services, but because he had been anticipated
by another man, he was given a post of merely secondary importance.
Later, at a Court banquet, when he was ordered by the Emperor to
write a poem on pomegranate blossoms, K'ung took the opportunity
to show his discontent by writing these lines:

        It is only because it came too late
        That its blossoms were not in time for Spring.

How this allusion would affect the interpretation of the poem we will
consider later. Meanwhile, let us proceed to the next couplet. Here the
imagery is both complicated and striking. The raindrops on the

peonies are compared to tears on jade plates, and the sound of the rain beating on the flowers is likened to zither (*se*) strings being abruptly plucked. Furthermore, these two images may be associated with two allusions. The image of tears on jade plates reminds one of the story about the mermaid whose tears turned into pearls on a jade plate. (See Part I, 4.) Thus, through this literary association, the raindrops are compared implicitly to pearls as well as to tears. The image of the zither strings may be associated with the Spirit of River Hsiang, who is said to play this instrument. According to legend, the two daughters of the sage Emperor Yao were both married to Emperor Shun, and when their husband died, the two sisters drowned themselves in the river Hsiang and became the goddesses of this river. Thus the "Spirit of River Hsiang" could refer to either of the two goddesses. Since in another poem (Poem 42) Li Shang-yin writes, "The rain beats on the fifty strings of the Spirit of River Hsiang," it is certainly not too fanciful to see an association between the comparison of the sound of the rain to that of the zither strings and this legend. Line 5 contrasts the gloomy surroundings of the present with the old garden from which the peonies have presumably been transplanted, and line 6 laments the passing away of time. In line 7 the poet develops the idea in the ancient song, "Dance of the Front Brook," in a different direction, by saying that after the peony has finished its dance in the wind and withered away completely, one will realize in retrospect that its beauty now, though damaged, is still fresh and worth watching. The word that I have translated as "you" is in fact ambiguous: in Chinese the word is *chün*, which can be used as a polite form of the second person pronoun or as a noun meaning "lord" or "sovereign". If we take it as a pronoun, it is still a little ambiguous, for it could be identified with the peony, or with the poet himself, or with some would-be interlocutor, although in each case the meaning would remain largely the same: "In the future, when you recall the present, you will realize that the peony's beauty [or, your beauty, if the words are addressed to the peony] is still fresh." If we take the word *chün* to mean "sovereign," then the peony would seem to be compared to a Court lady, with a pun on the words "powdery beauty," which in Chinese are the same as words that are used for "powdered beauty," and the poet would seem to be pleading on behalf of this metaphorical lady to the Emperor: "Favor her while her beauty still remains: otherwise, in retrospect, you may regret what you have missed." Like the preceding poem, the present one can also be taken on several levels. The ambiguity in the last two lines makes it possible to take the poem as a lament for a beautiful lady or ladies, though it is very doubtful if the jade plate and the zither refer to actual gifts the poet exchanged with the two Court entertainers Fei-luan and Ch'ing-feng, as Miss Su Hsüeh-lin suggested. Again, like the first poem, this one too can be taken as an expression of the poet's disappointment in life, and the peony can be regarded as a symbol of his frustrated genius. Taken on this level, the first couplet, with its possible allusion to the story about K'ung Shao-an, may be roughly paraphrased thus: "You may laugh at someone else who arrived too late on the scene and missed the boat, but what about yourself, who showed early promise but are now aging before your time?" The next two lines could either allude to unhappy love, through associations with tearful mermaids and tragic goddesses, or express sadness at the poet's own failure in life. Lines 5 and 6 bring out the contrast between the poet's present environment far from the capital and the good old days in the imperial city, while lamenting the passing of another wasted year. The concluding couplet pathetically expresses the wish that the Emperor, or the poet's patron, may yet relent and show some appreciation of his talents before it is too late. To sum up: it is not necessary to say dogmatically which of the three interpretations of these two poems is the correct one; all three are possible meanings, of varying degrees of consciousness in the poet's mind, perhaps. He may have been genuinely moved by the sight of peonies damaged by rain, and he could then have been reminded by this of his own unhappy life, and possibly also of some ill-fated beauty or beauties. Whatever made him write these poems, their effect is to make us sense the tragic waste of something precious and feel the pity of it all. The peony becomes for us a fused symbol of ravaged beauty (natural or human), wasted youth, and frustrated genius, just as in Guillaume Apollinaire's lines:

> O ma jeunesse abandonnée
> Comme une guirlande fanée

the faded garland becomes a symbol of all wasted youth, not merely of the poet's own. We may also compare these two poems with Thomas Moore's *Last Rose of Summer*, and note that, whereas the English poem is explicit and somewhat naïve and sentimental, the Chinese ones are oblique and sophisticated.

POEMS **4-5**

Without Title

4   *"Coming" is an empty word; going, you leave no trace.*

The moonlight slants over the roof; the bells strike the fifth watch.

Dreaming of long separation, I can hardly summon my cries;

Hurried into writing a letter, I cannot wait for the ink to thicken.

The candle's light half encircles the golden kingfishers;

The musk perfume subtly permeates the embroidered lotus flowers.

Young Liu already resented the distance of the P'eng Mountain:

Now ten thousand more P'eng Mountains rise!

NOTES

This is the first of four poems without titles given together in Li's collected poems, but I shall give only the first two, as the other two do not seem to be thematically related to these.

Line 2   Fifth watch. The night was divided into five watches, and "fifth watch" means dawn.

Line 4   Wait for the ink to thicken. The traditional way of preparing ink in China is to rub an ink-stick with water on an ink-slab, so that it takes some time for the ink to reach the desired degree of thickness.

Line 5   Golden kingfishers. Kingfishers' feathers mixed with gold to decorate the quilt. Chiang Yen (443–504) in his *Kingfishers* (*Fei-ts'ui Fu*) wrote, "Mix them with purple gold to form beautiful colors." (I am indebted to Professor Chow Tse-tsung for calling my attention to this quotation.)

Line 7   Young Liu. Probably Liu Ch'e, Emperor Wu of Han (157 B.C.–87 B.C.) P'eng Mountain. Also called P'eng-lai, fairy mountain in Taoist mythology. For further discussions on these two allusions, see commentary below.

COMMENTARY

These poems have been interpreted allegorically, but I prefer to take them as love poems, though not necessarily autobiographical ones. The speaker could be a man or a woman; on the whole, it seems to make better sense if we assume the former. Next, let us reconstruct a dramatic situation in the light of which the poems can yield a coherent meaning. In the first poem, let us imagine that the lover has waited all night for his beloved, who has failed to come. He now complains, "You said you would come, but this proved an empty word; and once you are gone, you leave no trace behind." Then (line 2) he sees the fading moonlight on the roof and hears the bells striking the fifth watch, announcing the arrival of dawn. Line 3 contains the highly ambiguous words, *t'i nan huan* (literally, "cry hard to call"). The word *huan* can mean "to summon" or "to call," and the three words together may mean, "I want to cry but can hardly summon any voice [that is, can hardly utter a cry]," or "I cry but find it hard to call you [that is, you will not answer my call]," or perhaps "I cry and can hardly be called up [aroused from my dream]." I have chosen the first possibility in the translation. Line 4 seems to imply the presence of someone else, who urges the speaker to write a letter in haste. This person cannot be the speaker's beloved, since she has not come. I suggest that this may be a messenger from the lady, and that he (or she) has brought a letter from her and asks for a letter in reply to be taken back in a hurry. After the messenger has gone, the speaker looks wistfully at the light of the candle, which half encompasses the kingfishers' feathers mixed with gold on the quilt, and smells the perfume, which has gradually penetrated the embroidered bed-curtain: all these elaborate preparations have been in vain! The allusions in the next couplet require further discussion. Some scholars take "young Liu" (*Liu lang*) not as an allusion to Emperor Wu of Han but as one to Liu Ch'en, who, in a story, had a love affair with a goddess but later failed to find his way back to fairyland, where he had met her. There are several reasons, however, for preferring to think that Emperor Wu is meant here. First, in the story about Liu Ch'en, the fairyland he visits is called T'ien-t'ai Mountain, not P'eng Mountain. Second, the poet Li Ho, who had considerable influence on Li Shang-yin, used the phrase "young Liu" in referring to Emperor Wu. Further, Li Shang-yin himself refers to Emperor Wu in other poems concerned with secret love affairs (for example, Poem 23). Finally, the story about Emperor Wu and Lady Li, one of his favorites, as told in *Anecdotes about Emperor Wu of Han* (*Han Wu ku-shih*), contains some details similar to those in the present poem: when Lady Li died, the Emperor missed her greatly and lamented her death. Li Shao-weng, a Taoist magician, said, "I can summon her spirit." Thereupon he set up a *curtain* and brightly lit *candles*, and prepared food and wine. He told the Emperor to sit behind another curtain, whence the Emperor could see Lady Li's spirit but could not get close to her. Later, Li Shao-weng was executed when his prayers did not produce any effect, but came back to life and said to one of the Emperor's messengers, "Tell His Majesty to look for me forty years hence at the *P'eng Mountain*."[1] In view of this story, and the fact that Li Shang-yin wrote several poems

---

[1] Once more I am indebted to Professor Chow Tse-tsung for calling my attention to this story.

on Lady Li, it is quite possible that he had Emperor Wu and Lady Li in mind. In that case, the heroine of the poem might be a palace lady, but we need not press the analogy too far, since there is no hint in the poem that the speaker's beloved is dead. Indeed, the last line seems to suggest that the lady is leaving for some distant place, so that the lover complains, "I already resented your being inaccessible; now you are ten thousand times more inaccessible!" If this is so, we may go back to the first line and see more meaning in it: the line would now seem to mean, "Not only have you failed to come as you promised, but you are going away, and I shall not be able to trace your movements."

---

5   *The east wind soughs and sighs as a fine drizzle falls;*

    Beyond the lotus pond there is the noise of a light thunder.

    The golden toad bites the lock through which the burnt incense enters;

    The jade tiger pulls the silk rope while turning above the well.

    Lady Chia peeped through the curtain at young Secretary Han;

    Princess Fu left a pillow to the gifted Prince of Wei.

    Do not let the amorous heart vie with the flowers in burgeoning:

    One inch of longing, one inch of ashes!

NOTES

Line 2   Thunder. This possibly alludes to *The Long Gate (Ch'ang-men Fu)* by Ssu-ma Hsiang-ju (179–117 B.C.), written on behalf of Empress Ch'en while she was living at the Palace of Long Gate after losing Emperor Wu's favor. In this piece of rhymed prose, the sound of the imperial carriage is compared to thunder. Cf. Poem 19, line 4.

Line 3   Golden toad. One explanation is that the toad was said to be good at holding its breath, and therefore locks were decorated with the toad motif to signify secrecy. Another explanation is that "golden toad" refers to a censer and "lock" refers to its knob.

Line 4   Jade tiger. Decorated pulley above a well.

Line 5   Lady Chia. Daughter of Chia Ch'ung (A.D. 217–82), prime minister of the Chin dynasty. She peeped through the curtain at her father's handsome young secretary Han Shou, and had a love affair with him. The affair was discovered by Chia Ch'ung when he smelt on Han's clothes a rare imported perfume which he himself had given his daughter. Thereupon the young lovers were allowed to be married.

Line 6   Princess Fu. Goddess of the River Lo. Legend has it that Ts'ao Chih (192–232), famous poet and prince of the Wei dynasty, was in love with a lady of the Chen family but was unable to marry her. She became instead the wife of his elder brother Ts'ao P'i, first Emperor of Wei. After her death the Emperor gave her pillow to Ts'ao Chih.

When Chih left the capital and reached the river Lo, he saw Empress Chen in a vision, in which their love was fulfilled. He then wrote his famous *Goddess of the River Lo* (*Lo Shen Fu*). This legend has been discredited by modern scholars as biography but is often alluded to in traditional literature.

Line 8   The heart is sometimes referred to as "square inch" (*fang ts'un*); the expression "ash-hearted" (*hui-hsin*) means despair.

COMMENTARY

The opening couplet recalls the scene of a secret rendezvous: "Amidst wind and rain, we met by a lotus pond, beyond which a light thunder sounded." Bearing in mind the possible allusion to *The Long Gate*, we may take the thunder as an indirect reference to the imperial carriage, in which case the scene would seem to be set in the palace and the woman involved would appear to be a Court lady risking grave dangers in coming to meet her lover. Even if we take the thunder literally, it still adds to the already menacing atmosphere created by the wind and rain, and emphasizes the desperate passion of the lovers by contrasting it with the harsh natural environment. The next two lines are puzzling, and I can only offer tentative interpretations. If we take "golden toad" to mean a lock on the door, line 3 would seem to mean that the woman is closely guarded, behind locked doors, in a secluded chamber where incense burns. Or perhaps the burnt incense that enters through the locked door represents messages that have managed to get through to her, despite locked doors. If we take "golden toad" to mean a censer, the line might mean, "The golden toad holds in the incense, just as the chamber keeps the woman in." In the next line, the jade tiger might represent a messenger commuting between the lovers: just as the pulley pulls the rope to fetch water from the deep well, so the messenger brings news of her from the deep recesses of her abode. In the following couplet, by alluding to Lady Chia's affair with Han Shou and Princess Fu's with Ts'ao Chih, the speaker is either drawing an analogy or pointing at a contrast: either he is saying, "You have shown your favor to me, as Lady Chia did to Han Shou and Princess Fu did to Ts'ao Chih," or he is saying, "I am not as handsome as Han, nor am I as gifted as Ts'ao: how can I hope to win your love?" In the last couplet, the lover apparently warns himself not to let his heart blossom forth with love, for he knows only too well what suffering this will bring, yet we sense that he cannot really help it. Such is the intensity of his passion that he cannot stop his longing but can only watch his heart being consumed by his unfulfilled desire until it turns to the ashes of despair.

POEM 6

Without Title

It is hard for us to meet and also hard to part;

The east wind is powerless as all the flowers wither.

The spring silkworm's thread will only end when death comes;

The candle will not dry its tears until it turns to ashes.

Before the morning mirror, she only grieves that her dark hair may change;

Reciting poems by night, would she not feel the moonlight's chill?

The P'eng Mountain lies not far away;

O Blue Bird, visit her for me with diligence!

NOTES

Line 7   P'eng Mountain. See Poem 4, line 7.

Line 8   Blue Bird. A messenger of the goddess Queen Mother of the West (Hsi Wang Mu). Cf. Poem 26, line 5.

COMMENTARY

Contrary to those commentators who take the poem as a veiled appeal to Ling-hu T'ao, I take it as an expression of love for a woman who lives within easy reach but with whom the poet cannot openly communicate. In the first line, the word "hard" (*nan*) is used in two slightly different senses: not only is it hard (difficult) for the lovers to meet, but once having met they find it hard (unbearable) to part. It is possible that the line has an additional meaning—that one of them is going away, and it is hard for them even to contrive to meet and say farewell to each other. In the second line, the powerless wind probably represents the poet, and the flowers represent his beloved: he is as powerless to prevent her youth and beauty from passing away as the wind is to stop the flowers from withering. At the same time, these images also serve the more immediate purpose of describing the actual scenery and indicating the season. In the next two lines, two more images are introduced. Just as the silkworm imprisons itself in the cocoon formed by its own endless silk, so does the poet enwrap himself in the endless sorrow of his own making, and just as the candle is consumed by its own heat, so is the poet by his own passion. These images are further enriched by auditory associations. In line 3, the word for "thread" (*ssu*, or *si*, as in T'ang pronunciation) is a pun on the word for "thinking" or "longing," and both the image and the pun seem to have been derived from one of the anonymous love songs known as "Midnight Songs" (*Tzu-yeh Ko*):[1]

> The spring silkworm is easily moved to change;
> Its silk-thread once more grows;

where "silk-thread" (*ssu-tzu*) forms a pun on "thinking of you" or "longing for you." We may also associate the word "thread" with the compounds "love-thread" (*ch'ing-ssu*), meaning "endless love," and "sorrow-thread" (*ch'ou-ssu*), meaning "endless sorrow," with a pun on "sorrowful thoughts." In line 4, the word for "ashes," *hui*, also means "gray," which adds to the gloomy atmosphere. The word may be further associated with the expression *hui-hsin* ("ash-hearted"), which, as I pointed out before, means despair. In the next couplet, the poet imagines how his beloved sits alone before the mirror in the morning, grieving that her beauty may fade away, or recites poetry at night, feeling lonely in the chilly moonlight. It is tempting to connect this picture of a woman alone in the moonlight with the lonely goddess of the moon (see Poems 28–35), and to accept Miss Su's theory that the poet's love was a Taoist nun. However, this is neither demonstrable nor important. What matters is that the poem has succeeded in embodying a frustrated passion through imagery, allusions, and verbal dexterity. There is nothing to prevent us from taking the justly famous images in lines 3 and 4 as universal symbols of heart-rending sorrow and hoping against hope, no matter how such feelings are induced.

---

[1] See Poem 43, line 2.

POEMS **7-10**

The Terrace of Yen

Spring

7   The light of spring gradually spreads over the roads, east and
     west;

     For several days her delicate soul has sought it, all to no avail.

     The winged visitor of the honeycombs is like her fragrant heart,

     Acquainted with all the wanton leaves and seductive twigs.

     The warm sun shines late west of the peach tree;

     Her tall topknot stands as high as the peaches' topknots.

     The male dragon and the female phoenix are gone—to what
     distant place?

     Heaven too is confused by the random catkins and numerous
     gossamers.

     She rises from a drunken sleep—the dim sun is like dawn;

[10]   Behind the sunlit curtain, a dream is broken, and fading words are
     heard.

     In sorrow she takes an iron net to enmesh the corals,

     But the sea is wide and the heavens are vast and she loses her
     bearings.

     Though the girdle has no feelings, it loosens or tightens;

     The spring mist is naturally gray, the autumn frost white.

     She grinds vermilion and breaks stones, but heaven is unaware:

     Would that she had a Heavenly Jail to lock up her wronged soul!

     Her lined gown is put away in a chest, replaced by thin silk;

     Her cool fragrant flesh sets off her tinkling pendants.

     Today, even the east wind cannot bear it any longer;

     It turns into a secret light and enters the western sea. [20]

NOTES

Title   The Terrace of Yen (Yen T'ai), also known as the Terrace of Gold
          (Huang-chin T'ai), was built by King Chao of Yen (reigned 312–

279 B.C.) to attract worthy men. For the possible significance of the
title, see commentary below.

Line 11   Iron net. It is said that in order to obtain corals one should first cast
an iron net into the sea, so that when the corals have grown in it,
they can be fetched up intact.

Line 15   This line alludes to the saying "Stones can be broken but their hardness cannot be removed; vermilion can be ground but its redness
cannot be removed."

Line 16   Heavenly Jail. Name of a constellation, but here apparently used in
the literal sense.

COMMENTARY

The title of this group of poems is puzzling. Chi Yün's idea
that the allusion to the Terrace of Yen, built by a famous patron of
worthy men, is an allegorical way of referring to one of the poet's
patrons, seems to me too farfetched. On the other hand, it is unlikely
that Yen T'ai is the name of a woman, as Chang Ts'ai-t'ien seems to
have taken it. Would the poet have given the game away so easily after
having couched the poems in highly obscure language? A third possibility is to regard the title as a clue to the geographical setting of the
poems, but here again difficulties are involved. The Terrace of Yen was
located near modern Peking, and as far as we know Li Shang-yin never
visited that part of the country. Besides, there are many references to
the south in these poems, which makes it even more improbable that
the scene is set in the north. Yet another explanation is offered by Feng
Hao: that the expression "Terrace of Yen" is a conventional way of
referring to a military governor, and that therefore the woman in the
poems must be a military governor's concubine. This might be true but
cannot be proved. It seems that the poet is being deliberately misleading, and perhaps we should regard the title as no more meaningful than
the label "Without Title," which Li Shang-yin is so fond of using.

Except for Chi Yün, most commentators agree that these are love
poems, although they differ in their interpretations of details in the
poems. On the whole, I agree with Professor Lao Kan that it is futile
and unnecessary to try to identify the woman involved, or to attach
much importance to the geographical references in the poems. However, it does seem to me desirable to analyze the poems closely, rather
than to rest content with a vague impression of rich imagery and
mysterious atmosphere.

The four poems, as Professor Lao aptly remarked, are like four movements of a musical composition and should be read as parts of a whole.
The first one, "Spring," presents the amorous longings of a woman in
this provocative season. As the light of spring (which often symbolizes
love in Chinese literature) spreads everywhere, the heroine pines for
love, but her soul fails to find it after a vain search (lines 1–2). In lines
3–4, the poet uses an inverted metaphor: instead of saying that the
heroine's heart is like a bee ("winged visitor of the honeycombs")

fluttering among flowers and leaves, he says the opposite. Further, "fragrant heart" (*fang hsin*) is a common expression for a beautiful woman's heart, but here the epithet is particularly appropriate since the heart is being compared to a bee gathering honey. The words "wanton" (*yeh*) and "seductive" (*ch'ang*, literally, "courtesan") in line 4 add to the erotic atmosphere, but I doubt if the whole line means, as Chang Ts'ai-t'ien suggested, "I have known all the courtesans but I have never seen this woman among them," for this would not follow the preceding line. It seems to me much better to take line 4 as continuing the metaphor introduced in line 3: her heart is like a bee that has visited all the enticing leaves and twigs of spring trees. Lines 5–6 picture her standing by a peach tree in the sun, the topknot of her hair as high as the peaches' "topknots" (probably tufts of budding leaves on top of the peach tree). Line 7 appears to mourn a bygone love, since the dragon and the phoenix (which, even without the adjectives "male" and "female," often represent man and woman) are gone and are nowhere to be found. In the next line, the random willow catkins and numerous floating gossamers, as they often do in Chinese poetry, suggest groundless, nameless, feelings of melancholy and ennui: they keep disturbing you and cannot be swept away, so much so that even heaven is confused by them. Lines 9–10 describe the woman getting up from an intoxicated sleep and seeing the dim light of the setting sun, which she mistakes for the light of dawn, for she is still half dreaming and talking (or listening) to her lover, who has appeared to her in her dream. The image of the iron net in the next line might be taken as another metaphor for her vain attempt to capture love: she has sunk her whole being into love, as the iron net is sunk into the sea, but she has failed to keep her precious loot and now feels bewildered and lost, as if alone on the wide, wide sea under an immense sky. The next two lines might be paraphrased, "Though the girdle is not sentient, it loosens or tightens as she loses or gains weight according to her moods, which change from time to time just as the seasons change." Or, if we wish to go deeper into these lines, we might interpret them as meaning, "It is as natural and inevitable for her to pine in sorrow for love and grow thin as it is for the girdle to loosen or tighten according to her changing waistline, for the spring mist to be gray, and for the autumn frost to be white"; in other words, everyone is doomed by his own nature, and there is no escape. Lines 15–16 reveal the strength of her love, which remains as unchangeable as the redness of vermilion or the hardness of stone; but alas, who knows? Not even heaven! In desperation she wishes for a "Heavenly Jail" in which to imprison her soul with its grievance for ever. Lines 17–18 indicate that spring is passing and summer is approaching, thus subtly preparing for the next poem, "Summer." This is further emphasized by the disappearance of the east wind, one of the signs of spring, in the last couplet; and the final lines also suggest that, unlike the wind, which flees to the sea when it is unable to bear its sorrow any longer, our heroine, being mortal, has no such means of escape.

Summer

8   *In the front room, the sorrow-laden curtain is not rolled up in
    the rain;*

    By the back hall, the frargant trees spread their dark, dark shades.

    The view in the Rocky City is like the Yellow Springs;

    *At midnight, the roaming youth in vain carries a crossbow of
    thorny wood.*

    The silk fan calls down winds from the gates of heaven:

    On the light curtains and green screens whirlpools rise.

    Has the lonely soul of the bird of Shu found a companion yet?

    *For several nights miasma-flowers have blossomed on the kapok
    tree.*

    *The Cassia Palace casts fleeting shadows; its light is hard to
    catch.*

[10] *Her sweet breath is like the orchid as she whispers soft words.*

    Would that the Silver River could fall into my bosom!

    But the Stellar Lady has not been sent to guard our meetings.

    *Why should the muddy river and the clear flow have different
    sources?*

    The Chi's water is clear but the Yellow River's is murky.

    How could I call up a thin mist around her light-yellow skirt,

    *That I might touch the cloud-awning of her carriage, calling
    "My Lady"?*

NOTES

Line 3   Rocky City. Shih-ch'eng, alluding to an anonymous ancient song
         about a girl called Sans Souci (Mo-ch'ou, literally, "Don't Worry"):
             Where does Sans Souci live?
             She lives west of the Rocky City.
             A light boat rowed by two oars
             Brings Sans Souci here fast.
         Another song, by Emperor Wu of Liang (reigned 502–49), also
         mentions a beautiful girl so named, who married into the rich Lu
         family but is unhappy for she regrets not having married a young
         man next door. (Cf. Poems 18, 92, 95.)

Yellow Springs. Huang-ch'üan, conventional phrase for the nether world.

Line 4   Crossbow of thorny wood. In Han times, many young men used crossbows of thorny wood to shoot birds.

Line 7   Bird of Shu. The cuckoo. See Poem 1, line 4.

Line 9   Cassia Palace. The moon. See Poems 29, 32.

Line 11   Silver River. The Milky Way. See Poems 28, 37, 39, 40.

Line 12   Stellar Lady. The Weaving Maid. See Poems 38–41.

COMMENTARY

The second poem seems to be written from the point of view of the man in love with the heroine of the first poem. I agree with Chang Ts'ai-t'ien that the speaker is imagining what his beloved is doing and not recalling an actual rendezvous, as Feng Hao and Professor Lao Kan think. The first four lines paint a gloomy night scene: the rain is falling, the lady sits alone in sorrow in her room, the whole atmosphere is like the kingdom of Death, and the lover feels as frustrated as a young dandy carrying a crossbow might feel when he finds he has no use for it at night. The mention of Rocky City is probably intended to suggest that the heroine is as beautiful as the girl Sans Souci in the ancient song, rather than as a geographical hint. (Chang Ts'ai-t'ien confused this Rocky City or Shih-ch'eng with Shih-t'ou-ch'eng, another name for Nanking, and concluded that the poet's beloved had been taken away to Nanking.) Lines 5–6 describe her fanning herself (thus indirectly suggesting the heat of summer) and the winds from heaven stirring the curtains and screens so that wrinkles like whirlpools rise on them. The speaker then asks if his beloved, like the lonely soul of the love-sick cuckoo, has found a new companion. The "miasma-flowers" on the kapok tree in the next line are rather strange; perhaps they are meant to indicate the climate of South China and add to the summery feeling. In line 9, the moon ("Cassia Palace") whose light is hard to catch may be taken as a symbol of elusive love, or it may represent the woman herself. Line 10 envisages her as whispering under the moon. Lines 11–12 I interpret as follows: "I wish she could fall into my bosom, but this is as impossible as it would be for the Milky Way to fall into my bosom; nor is there any kind deity to allow us to meet, as the Stellar Lady is allowed to meet her lover once a year across the Milky Way." (This is only a tentative interpretation, but it seems better than Chang's, that someone else has taken possession of the woman, or Feng's, that the speaker wishes to keep her in his bosom till autumn.) Lines 13–14 complain that the lover and his beloved are as different as the river Chi (which is clear) from the Yellow River (which is muddy) and therefore can never be happily united. This could mean that they belong to different social classes, or that they lived in two different worlds, but in any case there is an insurmountable barrier between them. In the last couplet the lover wishes he could conjure up a magic mist which would bring the lady to him, so that he could touch her carriage and speak to her. The expression that I have rendered as "My Lady" is *T'ai-chün*, which some take to refer to a goddess, though Professor Lao thinks it means the heroine's mother. I prefer to take the former explanation and regard the speaker as comparing the heroine to a goddess coming to him in a canopied carriage amidst clouds and mists.

Autumn

9   *The moon's waves dash across heaven; heaven's mansion is wet.*

When the cold moon has completely set, the widely scattered stars sink.

The cloud-screen stands still, sheltering lonely knit eyebrows;

Throughout the night, the iron bells at the western tower are blown hard by the wind.

She wishes to weave flowers of lovesickness and send them to someone far away;

All day long she is lovesick for him yet she resents him.

She only hears the sound of the Northern Dipper turning round,

But does not see the long River's water, clear and shallow.

A golden fish locks up the red cassia, cutting it off from spring;

[10] *Ancient dust fills the cushion embroidered with mandarin ducks.*

How sad that the little park has turned into a highway!

The jade trees show no pity for those who have lost their country.

The jasper-decked zither is silent, hiding the tunes of Ch'u;

The thin silk of Yüeh lies cold, heavy with splashed gold.

The parrot on the curtain-hook is aroused by the frost at night,

And calls up southern clouds to surround the Cloud-Dream Marsh.

A pair of tinkling ear-rings are tied to a foot of white silk,

On which is recorded the place where they met by the river Hsiang.

Her singing lips will be seen with rain all one's life;

[20] *Alas, that the fragrance should have faded from one's hands!*

NOTES

Line 2   The moon. Literally, "toad." See Poems 29, 35.

Line 3   Cloud-screen. *Yün-p'ing*, a screen made of *yün-mu* ("mother-of-clouds"), i.e. mica.

Line 4   Iron bells. *Feng-cheng*, literally "wind zither," also called "Iron Horses" (*t'ieh-ma*), iron bells hung under the eaves, which tinkle when blown by the wind. Feng Hao seems to have confused this with the kite, also called *feng-cheng*, which would not make much sense in the present context.

Line 8   River. The Heavenly River (i.e. the Milky Way).

Line 9   Golden fish. A golden lock made in the form of a fish.

Line 12   Jade trees. This alludes to the last ruler of the Ch'en dynasty, Ch'en Shu-pao (553–604), who wrote a song called "Jade Trees Blossoming in the Rear Courtyard". He lost his kingdom and tried to commit suicide by leaping into a well together with two favorite concubines.

Line 13   Ch'u. Ancient kingdom in central China, traditionally regarded as the "south."

Line 14   Yüeh. Ancient kingdom in southeast China, also considered part of the "south."

Line 16   Cloud-Dream Marsh. Yün-meng Tse, originally comprising two marshes, one called Cloud Marsh and the other Dream Marsh, in modern Hupeh.

Line 17   Foot of white silk. *Ch'ih-su*, conventional expression for a letter.

Line 18   Hsiang. River in modern Hunan province.

COMMENTARY

This poem expresses the mutual longings of the heroine and her lover. The first couplet sets the scene in an autumn night. As the moonlight inundates the sky, the mansion of heaven seems drenched by its waves. Then, when the moon has set, the widely scattered stars also sink. The word translated as "sink," is *ju*, literally "enter." Its meaning is ambiguous. Feng Hao takes it to mean that the starlight comes in the door after the moon has set, but since starlight does not seem strong enough to "come in the door," I prefer to think that it means the stars sink. When the sun sets, it is sometimes said to have "gone in" (*ju*). Lines 3–4 describe the lady sitting with knit eyebrows behind a screen all night, listening to the west wind blowing on the iron bells under the eaves. She wishes to send a love token to her lover far away, but she resents him (for having made her suffer so?) and yet longs for him all day in spite of herself. "Weaving flowers of lovesickness" might allude to the story about Su Hui (fourth century A.D.), who wove a palindromic poem in silk and sent it to her absent husband to express her longing for him. As day and night follow one another, and the seasons change, the heroine imagines she can hear the Northern Dipper turn round, but cannot expect to meet her lover again. Line 8 contains verbal echoes of a line from an anonymous poem (one of the so-called *Nineteen Ancient Poems*): "The River is clear and shallow." Since that poem is about the Weaving Maid and the Cowherd who are said to meet once a year across the Heavenly River (Cf. Poems 38–

41), the heroine seems to be contrasting her own lot with that of the Weaving Maid: the latter can at least meet her lover once a year! In the next line, the "golden fish" refers to a lock made in the shape of a fish, which locks her up so that she is cut off from love, like a cassia tree cut off from spring. Furthermore, because, in T'ang times, officials of the third rank and above wore the "golden fish" sash, this image might suggest that she is kept in the harem of a high official. The cushion embroidered with mandarin ducks (which often symbolize lovers) on which she used to sit or lie is now full of ancient dust, and the little park where she used to live has become a public highway. The allusion to the last ruler of Ch'en and his concubines in line 12 implicitly compares the heroine to these ill-fated ladies. Can Nature (as represented by the trees) be so indifferent to the sufferings of such beautiful ladies? Lines 13–14 I think mean that she now no longer plays her Ch'u tunes on the zither, and her southern dress, made of thin silk heavily decorated with gold, now lies discarded and cold. Feng takes these lines, together with the next two, to be a description of the lady playing the zither at night, wearing a silk dress. This ignores the words for "silent" (*an-an*) and "hiding" (*ts'ang*). It is true that the characters for *an-an* could be pronounced *yin-yin* and be taken to mean "calm", but this would still not explain why the tunes of Ch'u are *hidden*, if she is playing them. Feng further suggests that it is her playing that arouses the parrot and calls up the clouds, but the lines in question (15–16) can be construed as meaning that the parrot is aroused by the falling frost and it is the parrot that calls up the clouds. The "southern" clouds that surround the Cloud-Dream Marsh express her nostalgia. Moreover, the Cloud-Dream Marsh is associated with the Ch'u King's amorous dream of the Goddess of Mount Wu (Cf. Poem 18, line 3, and Poem 25, line 3.), since the King's palace of Kao-t'ang, where the dream occurred, was situated in the midst of this marsh. Thus she is not only nostalgic for her homeland but also hankering after a past love. Lines 17–18 more explicitly refer to her former love affair; she looks at the pair of earrings that he has given her (or perhaps that she is sending him as a souvenir), together with a letter (from her to him or vice versa), in which their first meeting by the Hsiang river is recalled. For the rest of his life (or for the rest of her life, for the original simply says "one lifetime") he will watch her singing lips with tears like rain (or she will shed tears like rain when she sings to please another man). What a pity that memories of their love are fading away, as traces of fragrance imperceptibly but inevitably fade from one's hands!

Winter

10   *The sun rises in the eastern heaven and sets in the west.*
      The hen-phoenix flies alone; the female dragon is widowed.
      The Blue Stream and the White Stone cannot see each other;
      The hall is farther away than the wilderness of Ts'ang-wu.
      On the frozen walls flowery frostwork stealthily rises;
      The fragrant root is broken in the middle; the incense-heart dies.
      Recklessly sailing in a painted barge, I recall the moon:
      The Goddess Ch'ang-o may not be a beautiful lady!
      The pipes of Ch'u and the strings of the southern barbarians
         bring nothing but sorrow;

[10] *In the empty city, the dance is over, only the waist remains.*
      Formerly they melted with joy in one's palms—
      The two sisters named Peach Leaf and Peach Root:
      Their chignons, falling on one side, braved the morning chill,
      Decked with white jade swallow-hairpins and golden cicadas.
      No wind-chariot or rain-horse will carry me away;
      The candle sheds red tears and complains till dawn.

NOTES

Line 3   Blue Stream. There is an ancient song about a goddess called Little Maid of the Blue Stream, who lives alone without a young man. (Cf. Poem 18, line 4).
           White Stone. There are two songs about an immortal called "White Stone Lad."

Line 4   Ts'ang-wu. Either the name of a prefecture or that of a mountain, signifying a remote place.

Line 7   The moon. Literally, "toad." (Cf. Poems, 29, 35.)

Line 8   Ch'ang-o. Goddess of the Moon. (See Poems 28–35.)

Line 11 This line may allude to Lady Swallow (see Poem 45, line 2), who was said to be so light that she could dance on one's palm.

Line 12 Peach Leaf and Peach Root. There is an ancient song about peach leaves and peach roots, and later legends invented two sisters so named. The phrase is often applied to sisters, especially singing girls.

Line 14 Swallow-hairpins. (See Poem 24, line 7.)

COMMENTARY

The fourth and last poem reiterates the theme of the previous poems in an even more forlorn tone. The first line, as some commentators have suggested, indirectly describes the shortness of the day: almost as soon as the sun has risen in the east, it already seems to set in the west. The meaning of the second line should be obvious and needs no comment. Line 3 compares the heroine to the lonely Little Maid of the Blue Stream, and her lover to the White Stone Lad, suggesting that they are separated. Hence, the hall in which she dwells seems to him farther away than the remotest corner of the known world. The harsh weather is indicated by the frostwork (in line 5), which may also symbolize hostile forces that are killing their love. In line 6, the fragrant root that is broken in the middle represents their disrupted relation, and the "incense-heart" (*hsiang-hsin*) probably involves a pun: the word *hsiang* means both "incense" and "fragrant," and *hsiang-hsin* therefore means both "incense-heart" and "fragrant heart" (that is, a beautiful woman's heart; see Poem 7). Thus, through this pun, her dying heart is likened to the incense burning to ashes. In lines 7-8 she is compared to the Goddess of the Moon. Sailing in a barge, the lover recalls first meeting her, and wonders if now, worn with sorrow, she is still as beautiful as she was. (Or perhaps line 8 means that, compared with her, even the Goddess of the Moon may not be called a beautiful lady.) Lines 9-10 contrast former happiness with present grief. Now that she is gone, the music brings nothing but sorrow; the whole city seems empty; her dance can no longer be seen, though her slender waist still remains. Lines 11-14 further recall former joys. The heroine and her sister were so light that they could have danced on one's palms, and they seemed to melt with joy as one held them in one's arms. Wearing precious ornaments on their hair, they stood in the chilly morning air. Such joy and such beauty are now all gone. The final couplet brings the lover back to the miserable present: he cannot get away in a wind-chariot or on a rain-horse to where his loved one is; he can only shed tears and complain until dawn, like the red candle dissolving in its own tears.

The four poems present variations on the same theme, accompanied by shifting moods. The first one expresses the heroine's longings for love and is dominated by a dreamlike atmosphere and a feeling of bewilderment. The second one shows her lover's frustration and wishful thinking, but he has not yet completely given up hope. In the third poem, the dominant mood is one of quiet resignation, as the lover mourns the absence of his beloved while she wistfully looks at the souvenirs of their love. The last poem is written in a tone of despair— her heart dies, and he laments all night. These poems are the offerings of a suffering heart on the altar of Love; no wonder they won the admiration of the girl Willow Branch, who inspired a new love, but also brought new sorrow to the poet's life. (See Poems 60-64.)

POEM **I I**

Without Title

At eight, she stole a look at herself in the mirror,
Already able to paint her eyebrows long.
At ten, she went out to tread on the green,
Her skirt made of lotus flowers.
At twelve, she learnt to play the small zither:
The silver plectrums she never took off.
At fourteen, she was hid among her relatives,
And, one imagined, not married yet.
At fifteen, she weeps in the spring wind,
Turning her face away from the swing.

NOTES

Line 3   Tread on the green. *T'a-ch'ing,* a custom in T'ang times of going out into the country or to the Meandering Stream in Ch'ang-an on the 3rd day of the Third Month.

Line 4   This line alludes to the *Songs of Ch'u* (*Ch'u Tz'u*), but also literally describes the lotus flowers embroidered on her skirt.

Line 5   Small zither. The *cheng* (*koto* in Japanese). It originally had twelve strings but in its modern version has sixteen.

Line 6   Silver plectrums. Literally, "silver finger nails" (*yin-chia*).

Line 7   Relatives. *Liu-ch'in,* literally, "six relatives." This has been explained in several ways, none of which seems particularly relevant, since the poet is using the expression for relatives in general rather than any specific group of relatives. In T'ang times girls often married in their teens. Hence the poet could say of a fourteen-year-old girl that she was "not married *yet.*"

Line 8   The meaning of this line is not clear. For further discussion, see Additional Note 10.

COMMENTARY

This seemingly simple poem has been interpreted in various ways. Feng Hao takes it to be an allegorical expression of the poet's disappointment at his lack of success despite his precocious talents, and cites a passage from one of Li's letters which contains verbal similarities:

"I began to study the Classics in my fifth year, toyed with the writing brush and the ink-slab in my seventh, and wrote essays in my sixteenth." This interpretation is plausible but not strictly necessary, for the poem is poignant enough taken at its face value as a lament for an ill-fated precocious beauty, who, at the early age of fifteen (Chinese reckoning), is either unhappily married or unhappy because she is not yet married, so that she has no further use for the swing, a symbol of youthful gaiety. Moreover, the phraseology of the poem can be considered a conscious imitation or an unconscious echo of some lines from the anonymous ancient ballad known as *The Peacock Flies to the Southeast*, which tells how a young man was forced by his mother to divorce his wife and how the young couple both committed suicide. In this ballad the young wife complains:

> At thirteen I could weave plain silk,
> At fourteen I learnt to make clothes,
> At fifteen I began to play the harp,
> At sixteen I knew the Classics,
> At seventeen I became your wife:
> My heart has often been filled with grief.

The resemblance of Li's poem to these lines makes it possible to take it as a description of an unhappy girl, without any allegorical significance. Another interpretation is offered by Miss Su Hsüeh-lin, who thinks that the poem alludes to the two Court entertainers Fei-luan and Ch'ing-feng, with both of whom the poet was allegedly in love. Thus, this poem can be taken on three different levels: as a description of an ill-fated beauty, as an allegorical self-lament, and as an oblique reference to a clandestine love. But its total significance transcends all three. Whatever the poet may have had in mind, the effect of the poem is to make us feel sadness at the loss of youth, beauty, and talent, no matter where and how such loss was incurred. We may compare this poem with Keats's *La Belle Dame Sans Merci*, which may be taken at its face value as a fairy tale, or as an expression of the poet's unhappy infatuation for Fanny Brawne, or as an allegory of his intoxication with Beauty, or as all three at once, for the total meaning of the poem transcends them all, though none of them needs be excluded.

POEM 12

High Noon

The doorknockers with tags of old brocade can be lightly pulled;
The jade key does not turn, the side door is locked.
Who is it that lies asleep inside the crystal curtain,
Her hair piled up like red peonies at high noon?
The floating fragrance ascends the clouds to complain to heaven
*   in spring,*
But oh, the twelve cloud-stairs and the ninefold gates!
What hope is there for one who takes life lightly?
The white moth dies stiff upon the folding screen.

NOTES

Line 1   Tags of old brocade. Doors in the palace had tags made of old
brocade tied to the knockers to make it easier to pull them open.

Line 6   Twelve cloud-stairs. There are supposed to be twelve jade towers
(which presumably have stairs of clouds) in the palace of the goddess
Queen Mother of the West.
Ninefold gates. The palace of Heaven is said to have ninefold gates.

COMMENTARY

Feng Hao takes this poem to be a veiled reference to the
Emperor, who is as hard to approach as heaven, and the moth to represent a loyal official risking death in his attempt to admonish the
sovereign. This seems too farfetched and does not fit all the details of
the poem. Chang Ts'ai-t'ien takes it as an allegory about the poet's
longing for the favor of Ling-hu T'ao and the latter's inaccessibility.
This too seems forced. A more likely interpretation is that the poem
describes a hopeless passion for some palace lady, whether this passion
is felt by the poet himself or imaginary. The door looks inviting enough;
it could be pulled open easily, yet the key does not turn, and the door
remains locked. The beauty lies tantalizingly within the transparent
curtain: one can see her but cannot come near. One would like to
complain to heaven (or perhaps she would like to complain to heaven),
but heaven is inaccessible with its manifold stairs and gates. Even if one
takes life lightly and does not mind risking death, what hope is there?

One can only despair and die like the moth that courts its own destruction by throwing itself against the screen. This image of the moth reminds one of Shelley's well-known lines:

> The worship the heart lifts above
>   And the Heavens reject not;
> The desire of the moth for the star,
>   Of the night for the morrow;
> The devotion to something afar
>   From the sphere of our sorrow.

Thus, the whole poem may be regarded as a symbol of a kind of romantic *désir de l'impossible*, of universal human aspirations for the unattainable, not merely as the expression of a personal longing for a particular woman or for the favor of a particular patron.

POEM 13

The Sun Shoots Its Beams . . .

The sun shoots its beams at the gauze window; the wind shakes the door.

She wipes her hands with fragrant silk; things have gone against her wish this spring.

The winding corridors on all sides enclose her solitude;

A green cockatoo faces the red roses.

COMMENTARY

The poem may be taken as a description of a lonely lady, as well as an expression of the poet's own solitude and disappointment.

POEM **14**

Screen

Its six zigzag panels, adjoining the green curtain, stand

In the tall mansion, at midnight, when one awakes from a drunken sleep.

How carefully does it shield the lamp and keep off the mist!

Yet it is unaware of the falling rain and the bright moon!

COMMENTARY

The poem seems to be an ironic comment on the efforts of some nobleman to keep guard on his harem. Despite his precautions, he is unaware of the clandestine love affairs which some of his concubines are carrying on.

POEMS **15–16**

Casual Lines

15 *In the small pavilion, an idle sleep dispels a slight intoxication.*

The mountain-pomegranate and the sea-cypress intertwine their branches.

By the amber pillow on the water-patterned bamboo mat

Lies a fallen hairpin with a pair of kingfishers' feathers.

16 *The pale moonlight is dim, the fragrant dew light;*

The rooms with winding corridors in the small courtyard have seen many meetings.

Amid the spring flowers, the birds will certainly nestle in pairs.

After the drinking party, do not walk with a red candle!

COMMENTARY

These two poems describe clandestine love affairs. The first one paints a day scene, and the second one a night scene. In the first poem, the imagery in line 2 has obvious erotic implications, and the word for "intertwine" in Chinese, *chiao*, is also used for sexual intercourse. Lines 3 and 4 obliquely suggest ardent love-making. In the second poem, the deceived husband is ironically warned not to walk with a candle at night, for if he did, he might find an unpleasant surprise!

POEMS 17–18

Without Title

17   *The fragrant silk, "Phoenix Tail," lies in thin folds;*
      The green-patterned round top is being sewn in the depth of night.
      Her fan, cutting the moon's soul, cannot hide her shame;
      His carriage, driving the thunder's noise, allowed no time for talk.
      In solitude she has watched the golden flickers grow dim;
      No news will ever come to announce the Red Pomegranate Wine!
      The piebald horse is always tied to a willow by the river;
      Where can one wait for the good southwest wind?

NOTES

Lines 1–2   These two lines describe the bed-curtain for the bridal chamber commonly used in T'ang times. "Phoenix Tail" is the name of a kind of silk.

Line 3   This line involves three possible allusions.
(a) The comparison of the circular fan with the moon is derived from a song of complaint by Lady Pan, a Court lady (1st century B.C.) who compared the fan to the moon, and herself, having lost imperial favor, to the fan discarded in autumn.
(b) There is a song called "White Circular Fan," which is said to have originated in the following manner. Wang Min (351–388) had a love affair with his sister-in-law's maid, named Hsieh Fang-tzu. One day, when the sister-in-law was caning the maid severely, Wang asked her to stop. Knowing that the maid was a good singer, the mistress demanded her to sing in lieu of further punishment, whereupon Hsieh sang:
      White circular fan!

The hardships and bitterness you've gone through
Have all been seen by your young man.
And again,
          White circular fan!
Haggard and worn, unlike in days of old,
You should be ashamed to see your young man!
(c) The line may also allude to the goddess of the moon. (See
Poems 28–35.)

Line 4   This line alludes to Ssu-ma Hsiang-ju's *The Long Gate*, where the
         Emperor's carriage is compared to thunder. (Cf. Poem 5, line 2.)
         For further discussion on lines 3 and 4, see Part III, 3.

Line 5   Golden flickers. A candle burning out, or perhaps incense.

Line 6   Red Pomegranate Wine. Wine for the wedding feast.

Line 7   Piebald horse. This alludes to an anonymous song about a young
         dandy on a piebald horse, roaming around without going home.
         Willow. "To pluck the willow branch by the Chang Terrace" is a
         common euphemism for visiting a courtesan.

Line 8   The line alludes to two lines from a poem by Ts'ao Chih (192–232),
         put in the mouth of a deserted woman:
         I wish to become the southwest wind
         To fly far away, into your bosom.

COMMENTARY

This poem and the following one have again been interpreted allegorically as expressions of the poet's wish to be restored to
the favor of Ling-hu T'ao, but I prefer to take them at their face value
as poems describing a lovelorn lady. In the first poem, the opening
couplet, by describing the elaborate bed-curtain for the bridal chamber,
which the lady is sewing at night, suggests her wish to be married soon.
In line 3, the allusion to Lady Pan's song evokes associations with
deserted ladies; that to Hsieh Fang-tzu's song adds the idea of shame to
that of desertion; the association with the goddess of the moon implicitly compares the beauty of the heroine with that of the goddess.
In line 4, the allusion to *The Long Gate*, which was written on behalf of
Empress Ch'en when she had lost the Emperor's favor, further emphasizes the idea of desertion. However, since the Emperor is said to have
been so moved that he restored the Empress to his favor, the allusion
would seem to indicate a hope for a similar return to favor. The
flickering candle or incense in line 5 may be taken both as a description
of a lonely night and as a symbol of despair. Line 6, by referring to the
wine for the wedding, harks back to the nuptial preparations carried
out by the lady hoping against hope, mentioned in lines 1–2. The
allusions in line 7 imply that the absent lover is wandering abroad and
that the lady suspects him of being detained in the company of some
courtesan. The last line, by borrowing from Ts'ao Chih, reiterates the
wish to be reunited with the lover.

18   *Deeply sheltered by double curtains is Sans Souci's chamber;*

Lying in bed, she feels the slow, slow passing of the quiet night.

The whole life of the goddess is really nothing but a dream;

Where the Little Maid lives, there's never been a young man.

The winds and waves do not believe the water chestnut's twigs are weak;

Under the moonlit dews, who could make the cassia leaves smell sweet?

You may say that it is completely futile to be lovesick,

But perhaps melancholic "clear madness" will not do any harm.

NOTES

Line 1   Sans Souci. Mo-ch'ou. (See note on Poem 8, line 3.)

Line 3   Goddess. Perhaps the goddess of Mount Wu, who appeared to the King of Ch'u in an amorous dream. (Cf. Poem 25, line 3.)

Line 4   Little Maid. Goddess of the Blue Stream. (See Poem 10, line 3). Although in the song about her, on which this line is based, she is said to live alone, without a young man, there is a story about her having a love affair.

Line 8   "Clear madness." *Ch'ing-k'uang*, which some explain as "seeming to be mad but not really so," and others as "looking calm but mentally dull."

COMMENTARY

This may be taken as a variation on the theme of the previous poem. The opening line suggests the deep seclusion in which the lady lives, and the name Sans Souci (Mo-ch'ou) strikes an ironic note by contrasting the literal meaning of the name with the reality of her life. Line 2 depicts her loneliness as she lies in bed alone. Lines 3 and 4, by evoking amorous goddesses, recall past love affairs, which are now gone like a dream. The expression "there's never been a young man" is ambiguous and may be taken to mean either or both of two things: first, she is pretending that she has never had a lover, as if trying to deny rumors; second, she is seeking to console herself with self-deception, now that her lover is gone, by saying, "Why should I miss him? There's never been a man in my life!" In line 5, the winds and waves may represent hostile forces that do not appreciate her delicate and sensitive nature; line 6 seems to express a wish for the impossible, while hinting (as suggested by A. C. Graham) at a comparison of the heroine to the goddess of the moon, who lives by a cassia tree (Cf. Poems 29, 32). In the last couplet, the poet suggests that the lady cannot help being lovesick, although she knows the utter futility of it. She is saying in effect, "I know that to be lovesick is no use, but perhaps to be just a little mad in love won't do any harm?" Like Hamlet, she is "but mad north-north-west," or so she thinks. Alternatively, if we accept the explanation that "clear madness" means "being outwardly calm but mentally dull," the last line would seem to mean, "perhaps being a fool in love won't hurt you?"

POEMS 19-20

Without Title

19 *Last night's stars, last night's wind—*

West of the painted pavilion, east of the cassia hall.

Our bodies have no colorful phoenix-wings to fly side by side;

Our hearts are linked to each other as if by the line in the magic horn.

As she passed the hook from another seat, the spring wine was warm;

Divided into teams, we guessed at riddles under the red candle's light.

Alas, I had to answer the call of duty when the drum sounded,

And ride my horse to the Orchid Terrace, like a tumbleweed in the wind.

NOTES

Line 4 Magic horn. *Ling-hsi*, horn of the "magic rhinoceros" which is said to have a white line running through, from the tip to the root.

Line 5 Hook. This refers to the game of "hiding the hook" (*ts'ang-kou*) which supposedly originated from the following story. Lady Hook (Kou-yi Fu-jen), one of the favorites of Emperor Wu of Han, was said to have been born with closed fists. When the Emperor opened them, he found a hook in one of her hands. In playing this game, the players were divided into two teams of equal numbers. One team would hide the hook and the other team had to guess in whose hand it was hidden.

Warm wine. It is a Chinese custom to serve wine warm.

Line 6   Riddles. *She-fu*, literally "shooting (i.e. guessing at) what is covered." The term was first used when Emperor Wu of Han asked some magicians to guess what was concealed under a vessel placed upside down.

Line 8   Orchid Terrace. Lan-t'ai, another name for the Imperial Library, where the poet worked in 839 and 842.

COMMENTARY

Some commentators think that this poem and the next one refer to a lady in the harem of the poet's father-in-law, Wang Mao-yüan, while others would have us believe that it was written for Li's future wife. Both theories are largely based on an allusion in Poem 22 (q.v.) to the Flute-player who married the daughter of Duke Mu of Ch'in, an allusion commonly used to refer to a son-in-law. However, neither theory is likely to be right, since in both 839 and 842, when Li was working in the Imperial Library (to which he refers in line 8), his father-in-law was away from the capital. In any case, it would have been very difficult for the poet to carry on a love intrigue either with one of his father-in-law's concubines or with his own fiancée. The poem can only be taken as an expression of regret over the necessity to leave a gay party graced by the presence of someone whom he admires and who seems to reciprocate his feelings. The tone of the poem is not as passionate as some of the other untitled poems (Poems 4, 5, and 6, for example) and does not suggest a serious love affair. The first couplet hints that a secret rendezvous has taken place before the party. The second couplet expresses the poet's wish to elope with the lady, and affirms his love in the face of obstacles. Of course it is possible that the poet is assuming too much—perhaps, when he declares that their hearts are linked to each other, he is indulging in self-deception in thinking that the lady fully reciprocates his feelings. Lines 5-6 describe the party, at which they could not reveal their true feelings. The last couplet expresses the poet's regret that he had to leave.

20 *I have long heard of Green-calyxed Bloom of Ch'ang-men;*

Years ago I used to gaze toward her, who seemed as far as heaven's end.

Who would have thought that the guest for one night in the Ch'in mansion

Would be able to peep at the flowers in the inner park of the King of Wu?

NOTES

Line 1   Green-calyxed Bloom. A goddess. See Poem 25, line 5.
Ch'ang-men. Another name for Soochow.

Line 2   Guest in Ch'in mansion. The flute-player, who married the daughter of Duke Mu of Ch'in. (See Poem 22, line 3.)

Line 4   King of Wu. Perhaps King Fu-ch'ai of Wu, to whom the two famous beauties Hsi Shih and Cheng Tan were presented by the King of Yüeh. (Cf. Poem 48, line 23.)

COMMENTARY

In spite of the allusion to the flute-player, we cannot be sure that the poem refers to the poet's fiancée or to a concubine of his father-in-law. We can only deduce from the poem that the poet is congratulating himself for having had the opportunity to meet some famous beauty whom he used to admire from a distance. The expression "guest for one night" and the tone of the whole poem both suggest a casual encounter rather than a serious love affair. The mention of Ch'ang-men possibly indicates the native city of the lady involved, although in the stories about the goddess Green-calyxed Bloom she is not said to come from this place. The King of Wu seems to represent a rich and exalted person, and the line harks back to Ch'ang-men, which is situated in Wu.

POEMS **21-23**

The Green Jade City

21   *Within the twelve green jade city walls with winding rails,*
A rhinoceros horn averts the dust, a jade averts the cold.
Letters from Lofty Park are mostly entrusted to cranes;
On Lady's-bed, phoenixes perch on every tree.
Stars sinking to the bottom of the sea can be seen at the window;
The rain over the river's source, viewed from another seat.
If the morning pearl were not only bright but also fixed,
One would always face the crystal plate all one's life.

NOTES

Title   The Taoist god Yüan-shih T'ien-tsun ("Primeval Heavenly Exalted-
one") is said to dwell in a palace surrounded by walls of clouds
colored like green jade.

Line 3   Lofty Park. Lang-yüan, dwelling of the immortals, who use cranes
as messengers.

Line 4   Lady's bed. Nü-ch'uang, a fabulous mountain on which phoenixes
rest.

Line 8   Crystal plate. Lady Swallow (Chao Fei-yen), favorite of Emperor
Ch'eng of Han (reigned 32 B.C.–7 B.C.), was said to be so light that
the Emperor ordered a crystal plate for her to dance on. The line
might also allude to Tung Yen, a lad who became the favorite of the
Princess of Kuan-t'ao, aunt of Emperor Wu of Han, and who
received a crystal plate from the Emperor.

COMMENTARY

The poems in this group are highly ambiguous and have
been variously interpreted. Chu Yi-tsun's suggestion that they are about
Emperor Hsüan-tsung and his concubine, the Honorable Consort Yang
(Yang Kuei-fei), is unconvincing. On the other hand, it is by no means
certain that these poems refer to the poet's own love affair with a
Taoist nun, for their tone is not passionate but rather ambivalent. It is
possible, as some commentators have suggested, that these poems are
satirical comments on princesses who had taken Taoist vows, but this
cannot be proved either. It seems best to read them dramatically, with-

out trying to identify the characters involved. In the first poem, the opening couplet describes the dwelling of the nuns, as luxurious and mysterious as the palace of the immortals. It is further possible, as Feng suggested, that the horn which averts the dust alludes to the nuns' having ostensibly left this "dusty world" (*ch'en shih*), while the jade that keeps away the cold obliquely refers to the warmth of their mortal passion. Line 3 refers to the messengers who carry letters between the nuns and their lovers; line 4, by mentioning the mountain with the highly suggestive name, reveals the licentiousness of the lovers, represented by the pairs of phoenixes. Lines 5–6, with their fantastic imagery, are the most difficult to explain. Some commentators take them simply as a hyperbolic way of saying how high the imaginary palace is: when one looks out of the window, one sees the stars below, as if they had sunk to the bottom of the sea, and the river's source, high in the mountains, now appears near by. Another explanation is offered by Feng: that line 5 alludes to the Three Magic Mountains (San-shen-shan) under water, and line 6 to the story about a man who sailed on a raft sent from heaven to the source of the Heavenly River (that is, the Milky Way) and saw the Weaving Maid there. This would leave the lines still puzzling, for it does not explain how the stars come to be at the bottom of the sea. Moreover, legend merely says that the Three Magic Mountains are in the eastern sea but does not mention a palace under water. And if it is under water, it cannot be high in the mountains at the same time. Yet another explanation is suggested by Mr. Takahashi, who quotes from the *Commentary on the Water Classic* (*Shui-ching chu*, a geographical work of the sixth century): "The waters on the Onion Range flow separately to the east and to the west: that which flows westward enters the great sea, and that which flows eastward is the source of the River [that is, the Yellow River]". Mr. Takahashi thinks that, in the lines concerned, "sea" and "river's source" represent "west" and "east" respectively, forming a contrast. This would still not explain why the stars should sink to the bottom of the sea, unless we connect these lines with the fact that the source of the Yellow River is called "Sea of Stars" (Hsing-su Hai). This name, however, is first mentioned in the *History of the Sung* and may not have existed in Li Shang-yin's time. It seems that the best we can do is to take the two lines as a description of a kind of upside-down world: the stars, instead of being high up in the air, sink to the bottom of the sea, and the river's source (or the Yellow River's source), instead of being far away, is near at hand. In spite of their ambiguity, these lines impress us with the power of the poet's imagination, which transports us to a dreamlike wonderland. The images have the qualities of things seen in a dream. They appear absurd when we stop to think, yet at the time of their appearance they seem to have a logic of their own, and their vividness compels us to accept them as valid symbols of real experience. In the final couplet, the morning pearl, I think, means the sun, or perhaps Venus, the morning star, although it has been taken literally to mean a precious pearl. It seems to me that either the sun or the morning star would make better sense than a real pearl: if the sun (or the morning star) were fixed and would stay still, one would gladly spend one's life facing the beautiful lady, who, like Lady Swallow, is light enough to dance on a crystal plate. Since that cannot be, however, one must leave this secret paradise when day comes. If we think the crystal plate alludes to Tung Yen, then it would be a hint that a princess is involved in the poem. Mr. Takahashi's suggestion that the crystal plate may refer to the moon is inappropriate, since it would contradict the "morning pearl" in the preceding line.

---

22 *Facing her shadow, hearing her voice, one already feels her loveliness.*

In the jade pool, the lotus leaves spread on the water.

Unless you meet the Flute-player, do not turn back your head,

Nor ever tap another Huge-cliff on the shoulder again.

The purple phoenix displays her charm, jade pendant in mouth;

The red fish dances wildly, plucking zither strings.

The night when the Prince of O gazed wistfully from his boat,

Beneath embroidered quilts, with incense burning, he slept alone.

NOTES

Line 3   Flute-player. Hsiao-shih, who, according to legend, married Nung-yü ("Playing-with-jade"), daughter of Duke Mu of Ch'in (7th Century B.C.) Later both became immortals.

Line 4   Huge-cliff. Hung-ya, name of an immortal. This line is derived from a poem on immortals by Kuo P'u (276–324), which contains the line, "On my right I tap Huge-cliff on the shoulder."

Line 5   Jade pendant. Literally, "Ch'u pendant." Probably an allusion to the story about Cheng Chiao-fu, who went to Ch'u and met a girl (or two girls, according to one version). Not realizing that she was a goddess, he made advances to her. She left him her pendant and then disappeared.

Line 6   Zither strings. The original has "Hsiang strings," that is, strings of the zither, with reference to the goddesses of River Hsiang, who play this instrument. The line may further allude to the legend that when Hu-pa played the zither, a huge fish came out to listen.

Lines 7–8   Prince of O. When this prince sailed in a boat, a woman of Yüeh sang a song to express her admiration and longing for him, whereupon he took her into his boat and covered her with embroidered quilts.

COMMENTARY

The opening couplet recalls a rendezvous by the pool. In the next couplet, the lover (who need not be identified with the poet) shows his fear that the woman he loves may fall in love with someone else. He compares himself to the lucky Flute-player, and a would-be rival to another immortal, Huge-cliff. The lines may be paraphrased thus: "Do not turn back your head to look at anyone unless I am the one you are meeting, nor ever flirt with another man again." In the next couplet, the purple phoenix and the red fish may be regarded as erotic imagery suggesting abandoned love-making, while at the same time the allusions arouse associations with romantic goddesses. But the last couplet seems to describe a disappointed lover: the speaker appears to be contrasting his own lot with that of the prince in the story, for instead of covering his beloved with quilts, he is now sleeping alone under them. This may seem inconsistent with the preceding couplet, but the apparent inconsistency can be resolved if we take the previous couplet to be a description of two happy lovers and the final couplet to refer to a jealous and frustrated onlooker. Whether the speaker is to be identified with the lucky lover or the disappointed spectator does not seem to make much difference to the dramatic situation implicit in the poem.

---

23   *On Seventh Night she came, as previously arranged;*

       The bamboo curtain of the bedchamber has never since been lifted.

       The hare in the Jade Wheel is beginning to grow a soul;

       The coral in the iron net has not yet put forth branches.

       Give her a magic recipe, and teach her to stay her youth!

       Take a piece of phoenix-paper and write down your longings!

       The Life of Emperor Wu *is plain for all to see:*

       Do not say that no one in the whole world knows!

NOTES

Line 1   Seventh Night. *Ch'i-hsi,* the seventh night of the Seventh Month, when the two stellar lovers, the Cowherd and the Weaving Maid, are supposed to have their annual reunion across the Heavenly River. There is also a story that the goddess Queen Mother of the West came to Emperor Wu of Han on this night.

Line 3   Hare in the Jade Wheel. In Chinese mythology, there is a hare preparing the elixir of life in the moon. "Jade Wheel" is a common metaphor for the moon.

Line 4   Coral in the iron net. (See note on Poem 7, line 11.)

Line 6   Phoenix-paper. Elaborate paper used in the palace, also used by Taoists to write prayers on.

Line 7   *The Life of Emperor Wu.* A story telling of the fictitious life of Emperor Wu of Han and his encounter with the Queen Mother of the West.

COMMENTARY

This poem appears to be concerned with an abortion. The first line recalls the lovers' meeting, and the second line hints that the woman has been confined to her bedroom since. Lines 3 and 4 refer metaphorically to the fetus which is growing but has not yet become fully formed. The "magic recipe" in line 5 is probably a euphemism for a prescription for abortion, although it could, of course, also help to fulfill its ostensible purpose of keeping the woman's youthful looks. The "phoenix-paper" in line 6 suggests that she is a Taoist nun in the palace. The last two lines point out that such scandals cannot be kept secret. I have avoided using the first person pronoun in the above three poems so as not to give the impression that the poet is describing his personal experience.

POEM 24

The Holy Lady's Temple

Pines and bamboos grow by the hall with an orchid-fragrant curtain;

A dragon protects the jasper windows, a phoenix closes the door.

Weightless, she is easily lost in the three-li-mist;

Immune from the cold, she always wears the five-hundred-grain gown.

In the human world, there must be a Ts'ui Lo-shih;

Up in heaven, there should be no Liu Wu-wei.

May I ask the pair of white swallows on the hairpin:

Every morning, when does she return from the hall of pearls?

NOTES

Title   The Holy Lady's Temple (Sheng-nü Tz'u) was situated on the Ch'in-kang mountain in Wu-tu district (modern Lüeh-yang in Hupeh province). On the side of a cliff was the image of a goddess who was credited with miracles and to whom people prayed. There are three poems on this temple in Li Shang-yin's collected works, but the order of their composition cannot be ascertained. I have placed them tentatively in the order in which they now appear.

Line 3   Three-*li*-mist. P'ei Yu of the Later Han period (A.D.25–220) was said to be able to produce mist extending three *li*.

Line 4   Five-hundred-grain gown. This alludes to the story about an immortal who called himself "The Boy from the Upper Pure Sphere" (Shang-ch'ing T'ung-tzu) and who wore a light gown weighing only five *shu* (each *shu* was the equivalent of one hundred grains of millet).

Line 5   Ts'ui Lo-shih. According to a story, Ts'ui (sixth century) met a lady who said she was the daughter of Wu Chih (177–230) and wife of Liu Yao. After the meeting, Ts'ui looked back and saw nothing but a grave.

Line 6   Liu Wu-wei. Liu Tzu-nan (first century A.D.), prefect of Wu-wei during the Later Han, received from a Taoist magician a "firefly pill" which supposedly made him invisible and invulnerable.

Line 7   Swallows on the hairpin. The story goes that in 116 B.C. a goddess appeared to Emperor Wu of Han and left a jade hairpin, which he gave to Lady Chao. Later, when other ladies opened the case containing the hairpin, they found only a pair of white swallows, which then flew away. This gave rise to the fashion of hairpins decorated with swallows.

COMMENTARY

The three poems on the Holy Lady's Temple are all highly obscure. They seem to be concerned with a Taoist nun or nuns, though we need not go so far as Miss Su Hsüeh-lin, who regards these as autobiographical poems. I shall interpret these poems as descriptions of secret love involving a Taoist nun, but on the understanding that the speaker need not be identified with Li himself.

The first poem describes the nun in terms of the goddess. The opening couplet evokes a picture of the Taoist temple. The next couplet suggests the fragile and delicate beauty of the nun, like a goddess wearing a flimsy gown flying in the mist. Line 5 hints that there must be a lucky lover who has met her, as Ts'ui Lo-shih met the female ghost in the story; line 6 seems to express the hope that there is no other lover in heaven (that is, within the secret confines of the temple, or perhaps among Taoist priests). The last couplet, with its courtly associations, may be taken to mean that the nun has been summoned to the palace and the speaker wonders when she will return.

POEM 25

Revisiting the Holy Lady's Temple

The white stone gate on the cliff is overgrown with green moss;
Banished from the Upper Pure Sphere, she is delayed in her return.
Throughout the spring, a dream-rain often flooded the tiles;
All day long, the spiritual wind has not filled the banners.
Green-calyxed Bloom comes from no fixed place;
Magnolia Fragrance has not been gone for long.
The Jade Lad, encountering this, becomes related to the immortals,
And recalls asking for the purple magic herb from the steps of heaven.

NOTES

Line 2   Upper Pure Sphere. One of the three "Pure Spheres" of Heaven in Taoist mythology. Cf. note on line 4 of preceding poem.

Line 3   Dream-rain. This alludes to the well-known story about King Huai of Ch'u, who had an amorous encounter with the Goddess of Mount Wu in a dream. Since she assumed the forms of cloud and rain, the expression "cloud and rain" became a common euphemism for sexual intercourse.

Line 5   Green-calyxed Bloom. O-lu-hua, a goddess described as a beautiful young girl, who appeared to Yang Ch'üan in A.D. 359 and taught him the art of immortality.

Line 6   Magnolia Fragrance. Tu-lan-hsiang, another goddess, who lived with Chang Shih as his wife and then vanished.

Line 7   Jade Lad. Yü-lang, a junior official in the Taoist hierarchy of immortals.

COMMENTARY

In this poem the speaker appears to be recalling a romantic encounter which took place here. The first line suggests that a long time has elapsed, since the stone gate is overgrown with moss. Line 2 could mean either that the nun, unable to free herself from human passion, is like an immortal banished from heaven, or that she has been delayed from her return to this temple. Lines 3 and 4 together might be paraphrased thus: "Throughout the spring she has had many amorous meetings with her lover(s), as the Goddess of Mount Wu made love to the King of Ch'u in his dream; and she has neglected her religious duties so that all day long there has not been sufficient spiritual wind to fill the banners." The next two lines, by referring to two other goddesses, again hint at romantic love affairs and further suggest the mysterious and unpredictable comings and goings of the nun. The last couplet means that the speaker, through his association with this nun, has "become related to the immortals" (that is, has been admitted to the society of nuns and their lovers), and that he himself has also studied Taoism.

POEM 26

The Holy Lady's Temple

Amid deep mists I encounter the goddess's footsteps,
While delayed on my vague and distant journey.
In what year did she return to the azure heavens?
This road leads to the imperial capital.
For news, I have to await the Blue Sparrow;
To meet her differs from meeting the Purple Lady.
My inside turns because of the dream of Ch'u;
My heart breaks for the shaman of the Han palace.
Her attendants rode on cold bamboo canes;
[10]   Her carriage went under the white elms.
Since the time the Stellar Lady left,
Has Sister Moon been here again?
The widowed crane is lost in the gray ravine;
The detained hen-phoenix blames the verdurous wu-t'ung.
It was only under the green peaches
That Fang So could be a "wild man".

NOTES

Line 5   Blue Sparrow. One of the messengers of the Queen Mother of the West. (Cf. Poem 6, line 8.)

Line 6   Purple Lady. Tzu-ku, goddess of the privy. She is said to have been a concubine who was persecuted by the principal wife and died on the 15th day of the First Month, which therefore became her feast day.

Line 7   Dream of Ch'u. See note on line 3 of previous poem.

Line 8   Shaman of Han Palace. I think this probably alludes to the story that a female shaman who dressed herself up as a man and became intimate with the Empress was killed by Emperor Wu of Han.

Line 9   Bamboo canes. Fei Ch'ang-fang, who studied magic with "Lord Pot" (Hu-kung), was given by the latter a bamboo cane which could be ridden on.

Line 10   White elms. Derived from an anonymous ancient poem, "What is there in heaven? Numerous white elms clearly planted," meaning stars.

Line 11   Stellar Lady. The Weaving Maid. (Cf. Poems 38–41.)

Line 14   *Wu-t'ung.* The only tree, it is said, on which a phoenix will perch.

Lines 15–16   Fang So. Abbreviated reference to Tung-fang So (154 B.C.–93 B.C.), a jester at the court of Emperor Wu of Han. In fiction, he is said to have been a banished immortal who had three times stolen the peaches of immortality from the Queen Mother of the West. The expression "wild man" refers to Tung-fang So's official biography, wherein he is described as having married and divorced many beautiful young girls and earned the reputation of being a "wild man." Furthermore, "wild man" could also mean "my simple husband," a term used in ancient times by women as a modest way of referring to their husbands.

COMMENTARY

The theme of the preceding poem is reiterated here. Revisiting the scene of their former rendezvous, the speaker asks when the nun left this temple and hints that she has been summoned to the palace (lines 3–4). Now he can only hope that a messenger ("Blue Sparrow") will bring news to her, but he cannot expect to meet her on the 15th of the First Month, the feast day of the Purple Lady. (Actually line 6 in the original is ambiguous: it merely says, "to meet [her] is different from [meeting] the Purple Lady," which seems to mean that the nun cannot be met on this day, or perhaps that she cannot be expected on any particular day.) Lines 7–8 more explicitly show the lover's sorrow, and, by alluding to the Goddess of Mount Wu and the shaman of the Han palace, further reveal that the nun has had love affairs in the past and is now in the palace. Lines 9–10 imaginatively re-create the scene of her departure from this temple: as her attendants rode away, as if on magic bamboo canes, she left in her carriage under the stars, which the ancients compared to white elms. In lines 11–12, the speaker refers to another nun, probably the first nun's sister, and wonders if *she* has visited this

place again. In line 13 the lover compares himself to a widowed crane
and imagines his beloved to be complaining in the palace like the hen-
phoenix being detained on a tree. The last couplet wistfully recalls the
past—it was only here that one could indulge in secret love, just as it
was only under the peaches that Tung-fang So could behave as a "wild
man." Several times in his poetry Li Shang-yin uses the story of Tung-
fang So's stealing of the peaches, to signify a clandestine love affair
(for example, Poem 35), and the expression "wild man," since it could
also mean "my husband," is possibly intended as a play on words, so
that the last two lines together also mean, "It was only here that one
could play the part of a husband."

POEM 27

Wind

It stirs the hairpin, bending the peacock,
And annoys the girdle, brushing against the mandarin ducks.
Who told it to come near the silk sleeping mat?
It is fasting time, and the secluded chamber is locked.

COMMENTARY

This poem appears to be an oblique description of a secret
rendezvous with a Taoist nun. The first three lines may be taken as
double entendre: it is the lover, as much as the wind, who is disturbing
the hairpin decorated with a peacock and handling the girdle embroidered with mandarin ducks (which represent happy lovers), and
who has come near the sleeping mat. Line 4 drops a hint that the heroine
is a nun by mentioning "fasting time" (*chai shih*); and the "secluded
chamber" (*tung-fang*, literally, "cave-room") seems deliberately ambiguous: the compound sometimes means "bridal chamber" but could also
refer to the secluded dwelling of a Taoist. Whether the poet himself is
to be regarded as the lover does not make much difference to the meaning of the poem.

POEM **28**

Ch'ang-o

Against the screen of "mother-of-clouds" the candle throws its
    deep shadow;

The Long River gradually sinks, the morning star sets.

Ch'ang-o should regret having stolen the elixir:

The green sea—the blue sky—her heart every night!

NOTES

Title   Ch'ang-o, also called Heng-o, stole her husband King Yi's elixir of
life and fled to the moon.

Line 1   Screen of "mother-of-clouds." Screen made of mica, with a pun on
the literal meaning. (Cf. Poem 9, line 3.)

COMMENTARY

In this poem and several others (Poems 29–34), Li Shang-
yin alludes to Ch'ang-o, goddess of the moon, who may be taken to
represent a Taoist nun, since, in the poem addressed to the Taoist nuns
named Sung (Poem 35), he also refers to this goddess. We may think
Miss Su is right in this instance. However, even here we still have to be
cautious. After all, the great Tu Fu (712–70) had already written about
the goddess's imagined loneliness:

> Imagine how the widowed Heng-o
> Can endure the cold in the depth of autumn!

and, so far as I know, no one has suggested that Tu Fu had a love affair
with a Taoist nun! On the other hand, to say that the poem expresses
the poet's self-pity or his regret over his marriage, as Ho Cho and
Chang Ts'ai-t'ien have done, is too farfetched. It seems best to regard
the poem both as a description of moonlight in terms of imagery
derived from mythology and as an oblique reference to a Taoist nun,
with whom the poet himself may or may not have had romantic relations. The poem shows considerable power of imagination. The
mythological scene is conceived in concrete detail: the screen, the
shadow cast by the candle, the Long River (the Milky Way) and the
morning star setting at dawn, and the solitary figure of the goddess
facing the immensities of the sea and the sky all night.

POEM **29**

Moonlit Night

The autumn insects under the grass, the frost on the leaves—
The vermilion balustrade presses down the light on the lake.
The hare is chilly, the toad cold, the cassia flower white:
On such a night, Heng-o would surely break her heart.

NOTES

Line 3   Hare, toad, cassia. The hare and the toad are both supposed to be the spirits of the moon. One modern scholar, Wen Yi-to, suggested that "hare" (*ku-t'u*) was a corruption of "toad" (*ch'an-ch'u*), though this is disputed by Su Hsüeh-lin. In some versions of the legend about Ch'ang-o, she is identified with the toad. There is also supposed to be a cassia tree in the moon, which a man called Wu Kang is for ever trying to cut down, in vain.

COMMENTARY

The theme of the preceding poem is reiterated here. Since even the hare, the toad, and the cassia are feeling the chill, the goddess herself must be feeling cold and lonely.

POEM **30**

Frosty Moon

As soon as the migrant wild geese are heard, the cicadas are silent;
The hundred-foot tower overlooks the water that touches the sky.
The Blue Maid and the White Lady both can endure the cold:
The one in the moon, the other in the frost, they compete in beauty.

NOTES

Line 3   Blue Maid. Ch'ing-nü, goddess of frost.
White Lady. Su-o, another name for Ch'ang-o.

COMMENTARY

Taken on the literal level, this is a description of moonlight over frost. The first line indicates the coming of autumn and the end of summer. The second line, which literally runs, "hundred-foot tower tall, water touches sky" (*po-ch'ih lou kao shui chieh t'ien*), has a variant reading, "to the south of the hundred-foot tower, water touches sky" (*po-ch'ih lou nan shui chieh t'ien*). If we adopt the latter reading, the line is straightforward. But if we adopt the former, as I have done, the line is ambiguous: we can take it simply to mean that the tower overlooks a river or lake which stretches as far as the horizon and seems to touch the sky, or we may take the water as a metaphor for the moonlit frost on the roof of the tower, which is so tall that it seems to touch the sky. As Feng Hao pointed out, there is an earlier line, "hundred-foot-tall tower touches the sky" (*po-ch'ih kao-lou yü t'ien lien*), of which the present line seems to be an echo. It is possible that, in the poet's mind, three images —that of the water which seems to touch the sky, that of the tower touching the sky, and that of the moonlit frost which looks like water— were fused into one. The last two lines can be regarded as merely a fanciful way of saying that the moon and the frost are vying with each other in beauty, but they can also be taken to be an indirect reference to two Taoist nuns, possibly the Sung sisters mentioned in the title of Poem 35.

POEM **3I**

Autumn Moon

Over the pond and beside the bridge,
Hard to forget and also lovely.
The curtain opens, revealing the brightest night;
The bamboo mattress is rolled up; it's already chill.
Where its light flows, rapid water-flowers rise;
When its beams issue forth, the cloud-leaves are fresh.
Heng-o has no powder or eyebrow-paint,
But proudly displays all her natural.charms.

COMMENTARY

This is another poem that can be taken both as a description of moonlight and as an indirect reference to a Taoist nun. The opening two lines could refer to the moonlight as well as to the nun. The four middle lines describe the actual scene and do not seem to involve any double meaning. "Brightest night" in line 3 indicates that the moon is full; "already chill" in the next line reveals the coming of autumn. Line 5 depicts the moonlight on flowing water, and line 6 describes its beams breaking through clouds and lighting them up. In the original, the subjects of "flows" and "issue forth" are understood; and there is a strict antithesis between "water-flowers" (that is, sprays) and "cloud-leaves," (clouds shaped like leaves). The final couplet seems to praise the natural beauty of the nun, who wears no make-up.

POEM **32**

Master Fang's Coral Powder

Heng-o's shadow is not to be seen:
She's guarding the moon's wheel in the cool autumn air.
Inside the moon, with leisurely mortar and pestle,
The cassia's seeds are pounded into dust.

COMMENTARY

Commentators have identified "Master Fang" with a certain magician of that name mentioned by two other poets who were Li's contemporaries. It has also been pointed out that "coral powder" was used both as an elixir of life and as a cure for eye diseases. However, I cannot see what all this has to do with the actual poem, which is about the goddess of the moon! It seems to me that the poem is concerned with an abortion. (Cf. Poem 23, where "coral" probably stands for the fetus.) In plain English, the poem seems to say, "The goddess of the moon [that is, a Taoist nun] is not to be seen, for she is confined to her chamber, where, with the aid of some medicine, an unborn child has has been reduced to nothing." The last line probably contains a pun: the words for "cassia's seeds" (*kuei tzu*) are homophonous with those for "precious child," and, indeed, the same word *tzu* is used for both "seed" and "child."

P O E M **33**

Stockings

I have heard that Princess Fu's stockings
Enabled her to tread on water like land.
Why not lend them to Ch'ang-o, that she
Could tread on the moon's wheel in the autumn air?

NOTES

Lines 1–2   Princess Fu. Goddess of the River Lo, made famous by the poet
Ts'ao Chih, who describes her as treading on the water in her stockings. (Cf. Poem 5, line 6.)

COMMENTARY

If the goddess of the moon again represents a Taoist nun,
then the speaker is expressing the wish that she could find some
miraculous means to come out and meet him. Some commentators
take the poem as an expression of the poet's wish to pass the examinations, for T'ang people sometimes referred to passing the examinations
as "plucking the cassia branch." But, since the poet does not mention
the cassia here, this interpretation does not seem plausible.

P O E M **34**

To Someone Far Away

There's no end to Heng-o's pounding of the drug,
Nor will the Jade Maid ever stop pitching her arrows.
O when will the seas all be turned into mulberry fields,
So that the Yi river can no longer flow to the east?

NOTES

Line 1   Heng-o and the drug. See Poem 32.

Line 2   Jade Maid. Yü-nü, a goddess who played the game of "pitching arrows into a pot" (*t'ou hu*) with the immortal Lord Prince of the East (Tung Wang Kung). When the latter missed, heaven opened its mouth and laughed.

Line 3   Mulberry fields. The goddess Ma-Ku remarked that she had thrice seen the Eastern Sea turning into mulberry fields. Hence, "the vast seas and the mulberry fields" is a common expression signifying the vicissitudes of life.

Line 4   Yi river. A possible pun on the pronoun *yi* ("he" or "she").

COMMENTARY

Two interpretations are offered by Feng Hao: first, that this is a love poem expressing the poet's wish to be free from the sufferings of separation from his beloved; second, that the poem refers to Ling-hu T'ao. Feng himself prefers the second interpretation but to me the first is far more plausible. Moreover, we can take the poem as a protest against Fate: when will all living beings, humans as well as immortals, be freed from their respective destinies? When can the goddess of the moon be freed from her task of preparing the elixir of life, or the Jade Maid from her eternal game, or the poet from his everlasting sorrows? Why cannot all seas run dry, so that rivers may cease to flow, and one's endless sorrows, which flow like the rivers, may also end?

POEM **35**

Again to the Sung Sisters of Hua-yang Temple, on a Moonlit Night

Stealing the peaches and pilfering the elixir cannot both be done.
Inside the twelve city walls the bright-colored toad is locked up.
One should enjoy it together with the Three Blooms,
But the jade tower is still behind the crystal curtain!

NOTES

Title   Hua-yang Temple. A Taoist temple in Ch'ang-an, formerly the mansion of the Princess of Hua-yang.

Line 1   Stealing peaches. See note on (Poem 26, lines 15–16.)
Elixir. (See Poem 28.)

Line 2   Twelve city walls. See Poem 21.
Toad. See Poem 29.

Line 3   Three blooms. *San-ying*, identified by commentators with the Three-pearled Tree (*san-chu-shu*), a mythical tree with leaves like pearls.

Line 4   Crystal curtain. (Cf. Poem 12.)

COMMENTARY

Miss Su Hsüeh-lin used this poem—together with another, addressed to the Taoist priest Yung, in which Li wrote, "You are now leaning against the Three-pearled Tree,/And no longer remember the time when leaves fell in the human world"—as evidence that there were three sisters called Sung, with one of whom the poet had a love affair, and that all the three sisters became Priest Yung's mistresses. I am not convinced by her arguments. For one thing, the "Three Blooms" or "Three-pearled Tree" need not represent three persons, but can be taken simply to signify a fabulous tree in fairyland. For instance, T'ao Ch'ien, in one of a series of poems called *On Reading the "Mountain and Sea Classic,"* mentioned the Three-pearled Tree, together with other fabulous trees and animals, as objects that delighted the goddess, Queen Mother of the West. Furthermore, the whole tone of the present poem is playful rather than serious. In the first line, by alluding to Tung-fang So's stealing of the immortal peaches (an episode that Li used several times in his poetry to represent clandestine love) and Ch'ang-o's theft of the elixir of life, the poet seems to be saying, "You cannot both indulge in secret love and pursue a religious life." The second line may mean, "You are locked up in the temple as the toad is locked up in the moon." And the last two lines may be paraphrased, "I should like to enjoy the moon with you, who are comparable to fabulous trees in fairyland, but your dwelling remains visible though inaccessible, as if it were behind a crystal curtain."

POEM **36**

Without Title

The immortal in the Purple Mansion is styled Precious Lamp;
The cloud-nectar, unconsumed, turns into ice.
How is it on a night when snow and moon mingle their lights,
You are still on the twelve-tiered Jasper Terrace?

NOTES

Line 1   Purple Mansion. Such a mansion is said to be in heaven, in Taoist
mythology.
Precious Lamp. There is no known Taoist deity of this name, and
the title seems to have been borrowed from Buddhism.

Line 4   Jasper Terrace. There are said to be twelve jasper terraces by the
K'un-lun Mountain, where the Queen Mother of the West dwells.

COMMENTARY

The immortal may again represent a Taoist nun, and the
cloud-nectar refers to wine: the speaker has prepared some wine in
anticipation of the nun's coming, but since she has failed to come, the
wine is left cold (it is a Chinese custom to warm wine before serving).
He then asks how she could stay, on such a beautiful night, in her
temple, which seems as far away as the Jasper Terrace.

POEM **37**

Playing the Pan-pipes under the Silver River

Wistfully gazing at the Silver River, I play the jade pan-pipes;

The pavilion is chilly, the courtyard cold, and dawn is drawing near.

Under the double quilt, a secret dream of former years is broken;

On another tree, a detained hen-bird was aroused last night.

In the moonlit arbor, an old fragrance is brought forth by the rain;

Behind the wind-blown curtain, the flickering candle is sheltered from the frost.

No need to follow recklessly the immortal on Mount K'ou—

The zither of Hsiang and the flute of Ch'in have enough feelings of their own.

NOTES

Title   Pan-pipes. The *sheng*, a kind of mouth organ resembling the pan-pipes.
Silver River. Another name for the Heavenly River (Milky Way).

Line 7   Mount K'ou. According to mythology, Prince Chin (also called Prince Ch'iao), son of King Ling of Chou (reigned 571–545 B.C.), was an expert player of the *sheng*. He became an immortal and ascended to heaven from Mount K'ou, riding on a white crane.

Line 8   Zither of Hsiang and flute of Ch'in. See notes on Poem 22, line 6 and line 3.

COMMENTARY

Some commentators think that the poem is written in memory of the poet's deceased wife, and others think that it refers to a Taoist nun. Neither interpretation, of course, can be proved. It is not even clear whether the speaker is a man or a woman, for the reference to a hen-bird makes it possible that the dramatis persona is a woman. In any case, the poem describes with great delicacy and sensitivity the lonely feelings of someone recalling a past love. Having been woken from a dream of former happiness, the speaker rises and plays the pan-pipes, gazing wistfully at the Heavenly River and probably thinking of the mythological couple, the Weaving Maid and the Cowherd, who are said to be reunited annually across this river. Or perhaps it is the sound of someone else playing the panpipes that has woken up the speaker, for in the original the subject of the verb "play" is not identified. He or she, then, sees a solitary bird that has apparently lost its mate and has been aroused from its sleep, like the speaker. The rain brings forth the faint trace of a once-familiar fragrance or perfume, as elusive as memories of bygone happiness, and the all-but-burnt-out candle, barely protected from the wind and the frost by a flimsy curtain, still flickers, like the embers of love. Why should one wish to become an immortal like Prince Chin, who played the panpipes and left the world? It is enough to be human and to know the taste of love, as the goddesses of River Hsiang and the Flute-player and his wife can testify.

Incidentally, since the Weaving Maid and the Cowherd are said to have their annual reunion across the Silver River on the seventh night of the Seventh Month, and Prince Chin is also supposed to have left Mount K'ou on this day, it is possible that the poem was written on Seventh Night, which seems to have had special sentimental associations for Li Shang-yin. (Cf. Poems 38–41.)

POEM 38

Written Casually on Seventh Night

The Precious Lady shakes her pearl pendant;
Ch'ang-o shines with her jade wheel.
The Spirit returns to her spouse in heaven,
And bequeaths her skill to mortals on earth.
The fragrance of flowers and fruit pervade a thousand doors;
The sound of pipes and reeds overflows the neighborhood.
Tomorrow, the "calf's-nose" breeches will be hung out in the sun:
Only then will they believe young Juan is poor!

NOTES

Title   Seventh Night. See Poem 37, Commentary.

Line 1   Precious Lady. Pao Wu or Wu-nü, name of a constellation near the Weaving Maid.

Line 2   Ch'ang-o. See Poem 29.

Line 3   The Spirit. The Weaving Maid.

Line 4   This refers to the custom among women of offering fruit to the
            Weaving Maid on Seventh Night and praying for skill in needle-
            work.

Lines 7–8 These lines allude to the story that Juan Hsien (third century A.D.), a
            "bohemian" literary man and nephew of the famous poet Juan Chi,
            hung out his "calf's-nose" breeches in the sun on the seventh day of
            the Seventh Month, when his wealthy kinsmen put out their finery
            to be sunned.

COMMENTARY

The poem seems to be partly a description of the Seventh
Night festival and partly a comment on the poet's own poverty. The
first two lines imaginatively picture the neighboring constellation and
the moon as companions of the Weaving Maid; the next two lines show
her going back to heaven to be reunited with the Cowherd, and blessing
mortal women with her skill; the third couplet describes actual festivi-
ties; and the last couplet, by alluding to the unconventional Juan Hsien,
reveals that Li Shang-yin too is not ashamed of his poverty.

POEM 39

Seventh Night of the Year Hsin-wei

I fear that the gods delight in keeping lovers apart,

And have purposely delayed the happy date of reunion.

As always, by the Silver River in the azure sky,

She eagerly awaits the time of the golden wind and jade-like dew.

*As the water-clock gradually drips away, she has long been
looking for him;*

*The tiny clouds have not yet touched each other—how late is the
crossing!*

How can she not wish to repay the magpies,

But only lend the spider her skill in weaving silk?

NOTES

Title   The year *hsin-wei* corresponds to 851.

Line 4   She. The Weaving Maid.
         Golden wind. *Chin-feng*, which means autumn wind, since autumn
         is supposed to correspond to *chin* (gold or metal in general), one of
         the Five Elements (*wu-hsing*). Normally I would have translated the
         phrase simply as "autumn wind," but here I have translated it liter-
         ally so as to preserve the verbal contrast between "golden wind"
         and "jade-like dew."

Line 7   Magpies. These are said to form a bridge across the Heavenly River
         for the Weaving Maid and the Cowherd on Seventh Night.

Line 8   Spider. When a woman prayed to the Weaving Maid for skill (see
         Poem 38), her prayer was considered answered if a spider made a
         web on the fruit she was offering to the goddess.

COMMENTARY

The poet puts himself in the position of the Weaving Maid.
As she waits impatiently for the Cowherd to come and meet her, she
cannot help feeling that the gods must take a positive pleasure in separ-
ating her from her lover and making her suffer. The four middle lines
emphasize her solitude and impatience, while the last two lines suggest
that she should not forget the magpies, who make it possible for her to
cross the River. The whole poem may be taken as a complaint against
the fate of all separated lovers, and the magpies perhaps represent
messengers who act as go-betweens. But it is also possible to take the
poem allegorically as referring to the poet's wish for greater reward in
official life, as Feng suggested.

POEM 40

Seventh Night of the Year Jen-shen

She has already mounted her seven-perfumed carriage;
Her heart and his both await the colorful sunrise clouds.
The wind is light, just enough to tinkle her pendants;
The moonlight is pale, not lending charm to the flowers.
The tender cassia blossoms spread their fragrance far;
The tall elm trees cast their slanting shadows.
When passing the fortune-teller's shop in Ch'eng-tu,
I once envied his knowledge about the magic raft.

NOTES

Title   The year *jen-shen* corresponds to 852, one year after the date of the previous poem.

Line 2   Her heart and his. The original simply repeats the word "heart," which I take to refer to the two mythical lovers' hearts, and not just to lend emphasis to the word.
Sunrise clouds (*hsiao hsia*). I suspect this is a misprint for "sunset clouds" (*wan hsia*), since it would make better sense if the Weaving Maid and her lover are waiting impatiently for the evening when they can have their annual reunion, rather than waiting for dawn. In fact, "moonlight" in line 4 is an emendation for "sunlight," suggested by Ho Cho and accepted by Feng Hao. If we emended "sunrise" in line 2 to "sunset," the poem would gain in consistency.

Lines 5–6   Cassia and elms. The cassia in the moon (see Poem 29) and the stars likened to elms (see Poem 26, line 10).

Lines 7–8   The fortune-teller refers to Yen Chün-p'ing (1st century B.C.), a wise man who kept a fortune-teller's shop in Ch'eng-tu. The story goes that when Chang Ch'ien went in search of the source of the Yellow River, he reached a place where he saw a woman weaving and a man giving his cow a drink by the river. When he asked where this was, he was told to consult Yen Chün-p'ing. Later, Chang asked Yen, who told him that on such and such a day a "guest star" invaded the spheres of the constellations the Weaving Maid and the Cowherd. Another version of the story does not mention Chang by name but only says that a man sailed up the Heavenly River in a raft sent from heaven. Li Shang-yin appears to have combined both versions.

COMMENTARY

On the literal level, the poem once more describes the Weaving Maid waiting to be reunited with her lover. In the first two lines, the lovers are imagined to be waiting impatiently for nightfall so that they can meet (hence, "sunset" would be more appropriate than "sunrise"). Then, the Weaving Maid is shown to be still waiting after night has fallen: she is standing in the moonlight (hence the necessity for the emendation of "sunlight" to "moonlight" in line 4.) In the next couplet, the fabulous cassia tree in the moon and the metaphorical elm trees are described as if they were real. The last couplet might be paraphrased thus: "Formerly I envied Yen Chün-p'ing for his knowledge about the Weaving Maid, but now I myself am going to meet her." On a symbolic level, the poem may be read as a description of a secret love, although some commentators inevitably interpret it as yet another veiled reference to Ling-hu T'ao.

POEM 41

Seventh Night

The pheasant fans slant apart; the phoenix curtain opens.
The starry bridge spans the River; the magpies fly back.
Would that one could exchange endless separations in this world
For the reunion that comes once every year!

NOTES

Line 1   Pheasant. The original has *luan*, another species of "phoenix," but I have changed it to "pheasant" to avoid repetition.

Line 2   Magpies. See Poem 39, line 7.

COMMENTARY

Here the poet contrasts the indefinite separations in human life with the annual reunion of the Weaving Maid and the Cowherd in heaven. It is not necessary to say, as some critics do, that the poem mourns the death of the poet's wife, for it can apply to separation in life as well. Cf. Tu Fu's lines

The Cowherd and the Weaving Maid need not grieve,
At least they can cross the River in autumn!

POEM **42**

Written after a Dream, while Listening to the Rain together with Candidates Wang and Cheng, on the 28th Night of the Seventh Month.

First I dreamed of the Dragon Palace, where treasures shone like flames,

And auspicious, colorful clouds filled the sunny sky with their brilliance;

In a moment, I was drunk, leaning against a tree on P'eng-lai,

And there was an immortal who tapped me on the shoulder.

Soon I heard the sound of pipes coming from far away,

But I could not see the players, separated by flying mists.

As I lingered, over the Hsiao and the Hsiang it rained again,

And the rain beat on the fifty strings of the Spirit of River Hsiang.

I had a glimpse of the Water God, who looked wistful;

[10] *Sell the mermaid-silk no more, for the sea has turned into fields!*

I also met the Hairy Maid, who was very listless,

And the Dragon Earl, who held aloft the Lotus Peak of Mount Hua.

Everything was vague and confusing—bright one moment, dark the next;

The indistinct forms emerged endlessly—broke up, then continued.

When I awoke, the rain was falling on the steps outside;

Alone, with my back to the cold lamp, I had been sleeping, pillowed on my hand.

NOTES

Title   For textual notes, see Additional Note 11.
Candidates. *Hsiu-ts'ai*, literally, "Budding Talent." Strictly speaking, the term referred to the "Budding Talent" examination (see *Biographical Sketch*), but in Li Shang-yin's time this examination had

long ceased to be held regularly, and the term was applied loosely to candidates for the Literary Examination.

Line 1   It was believed that the Dragon King's palace was full of treasures.

Line 3   P'eng-lai. Mountain in Taoist fairyland. Cf. Poem 4, line 8, and Poem 6, line 7.

Line 4   See Poem 22, line 4.

Line 7   Hsiao and Hsiang. Two rivers in modern Hunan.

Line 8   See Poem 1, line 1, and Poem 22, line 6.

Line 9   Water God. P'ing Yi, sometimes described as a water god, and sometimes identified with the god of the Yellow River.

Line 10   Mermaid-silk. Mermaids were said to spin fine silk and sell it to humans.
Sea turned into fields. Cf. Poem 34, line 3.

Line 11   Hairy Maid. Mao-nü, described as a girl covered with hair, who was at first a palace lady at the Court of the First Emperor of Ch'in and then became an immortal on the Lotus Peak of Mount Hua (mentioned in the next line).

Line 12   Dragon Earl. Lung-po. This name can be taken literally, in which case it seems to refer back to the Dragon Palace in Line 1; or as a reference to the fabulous country called Lung-po, where the inhabitants are supposed to be three hundred feet tall.

COMMENTARY

Feng and Chang take the poem as an allegory of the poet's political life, whereas Miss Su takes it as a veiled expression of his amorous adventures in the palace. Although the allusions and imagery in the poem can be ingeniously interpreted to fit either theory, or any other theory for that matter, attempts to do so are doomed to end in frustration. It would be better to take the poem simply as a description of a dream or fantasy. The images follow each other in a stream without any apparent connection, as they do in actual dreams or in "free association." Again, as in a dream, things which should be apart are brought together: the Dragon Palace under water is juxtaposed with the sunny sky above, and the Dragon Earl who lives under water (or, a giant from the fabulous country called Lung-po) is holding the peak of the Hua Mountain. The poem defies logical analysis, and should be approached on a sensuous level—the fantastic images pass on in a dreamlike sequence and evoke vague feelings of excitement and sadness in turn. The allusions to Taoist immortals and to other mythological figures add further associations. For instance, the mention of mermaid-silk in line 10 reminds us of the story about the mermaid who shed tears that turned into pearls (see note on Poem 1, line 5) and thus deepens the note of sadness; the allusion to the story that the sea has many times turned into fields suggests that life is full of vicissitudes. We can no doubt read many more ideas and Freudian associations into the poem if we wish, but for my own part I shall go no further.

POEM **43**

Thoughts during Separation

My breath is exhausted by the Dance of the Front Brook;
My heart aches at the Midnight Song.
I seek but cannot find the cloud from the Gorge;
What am I to do with the water in the ditch?
The northern wild goose has ceased to bring letters;
The bamboos by the Hsiang are stained with many tears.
I have no means of getting to see your face,
But let me still entrust the tiny ripples with a message!

NOTES

Line 1   Dance of the Front Brook. See Poem 3, line 7.

Line 2   Midnight Song. *Tzu-yeh Ko*, a song named after a singing girl called Tzu-yeh ("Midnight"), who is said to have lived some time before the fourth century. Many later love songs are also called Midnight Songs.

Line 3   Clouds from the Gorge. This alludes to the Goddess of Mount Wu, who assumes the form of a cloud in the morning. (Cf. Poem 25, line 3.) The Gorge refers to the Wu Gorge, one of the three famous gorges on the upper Yangtze River.

Line 4   Water in the ditch. Allusion to the following lines from the *Song of White Hair* by Chuo Wen-chün, the rich young widow who eloped with the poet Ssu-ma Hsiang-ju, written to express her fears that she might be deserted when she grew old:
    To-day, we meet with a gallon of wine;
    To-morrow, I shall be alone by the ditch water.

Line 5   Northern wild goose. When Su Wu (140 B.C.–60 B.C.) was detained by the Hsiung-nu tribes, a Chinese messenger told the Khan that the Chinese Emperor shot down a wild goose with a letter tied to one of its legs, informing the Emperor of Su's whereabouts. Su was consequently released.

Line 6   Bamboos by the Hsiang. Legend has it that when the sage Emperor Shun died, his two wives became goddesses of the river Hsiang (see Poem 3, Commentary) and shed tears on the bamboos, which turned speckled. (The species of bamboo with speckles is still called *Hsiang-fei chu* or "Princess of Hsiang" Bamboo.)

Line 8   This line is derived from Ts'ao Chih's *Goddess of the River Lo* (see note on Poem 5, line 6):

> I entrust the tiny ripples with my message.

COMMENTARY

Although in the original poem no pronouns are used and none of the subjects of the verbs is identified, the meaning makes it clear that the speaker is a woman. Some commentators would go further and regard her as an allegorical representation of the poet himself, but this does not seem to me necessary. We can take the poem simply as a description of the feelings of an imaginary woman separated from her lover. The first two lines suggest that she is a professional dancer and singer; the next two express her lovesickness: "I seek but cannot find traces of our former love, and I fear I am deserted." (The allusion to the Goddess of Mount Wu, who appeared to the King of Ch'u in an amorous dream, arouses erotic associations, while the allusion to Chuo Wen-chün's song strikes a pathetic note.) Lines 5–6 might be paraphrased, "I have had no news of you, and the bamboos are stained with my tears." The last two lines mean, "Although I have no way of getting to see you, I will not complain but will still try to send a message to you." Thus, by alluding to ill-fated singing girls, romantic goddesses, widowed queens, and deserted wives, the poet conjures up the picture of a lonely woman who fears she is deserted by her lover.

POEM 44

Parting at Dawn by the Wooden Bridge

Looking back at the high city walls, you see the Heavenly River set at dawn;

The windows of the post-pavilion overlook the tiny ripples.

The Water Sprite is about to leave, riding on a carp;

All night long, many red tears have been shed on the lotus flowers.

NOTES

Title   Commentators point out that there was an especially famous wooden bridge, where an inn was kept by a certain Third Lady, outside the city of Pien-chou. The poem could have been written there.

Line 2   Post-pavilion. A pavilion by the road for couriers to rest and change horses.

Line 3   Water Sprite. A man called Ch'in-kao is said to have disappeared into the Cho river and later to have emerged riding on a red carp.

Line 4   Red tears. Hsüeh Ling-yun, who became a concubine of Ts'ao P'i, Emperor Wen of Wei, shed tears which turned red like blood when she took leave of her parents.

COMMENTARY

The poem describes a parting of two lovers at dawn after a night of romantic love. The first two lines indicate the time and place of the parting; line 3 refers to the man, who is going away; line 4 expresses their parting sorrow.

POEM 45

Presented to His Excellency Ling-hu at an Official Banquet Held in T'ien-p'ing

Having ceased to hold the rainbow banners, they mount the altar:
They look like slender trees, and light enough for a crystal plate.
As night wears on, their moth-eyebrows knit in complaint;
In their thin garments, their jade-like beauty feels the chill.
The white-footed Buddhist monk is in danger of breaking his vows;
The dark-robed imperial censor wishes to retire from office.
Although I too am a guest of the general,
I dare not openly take a close look at them!

NOTES

Title   This poem was written about 830 when Li Shang-yin was on the staff of Ling-hu Ch'u, military governor of T'ien-p'ing Region. (See Part I, 2.) For the expression "His Excellency," see Additional note 12.

Line 2   Crystal plate. Allusion to Lady Swallow, who was said to be so light that the Emperor ordered a crystal plate made for her to dance on. Cf. Poem 21, line 8.

Line 3   Moth-eyebrows. A cliché derived from the *Book of Poetry*, where a beautiful woman's eyebrows are compared to the antennae of a moth.

Line 5   White-footed Buddhist monk. The monk Hui-shih (fifth century) was called "White-footed Master" because it was said that his feet remained white and clean even after he had trodden on dirt.

COMMENTARY

This is a description of Taoist nuns, some of whom were no better than courtesans. Their very presence at an official banquet, together with the whole irreverent tone of the poem, indicates that they were not devout and respectable. According to a note by the poet himself, the fifth line refers to Ts'ai Ching, who had once been a Buddhist monk. Since Ts'ai later became an imperial censor, it is possible that line 6 also refers to him. However that may be, the two lines together constitute a joke: the nuns are so charming that even a saintly monk would break his vows for them, and an imperial censor, custodian of public morals, would give up his post for their sake. In the last two lines, the poet turns the joke against himself: as a junior member of the staff and a mere youth of about seventeen, he dare not look too closely at the nuns himself. The tone of the poem is playful, if not sarcastic, and there is no suggestion that the poet is falling in love with any of the nuns.

POEM **46**

Spring Outing

On the steep bridge the piebald horse gallops;
Over the long river the white birds soar.
The mist is light, barely moistening the willows;
The wind is wild, about to blow on the peaches.
Leaning on the balcony of the three-tiered tower,
I caress my sword bedecked with seven jewels.
Master Yü is the youngest of them all;
The green grass envies his spring gown.

NOTES

Line 7   Master Yü. Yü Yi (305–45), a talented and handsome young man, who achieved military successes as well as literary repute.

COMMENTARY

This poem shows Li Shang-yin in a rare mood of happiness. Judging by its tone of carefree gaiety and youthful confidence, it must be an early work. Although in the original no pronoun is used and it is not clear who is being compared to young Yü, such an omission is common practice in Chinese poetry, and it seems safe to assume that the poet is speaking of himself. Feng Hao takes the allusion as a reference to some colleague younger than the poet, and dates the poem 847, when Li left the north, in spring, for Kweilin (see Part I, 2). Chang Ts'ai-t'ien argues for an earlier date, 834, when Li may have taken a spring trip. Both, in their eagerness to pin the poem down to an exact date, seem to me to err in taking the title "Spring Outing" (*ch'un yu*) to mean a trip undertaken on official business.

POEM 47

Sunset Tower

The flowers are bright, the willows dark, the heavens surrounded with sorrow.

Having climbed the double city walls, I climb the tower.

I wish to ask the lonely wild goose whither it is flying,

Not knowing that my own destiny is just as vague as his!

POET'S NOTE

The tower is situated in Ying-yang, and the poem was written when my friend, the present Vice-Minister Hsiao of Sui-ning, was prefect there.

TRANSLATOR'S NOTE

We know that Hsiao Huan was prefect of Ying-yang (another name for Cheng-chou, Li's home) in 833, and later became Vice-Minister of Justice. In 836 he was demoted and banished to Sui-chou (Sui-ning, in modern Szechwan) where he died in the same year. The poem, therefore, must have been written in 833, and not in 836 as Chang Ts'ai-t'ien stated.

POEM 48

Painting of Pine-trees, A Gift From Li Hung

The ten thousand grasses are already cool with dew,
As I open the scroll and unfold the ancient pines.
Among blue mountains that stretch by the vast sea,
On which peak are these trees growing?
Their solitary roots spread far, relying on nothing;
They stand straight, pillaring the primeval air of nature:
Upright as the persons of true gentlemen,
Erect as brave knights with chests thrust forward.
Their low-bending branches stretch powerfully,
[10]   Suddenly twisting upward as if to reach the sky.
Again, they are like dragons running in surprise,
Silently encountering rushing clouds.
Their offshoots give forth tiny leaves
As soft as a fine fox fur coat,
Or the thick tufts of hair on top of a child's head,
Or the dense dark eyebrows of a beautiful lady.
After looking at them for a long time, my eyes are dazzled;
Quickly and suddenly, their appearance changes:
Just now they stood lofty and straight,
[20]   In a moment their graceful branches seem to be pulled.
Then I seem to be in a cool secluded chamber,
Where a green coverlet spreads like the vault of heaven,
Or watching the maidens from the Wisteria Hill
Making up their faces early in the morning.
The fine twigs, I suspect, have obtained the primordial essence;
The fierce trunks seem to compete with the works of the gods.
Though the swallows and sparrows are silent,
The mists and dews frequently appear in abundance.

The fragrant orchid is ashamed that it ages so soon,

[30]   The green bamboo that it is empty inside.

These pines may assemble auspicious phoenixes,

And are worthy to shelter rain-making dragons.

As for the twisting cassias of the Huai mountains,

Or the shady mulberry tree of the land of Shu,

Though their branches are bright and their twigs tender,

How can they possess the same spiritual power?

Formerly the story of the Emperor of Hsien-yang was heard;

Of late, people have been talking about the man of Mount Hsi.

Once the pine received the title of "immortal,"

[40]   Another time it was given the rank of a high minister.

The Chung-nan Mountain and the Pure Capital

Communicate with each other from afar, through mist and rain.

Who knows whether, by wishing it night after night,

One could raise the southwest wind or not?

Formerly a fine person of elegant tastes

Cherished the painting as if it had been the Lunar Bell,

Placed it among a handful of treasure boxes,

Enwrapped in thousands of layers of fragrant red silk.

But one day the demons cast their eyes on his chamber,

[50]   And manifold nets and snares were thickly spread;

A red-feathered arrow hit a fatal point—

Right and wrong were all over in a moment.

In life he was like the moon over the blue sea;

In death he was trampled like grass in the frosty countryside.

The things he used to handle and enjoy in his lifetime

Were scattered and passed into the hands of his servants and slaves.

I have heard that a monster-reflecting mirror,

As well as a sword of supernatural powers,

Will find its own proper dwelling place,

[60]   And will not be obscured by common objects.

When my friend held this painting in his hand,

He looked around for the right owner.

Who am I that he should have chosen me?

Happily I took the work of marvel in both hands.

I repaid his kindness with a lacquered zither;

I hung it up behind a curtain of pearls.

At that time it was the height of summer,

Yet the room felt as cold as the depth of winter.

I recall when I declined to see visitors

[70]   *And studied immortality east of the Yü-yang Mountain,*

There were a thousand trees all like these,

Lining the road that led to the Jade Palace.

The Song of Dark Clouds issuing from my mouth,

I held golden lotus flowers in my hands.

Thick mists surrounded my rainbow-colored sleeves

Whose brightness mingled with that of the bamboos.

Alas, that I should have fallen into the net of this world,

And left all that behind like the lost bow!

My form and spirit mount the Heavenly Altar,

[80]   *And I gaze at the sun rising high above the sea.*

Finally I hope to return on a purple phoenix,

And send this to the Old Man of Fu-sang.

NOTES

Title   The original title also contains the words, "written on two sheets of paper, altogether forty rhymes" (actually there are forty-one rhymes). Li Hung is the man who passed, as "Top of the List," the Literary Examination at the same time as Li Shang-yin, in 837. The poem seems to have been written before that date.

Line 2   Scroll. The original simply says "picture" (*t'u*), but I have used the word "scroll," for otherwise the verb "open" would not make sense. Chinese paintings are, of course, generally mounted on scrolls.

Line 6   Primeval air of nature. *Hung-meng*, literally "vast and vague", a term taken from the Taoist work *Chuang Tzu*.

Line 13   Offshoot. *Sun-chih*, literally "grandson branches," originally used to describe the rhizomes of bamboos.

Line 15   This line may be textually corrupt and is obscure in meaning. My translation follows the emendation suggested by Yao P'ei-ch'ien. See Additional Note 13.

Line 20   This line is translated in accordance with Feng Hao's emendation. See Additional Note 13.

Line 22   Vault of heaven. For a different interpretation, see Additional Note 13.

Line 23   Maidens of Wisteria Hill. The original line has "maidens of Chi-
            Lo," alluding to Hsi Shih and Cheng Tan, two famous beauties of
            the fifth century B.C., who came from the Chu *Lo* Hill ("Hemp and
            Wisteria Hill") in Chu-*chi* district in the kingdom of Yüeh (modern
            Chekiang). They were presented by King Kou-chien of Yüeh to his
            enemy King Fu-ch'ai of Wu, and brought about the latter's down-
            fall.

Line 25   Primordial essence. *Ch'i-mu*, literally "mother of air," a term taken
            from the *Chuang Tzu*, where it is explained by commentators to
            mean the essence of the primordial force of nature.

Line 33   Cassias of Huai mountains. This alludes to the lines
                The cassia trees grow in clusters on the secluded mountains,
                Their twisting and linking branches intertwine,
            from "Summons to a Recluse", attributed to Liu An, Prince of
            Huai-nan (179–122 B.C.).

Line 34   Mulberry tree of Shu. When Liu Pei (162–223), future founder of
            the Shu-Han dynasty, was a boy, a mulberry tree grew outside his
            house, measuring some fifty feet and with a shady top that looked
            like a canopy. This was regarded as a good omen. Strictly speaking
            the allusion is not accurate, for Liu Pei's native district was not in
            Shu, although he became Emperor there.

Line 37   Emperor of Hsien-yang. The First Emperor of Ch'in (reigned 246–
            210 B.C.) whose capital was Hsien-yang. The story is alluded to in
            line 40.
            Man of Mount Hsi. This has not been satisfactorily identified.

Line 40   High minister. When the First Emperor of Ch'in sacrificed to the
            sacred T'ai Mountain, a storm came. He found shelter under a pine
            tree which he subsequently made a "high minister."

Line 41   Chung-nan Mountain. A mountain to the south of the T'ang
            capital Ch'ang-an.
            Pure Capital. Ch'ing-tu, dwelling of the Emperor of Heaven in
            Taoist mythology.

Line 44   Southwest wind. Wind from the gates of heaven.

Line 46   Lunar Bell. *Yüeh-chung*, possibly alluding to the story that the god-
            dess Lu Miao-tien had a bell shaped like a crescent moon, given to
            her by a god.

Line 49   This line alludes to the saying, "in the house of a noble family,
            demons cast their eyes on the chambers," meaning that a rich and
            noble family is the object of envy of demons as well as of humans.

Line 57   Monster-reflecting mirror. Emperor Hsüan of Han (reigned 73–
            49 B.C.) had a magic mirror which was said to be able to reflect the
            forms of monsters. When he died, the mirror disappeared of its own
            accord. In later stories, "monster-reflecting mirror" became a
            common object.

Line 58   Sword of supernatural powers. King He-lu of Wu (reigned 513–
            495 B.C.) had a sword which flew away to the King of Ch'u, because
            the latter was more virtuous!

Line 69   Visitors. The original has "four horses" (*ssu chi*), the meaning of
            which is not clear. I have followed Feng Hao's suggestion that this
            refers to visitors coming on horseback from all directions.

Line 72   Jade Palace. A Taoist temple.

Line 73   Song of Dark Clouds. A song sung by one of the ladies-in-waiting of the goddess Queen Mother of the West.

Line 78   Lost bow. King Kung of Ch'u (reigned 589–557 B.C.) lost a bow and refused to search for it, saying, "A man of Ch'u lost it, a man of Ch'u will find it. Why search for it? (In other words one man's loss is another's gain.)

Line 79   Heavenly Altar. T'ien-t'an, name of the highest peak of the Wang-wu Mountains, of which the Yü-yang Mountain is a branch.

Line 82   Old Man of Fu-sang. The god Lord Prince of the East (Tung Wang Kung), who is said to rule over Fu-sang, an island in the sea. The name Fu-sang literally means "supporting mulberries" and refers to the story that on this island there are two giant mulberry trees supporting each other, whose berries bestow immortality. The name Fu-sang is sometimes used for Japan.

COMMENTARY

This long poem may be divided into five sections. The first section (lines 1–28) is a description of the painting of pine trees. The second section (lines 29–40) consists of a eulogy of the pine in symbolic and allusive terms. Section 3 (lines 41–44) at first sight appears irrelevant but on closer examination is seen to be an anticipation of section 5, since it alludes to the Taoist heaven. Section 4 (lines 45–68) gives an account of the previous history of the painting and how it came into the poet's possession. Section 5 (lines 69–82) develops the hint dropped in section 3: the poet shows how the painting reminds him of his study of Taoism, and expresses the wish to withdraw from the world and go to the dwelling of Taoist immortals.

Let us now examine the poem more closely, section by section. In the first section, the opening line indicates the time when the poem was written, some time after the painting was given to the poet by his friend in the summer (see line 67). As the poet gradually unfolds the scroll, his eyes roam over the painting, and what a wonderful world is revealed to him! (Lines 3–26). In describing the painted pine trees, he almost exhausts all available vocabulary and makes abundant use of imagery: the pines are compared to upright gentlemen, brave knights, and running dragons (with obvious symbolic implications); their tiny new leaves are likened to fox fur, a child's hair, and a lady's eyebrows; and their foliage is compared to a green coverlet (which in turn is compared to the vault of heaven), and to beautiful maidens at their morning toilet. The description ends with a couplet (lines 27–28) which indirectly pays tribute to the painter's skill: as you look at the painting, you almost expect to hear swallows twitter and sparrows chirp, and feel the presence of abundant mists and dews.

In the next section (lines 29–40) the poet eulogizes the virtues of the pine. Compared with it, the orchid, though fragrant, is too short-lived, and the bamboo, though enduring, is empty inside and not solid. As a matter of fact, all three are common symbols of virtue and moral integrity in Chinese literature and art, but the poet here praises the pine at the expense of the other two. Further, he alludes to the cassia trees celebrated by the Prince of Huai-nan in connection with the life of a recluse, and the mulberry tree that prophesied the future greatness of Liu Pei, and concludes that even these are inferior to the pine in spiritual power. Then, in lines 37 and 40, the poet alludes to the story that a pine tree was given the rank of high minister for having sheltered the First Emperor of Ch'in from a storm, perhaps implicitly contrasting the happy lot of the tree with the fate of virtuous men who receive no such recognition from the ruler. Lines 38 and 39 are obscure. The "man of Mount Hsi" in line 38 has not been satisfactorily explained: none of the stories cited by commentators seems to fit. In fact, the word that I translated as "man" is ambiguous: in Chinese the word is *nung*, which is commonly used as a pronoun ("I" or "you") and is therefore of uncertain gender. Line 39 is equally puzzling. Because line 40 refers back to line 37, line 39 should refer to the same story as line 38, so that two stories are alluded to in the four lines. Since we do not know what story is being alluded to in line 38, we are in no position to interpret the meaning of line 39. Also, in some editions, line 39 has *chia-jen* ("beautiful lady") instead of *hsien-jen* ("immortal"), but once again, not knowing the story alluded to, we cannot decide which is the correct reading, though the latter seems more appropriate.

The brief third section (lines 41–44) foreshadows section 5 by alluding to the Taoist heaven and hinting at a wish to go there, riding on the southwest wind. Since the Chung-nan Mountain is near the capital Ch'ang-an, it seems to represent the hub of this world, in contrast to the Pure Capital where the Emperor of Heaven lives. Lines 41–42 therefore may be interpreted as meaning: "Although the capital of this world and that of the gods are far from each other, there can be communication between them." The "southwest wind" in line 44 I take to refer simply to the wind from the gates of heaven, such as mentioned in a poem by Kuo P'u (276–324), and I do not find it necessary to connect this line, as Feng did, with a line from Ts'ao Chih, to which Li Shang-yin alludes in another poem (Poem 17), and to take it as a veiled reference to the Emperor.

In the fourth section (lines 45–68), Li Shang-yin relates the sad story of the painting's previous owner in highly abstruse terms. In the first place, what I have translated as "fine person" in line 45 is an ambiguous expression, *mei-jen*, which usually means "beautiful lady" but could mean "virtuous man." I have therefore used the noncommittal "person." (though later, in Line 49, I have had to use "his.") In any case, this person of elegant tastes cherished the painting as if it had been some celestial treasure, until one day, the demons jealous of his possessions struck, and he fell into the snares of his enemies and was killed by a red-feathered arrow. All was over in one moment—what was the good of discussing who was right and who was wrong any more? He who had been looked up to like the moon above the sea was now trampled like grass. His treasured objects of art now became scattered, and were owned by his former servants and slaves. But a marvelous work of art, like a magic mirror or a supernatural sword, will find its right owner, and so this painting eventually found its way to Li Hung, who then, after a careful choice, presented it to the poet, as a man worthy of such a rare picture.

In the last section (lines 69–82) the poet shows how the painting reminds him of the time when he withdrew from society and studied Taoism in the mountains. He recalls the happy days when he felt like an immortal, and laments the fact that he has fallen into the net of this dusty world and left his Taoist paradise behind, like the bow lost by the King of Ch'u, and he hopes that someone else may have found that paradise. Finally, the poet expresses his wish to roam freely and return to his Taoist paradise, riding on a phoenix, and then show this painting (or perhaps this poem) to the god of the fairy island in the sea.

Our analysis of the poem enables us to follow the poet's train of thought. His mind first dwells on the painted pine trees, then turns to contemplate the pine itself as a symbol of virtue, recalling its many noble associations. Next, it turns to thoughts of otherworldly things, of the dwelling of the gods. But these thoughts are momentarily suppressed; instead, the poet turns to recall the tragic life of the previous owner of the painting. Realization of the vicissitudes of fortune, exemplified by this tragic life, reinforces the poet's desire to withdraw from the world and go to the Taoist paradise.

This poem is a truly remarkable *tour de force*, especially when we remember that it was probably written by Li Shang-yin in his early twenties. Not only does it describe the painting and reveal the power of art to inspire lofty otherworldly feelings, but it also praises the pine tree as a symbol of moral integrity and indirectly pays a compliment to Li Hung and to the poet himself. Li Hung, by choosing such a painting as a gift and choosing the poet as its recipient, shows his discrimination and his appreciation of the spiritual qualities which the pine symbolizes and the two friends both possess. The poet, having been chosen to own such a work, implicitly admits his own suitability to be its guardian, since he is spiritually and artistically attuned to it. The poem ends with a glorious vision of the poet triumphantly returning to paradise and proudly displaying to the smiling gods this painting and the poem he has just written.

POEM **49**

To Ts'ui Yung and Ts'ui Kun, while Staying at Lo's Pavilion

The bamboo bank is dust-free, the water beneath the railings clear;

My thoughts of you travel far, over many towns.

The autumn gloom does not disperse; the frost flies at night.

I've kept a few withered lotuses to listen to the rain.

NOTES

Title   Ts'ui Yung and Ts'ui Kun were sons of Ts'ui Jung, under whom the poet served. The poem was written after Ts'ui Jung's death in 834. The "Lo's Pavilion" cannot be identified with certainty.

COMMENTARY

The strength of the poem lies in the last line, which, by its reference to listening to the rain, suggests that the poet has been lying sleepless at night, thinking of his friends. Moreover, the idea of keeping withered lotuses so as to listen to the rain beating on them might contain a symbolic message: even withered lotuses are useful, for they add to the music of the rain; so are old ties of friendship, which should not be severed. (Cf. the common expression "*ou tuan ssu lien*" or "the lotus root is cut asunder but the filament remains unbroken," which is used to describe two people who have severed relations but cannot forget each other completely.) The poem shows that Li Shang-yin remained grateful to his former patron and still cherished friendly feelings for Ts'ui Jung's sons.

POEM **50**

The Tower on the City Wall of An-ting

The high city wall stretches far; the tower stands a hundred feet.

Beyond the green willow branches, I see nothing but banks and islets.

Master Chia in his youth in vain shed tears;

Wang Ts'an in spring once more went on a distant journey.

For ever remembering the rivers and lakes to which I would return, white-haired,

I yet wish to turn round heaven and earth before entering a tiny boat.

Not knowing the rotten rat was considered tasty,

The phoenix unwittingly aroused endless suspicions!

NOTES

Title   An-ting is another name for Ching-chou, where the poet stayed in 838.

Line 3   Master Chia. Chia Yi (201–169 B.C.), famous scholar of the Han dynasty, who in his youth memorialized the throne several times, saying that there were things in the government that deserved weeping about. See also Poem 98.

Line 4   Wang Ts'an (177–217), celebrated poet, particularly well known for his piece called "Climbing the Tower," which expresses home-sickness.

Lines 7–8   These lines allude to the following fable in the Taoist work *Chuang Tzu:* Master Hui was prime minister of Liang and Master Chuang went to see him. Someone said to Master Hui, "Master Chuang's intention, in coming here, is to replace you as prime minister." Master Hui was afraid and searched the kingdom for three days and three nights. Master Chuang went to see him and said, "In the south there was a bird called *yüan-ch'u* (phoenix); it set out from the south sea to fly to the north sea; unless it was a *wu-t'ung* tree, it would not rest on it; unless it was the fruit of bamboo, it would not eat; unless it was the water from a sweet spring, it would not drink. Then there was an owl that had got hold a of rotten rat, and when the phoenix flew past it, it looked up at the phoenix and cried, 'Ho!' Now, do you, sir, wish to *ho* me with your kingdom of Liang?"

COMMENTARY

As the poet stands in the tower on the city wall, he surveys the scene and expresses his feelings. The opening couplet describes the actual scenery. In the second couplet he compares himself to two earlier writers: "Like Chia Yi, I too shed tears in vain over the deplorable conditions of the government, and like Wang Ts'an, I am constantly traveling from one place to another." The next couplet may be paraphrased thus: "Though I always bear in mind my ultimate wish to withdraw from the world and roam freely over rivers and lakes in a tiny boat, I would only do so in my old age, having accomplished the task of setting the world right." He then alludes to the fable about the phoenix and the owl: "Official positions mean no more to me than the rotten rat means to the phoenix, but others, judging me by their own standards, suspect me of having political ambitions, as the owl suspects the phoenix of wishing to rob it of its rotten rat." Though the sentiments in the poem are commonplace and perhaps none too sincere, they are expressed with remarkable force. The third couplet is particularly impressive as the work of a young man, for it calmly announces the poet's ambition to set the world right and anticipates the distant future when, his task done, he will withdraw from the world and lead a life of freedom—the professed ideal of every traditional Chinese scholar. It is said that the Sung poet and statesman Wang An-shih (1021–86) was especially fond of this couplet, because it summed up his own life ambition.

POEM 5I

Reflections

To dally halfway is what I seem to excel in!
Since ancient times, fate and talent have been at loggerheads.
Let me advise you not to add feet when drawing a snake;
He who did so missed the goblet of fragrant wine!

NOTES

Lines 3–4   These lines allude to the following story. A man gave a goblet of wine to his attendants, who agreed among themselves that whoever first finished drawing a snake should have it. One of them finished his drawing first but added feet to it, so that he missed the prize which he should have won. This fable gave rise to the common expression "adding feet when drawing a snake" (*hua-she t'ien-tsu*).

COMMENTARY

Feng Hao suggested that this poem was written in 839, when Li Shang-yin was transferred from the Imperial Library to the district of Hung-nung. According to Feng's interpretation, Li is showing regret over his marriage, which has not helped his career but has incurred the resentment of Ling-hu T'ao. The poet now feels that his whole effort to gain advancement through marriage has been as foolish as "adding feet to the snake" and has cost him his position at the Imperial Library, the much envied "goblet of wine." This interpretation is ingenious but not really convincing. For one thing, there is no evidence that Li lost his post at the Imperial Library through Ling-hu's intervention. Secondly, the poem contains no allusions to marriage. The only allusion in the poem can refer to any overzealous effort that defeats its own purpose. I prefer, therefore, to take the poem in more general terms, as an expression of discontent followed by resignation to fate. The poet begins by mocking himself for being such an expert at making no progress in his career; he then tries to console himself with the thought that he is not alone in this—since ancient times, many talented men have suffered a similar fate. Finally he warns himself against overeagerness in promoting his career, the very fault with which he has been charged by later historians and commentators.

POEM *52*

Lament for Liu Fen

The Heavenly Emperor's palace is deeply enclosed within nine gates;

The Great Shaman does not descend to inquire about your wrongs.

Since we parted at Huang-ling, spring waves have kept us apart;

Now a letter comes from the bank of the P'en as the autumn rain falls.

Only An-jen could have written a fit funeral ovation;

Who says Sung Yü knew how to summon the soul?

A lifelong teacher and friend—this you were to me:

I dare not mourn you outside the door of the inner chamber.

NOTES

Title   For Liu Fen, see Part I, 2.

Line 1   See Poem 12, line 6.

Line 2   Great Shaman. Wu-hsien, a legendary figure, described as chief of the shamans of remote antiquity. See David Hawkes, *Ch'u Tz'u, Songs of the South,* p. 31.

Line 3   Huang-ling. A place in modern Hunan province.

Line 4   Bank of the P'en. The P'en is a river in Kiangsi province. The expression "bank of the P'en" (P'en-p'u) can also be taken as the name of the town at the mouth of the P'en river.

Line 5   An-jen. Courtesy name of P'an Yüeh (or Yo; 247–300), who excelled in writing funeral ovations (*lei*).

Line 6   Sung Yü. A poet of the third century B.C., about whom little is known. Traditionally he is said to have written the "Summons to the Soul" to summon the departed soul of his master, the great poet Ch'ü Yüan. See Hawkes, p. 102.

Line 8   Confucius is recorded to have said, "For the death of a teacher, I cry in the inner chamber; for the death of a friend, I cry outside the door of the inner chamber."

PARAPHRASE

The palace of our Emperor, like that of the Emperor of Heaven, is remote and inaccessible, and no messenger has been sent to investigate the wrongs you suffered. Since we parted at Huang-ling, we have been separated by rivers and hills; now a letter comes from the bank of the P'en to tell me you are dead, on this gloomy, rainy autumn day. I cannot express my feelings: only a P'an Yüeh could have written a fit elegy for you. I wish I could summon your soul back, as Sung Yü is said to have summoned Ch'ü Yüan's, but can one believe in such things? You were to me both a teacher and a friend; I would not presume to mourn you as a friend, yet to mourn you as a teacher would make our relation seem too formal. I am thus reduced to mourning you in silence.

COMMENTARY

This is one of four poems mourning the death of Liu Fen, in Li Shang-yin's collected poems. (There is another one addressed to Liu in his lifetime.) The exact time and place of Liu's death, as well as those of his last meeting with Li, are matters of controversy and do not concern us here. Suffice it to say that in lamenting Liu Fen the poet is not only expressing grief at the death of a friend but also voicing his indignation against the circumstances that led to Liu's exile and death. The allusions to the Great Shaman, mentioned in Ch'ü Yüan's "On Encountering Sorrow" (*Li-sao*), and to the "Summons of the Soul," implicitly compare Liu to Ch'ü, the archetype of the virtuous and loyal official wrongly banished from the Court.

POEM **53**

Lament for Registrar Liu Fen

Living apart, we watched the stars and years change;
All hope gone, we are separated by life and death.
The cinnamon lees gather in the wine jar;
The old rue leaves lie cold on the book labels.
The river wind blows hard on the wild geese;
The mountain trees, sheltering cicadas, stand in the setting sun.
A single cry, a thousand times turning back the head—
But heaven is high and does not hear!

NOTES

Title   Registrar. *Ssu-hu*, a junior provincial official in charge of registration of households, revenue, etc. Liu Fen was banished to Liu-chou to be the registrar there, but it is not known for certain whether he died on his way to exile or after he arrived at his destination. It was customary to refer to a man by his official title even if it was a humble one.

Line 3   Cinnamon. Cinnamon wine is mentioned in a song in the anthology *Ch'u Tz'u* (see Hawkes, p. 36). Here it is merely a poetic touch, rather than a realistic detail.

Line 4   Rue leaves. These were placed in books to keep away worms. Book labels. Chinese books bear labels on the front cover for writing the titles on.

COMMENTARY

This poem is more passionate than the preceding one. The poet says, "Formerly, although we were living apart, we could still hope to see each other again, but now all such hope is gone, for we are separated for ever, the living from the dead." In lines 3–4, he conjures up a vivid picture of the few personal belongings that his friend may have left behind: a wine jar with only dregs left, and some books on which the rue leaves lie cold. In the next two lines, he seems to imagine the soul of his friend wandering like a wild goose blown by the wind, or crying sadly like a cicada at sunset. The subject in line 5 is not identified, so that we cannot tell whether it is the poet who is crying and turning back his head to look at his friend's abode, or the soul of the friend who is crying and looking back at his home. But in either case the last two lines remain effective: heaven does not hear the cries of anguish and protest of mortals, just as the Emperor does not hear the cries of his suffering subjects.

POEM 54

Listening to the Drum

Above the city wall, a drum repeatedly sounds;
Beneath the city wall, the evening river is clear.
I wish to ask for the "thrice-repeated Yü-yang beat",
But there is no Ni Cheng-p'ing in the world to-day!

NOTES

Line 4   Ni Cheng-p'ing. Courtesy name of Ni Heng (173–198), a proud
scholar who was summoned by the prime minister Ts'ao Ts'ao to be
a drummer as an insult. Ni played the "thrice-repeated Yü-yang
beat" in a heroic manner and took off his clothes to insult Ts'ao
before his assembled guests. The story is still presented on the stage,
and Ni's name has become a synonym for intrepidity.

COMMENTARY

It is possible that in writing this poem Li Shang-yin had in
mind the fearless and outspoken Liu Fen. I am therefore placing it
immediately after the two elegies for Liu.

POEM 55

Early Rising

Light breeze and dew in the early morning—
By the curtains I rise, all alone.
The oriole cries while the flowers smile:
Who owns this spring after all?

POEM **56**

Spring Wind

Though the spring wind is naturally fine,
Things in spring are too luxuriant.
If only spring had feelings, she should
Send flowers to one twig alone.
My feelings differ from spring's feelings:
Before spring, I am already heartbroken.

COMMENTARY

When one is in a sad mood, the bounties of nature can become oppressive. Therefore the poet wishes that spring would allow only one twig to have blossoms.

POEM **57**

Fallen Flowers

From the tall pavilion the guests have all departed;
In the little garden flowers helter-skelter fly.
They fall at random on the winding path,
And travel far, sending off the setting sun.
Heartbroken, I cannot bear to sweep them away;
Gazing hard, I watch them till few are left.
Their fragrant heart, following spring, dies;
What they have earned are tears that wet one's clothes.

COMMENTARY

The first line suggests the inevitability of parting and the passing of time, and hence foreshadows the sad mood of the rest of the poem: just as parties have to come to an end and guests have to go, so flowers have to fall, the sun has to set, and spring has to pass away. As the poet watches the fallen flowers, he identifies himself completely with them, so that the heart that dies and the tears that wet his clothes belong as much to the flowers as to the poet. The poem is thus a remarkable example of empathy.

POEM *58*

Being Intoxicated beneath the Flowers

While searching for fragrance, I became intoxicated with the "Streaming Cloud" unawares;

As I slept soundly, leaning against a tree, the sun had already set.

After the guests have dispersed and I have woken up deep in the night,

I still hold a red candle to enjoy the few remaining flowers.

NOTES

Line 1   "Streaming Cloud." *Liu-hsia*, a fancy name for wine, based on the story about a man to whom the immortals gave "streaming cloud" to drink.

POEM 59

Drinking Alone in a Small Garden

Who could have knit the willow's belts?
The flower buds are unwilling to open yet.
Only a pair of dancing butterflies are left;
Not a single person has come here.
I half unfold the dragon-whisker mat,
And lightly pour into the horse-brain cup.
Every year the arrival of spring is uncertain;
I have been deceived by the early blooming plum!

NOTES

Line 5   Dragon-whisker. *Lung-hsü*, a kind of grass.

Line 6   Horse-brain. *Ma-nao*, Chinese name for agate, so called because the veins of the agate were supposed to look like horse brains.

POEMS 60-64

Willow Branch

Preface

Willow Branch was a girl who lived in a street in Lo-yang. Her father, a wealthy merchant, died in a storm over a lake. The mother paid little attention to her sons but lavished her care on the girl. Having reached her seventeenth year, Willow Branch was so restless that whenever she was making up her face or dressing her hair she would get up before she had finished. Sometimes she would tune the strings, or play the stops of the pipe, to produce music like the winds from heaven and the waves of the sea, or melodies suggesting secret memories and heartbreaking grievances.

Those who lived near their house and were friends with the family, having heard her play for ten years, all suspected her of living in an intoxicated dream, and no one wanted to be betrothed to her. My elder cousin Jang-shan lived close to her house. One cloudy spring day, Jang-shan dismounted from his horse by a willow to the south of Willow Branch's house, and recited my "Terrace of Yen" poems.[1] Willow Branch asked in surprise, "Who wrote these? Who did these?" Jang-shan told her. "These are by a young cousin of mine." Willow Branch broke a long girdle with her own hands, tied a love knot, and gave it to Jang-shan, saying, "Give this to your cousin and beg him to write a poem for me!" Next day, I rode to her street. Willow Branch had finished her make-up, with her hair done up in two buns, and stood there holding a fan, as the wind lifted one of her sleeves. Pointing at me, she said, "So you are the young cousin! Three days later I shall go with some neighbors to splash our skirts by the river,[2] and I shall take a Po-shan censer[3] and wait for you there." I agreed. But it so happened that I was due to leave for the capital with a friend, and this friend, in jest, stole my luggage and left first, so that I was unable to stay. Later, Jang-shan came in the snow one day and said, "She has been taken away by a lord from the east!" Next year, Jang-shan again was going to the east, and we parted by the Hsi river. I therefore wrote the following poems to be put up where she used to live.

Notes

1   See Poems 7–10.

2   "Splash our skirts." It was a custom for women to go to a river and splash their skirts with water so as to ward off evil spirits, usually on the third day of the Third Month, in observance of the Purification Festival.

3   "Po-shan censer." A censer made in the form of a symbolic mountain, with a tray underneath filled with water to symbolize the sea. Its mention here contains an allusion to a love song:

> My love is the incense that sinks in water,
> And I am the Po-shan censer.

---

60   *By the flower pistils and honeycombs,*

        A male bee and a female butterfly—

        Living at the same time but not of the same kind,

        How can they still long for each other?

COMMENTARY

The symbolism in this poem is obvious, but the poem itself could be written from the poet's point of view or from the girl's. Either he is complaining, or she is imagined to be complaining, that they belong to two different worlds.

61   *She is a lilac tree whose twigs*
      Have just put forth knot-like flowers.
      The t'an-ch'i *board made of jade*
      Is not level at its center.

NOTES

Line 3   T'an-ch'i. Literally, "snap-chess," a game for two played with six white and six black pieces, on a board with a raised center. Each player would snap his fingers against one of his own pieces so as to hit one of his opponent's.

Line 4   This line involves two puns. The word for "level" (p'ing) also means "fair" or "just," and the word for "center" (hsin) also means "heart." Therefore, "not level at its center" puns on "feels injustice in one's heart."

The effect of the puns is, of course, lost in the translation, but in the original, the poem is ingenious. The comparison of the heart that feels injustice to a *t'an-ch'i* board with an uneven center is far-fetched but interesting. We may perhaps compare it with Donne's famous "Metaphysical conceit," which likens two lovers' souls to a pair of compasses. Again, although the two halves of the poem do not seem to bear any relation to each other, their juxtaposition is no more startling than in Donne's:

> Goe, and catche a falling starre,
> Get with child a mandrake roote,

or in Eliot's:

> Garlic and sapphires in the mud
> Clot the bedded axle-tree.

Of course I am not suggesting that the three poems explore similar worlds of experience; I am only pointing out a certain similarity in artistry.

62   *The fine melon stretches its long tendrils;*

Its green jade freezes in the cold water.

Though its five colors shine at Eastern Mound,

How can one bear to bite its fragrant flesh?

NOTES

Line 2   This line involves an allusion to a song, which in turn involves a play on words. The song is about a girl named Green Jade and contains the lines:

> When Green Jade breaks the melon,
> Her young man is mad with love.

"Break the melon" (*p'o-kua*) is a common substitute for "in her sixteenth year," since the Chinese character for "melon" (*kua*), when split into two halves, looks more or less like the character for "eight" (*pa*) repeated. Thus, "break the melon" = "twice eight" = sixteen. It may be noted that Chinese heroines of love romances tend to be girls in their teens.

Line 3   Eastern Mound. This alludes to Shao P'ing (third century B.C.), Marquis of Eastern Mound (Tung-ling) under the Ch'in. After the fall of the Ch'in, he became a commoner and sold melons outside the Green Gate (Ch'ing-men) of Ch'ang-an. His melons were said to have five colors and were known as "Eastern Mound melons" or "Green Gate melons." A poem by Juan Chi (210–263) begins:

> I have heard the Eastern Mound melons
> Grew outside the Green Gate;
> Their five colors shone in the morning sun;
> Worthy guests gathered from all sides.

The allusion is usually used to illustrate the vicissitudes of worldly power and glory but here it hints at the "lord from the *east*" mentioned in the preface.

COMMENTARY

This short poem, in spite of its simple language, has a complex underlying structure of meaning. In the first line, the melon represents the girl's beauty. In the second line, the "green jade," while describing the melon's beauty, at the same time identifies our heroine with the girl called Green Jade in the ancient song, which in turn hints at her youth and the poet's love for her. In the last two lines, by alluding to the Marquis of Eastern Mound, the poet obliquely refers to the girl's fate and shows his pity for her: she has been taken away by a powerful lord, and this is as unbearable for him as to see someone sink his teeth into the delicate flesh of a melon. In this way the poem returns to the image introduced in the first line. The sequence of associations may be shown as follows: girl named Willow Branch—melon—green jade—girl named Green Jade—breaking melon—in her sixteenth year—beloved—taken away by lord from the east—ravaged like melon being eaten.

63   *The willow branches twine above the well;*

The lotus leaves dry upon the shore.

The brocade-like scales and the embroidered feathers

Suffer injuries in water and on land.

COMMENTARY

The pun in the first line on the girl's name is obvious. It suggests that the girl is not living in her element, since the willow should not grow above a well. The idea is reiterated in the second line, which further suggests that she is pining away for lack of love, as the lotus leaves dry up for lack of water. The fish with brocade-like scales and the bird with embroidery-like feathers represent the poet and the girl (it does not seem to matter which represents which); they both suffer, though each is in a different place.

64   *The painted screens and embroidered curtains*

Naturally form pairs, like everything else.

How is it when I gaze on the lake,

I can only see mandarin ducks?

NOTES

Line 4   Mandarin ducks. *Yüan-yang*, the male and female of which symbolize conjugal happiness.

The poem reminds one of Shelley's lines:

Nothing in the world is single,
All things by a law divine
In one another's being mingle—
Why not I with thine?

All the five poems in this group stylistically resemble the anonymous love songs of the Six Dynasties (third to sixth centuries) in their simplicity of language, their charming naïveté, their juxtaposition of images, and their use of puns.

POEM 65

Marshes of Ch'u

After the setting sun has gone its way,
In the frosty countryside all sounds dry up.
Gathering birds fly around the fishing boats;
A fading rainbow brushes past the horse's saddle.
Liu Chen was always full of sickness,
Yü Chi several times declined office.
My white lined gown has been rolled up for a year;
Now, coming west, I feel the early chill.

NOTES

Line 5   Liu Chen (*ob.* 217), famous poet of the Han period.
Line 6   Yü Chi (510–79), high-minded scholar of the Liang and Ch'en dynasties.

COMMENTARY

This is a rather uneven poem. The first half, with its sensitive observations and original expressions, is fresh and delightful. The second half, by contrast, is almost perfunctory. One feels as if the poet had suddenly grown tired and could not be bothered to probe more deeply into his mind, so that he was content with striking a conventional pose.

POEM **66**

Yüeh-yang Tower

Wishing to disperse for once the sorrows of a lifetime,
I mount the Yüeh-yang Tower above the Tung-t'ing lake.
Over ten thousand miles I could have sailed in high spirits,
But alas, there are dragons who know how to upset the boat!

NOTES

Title   The Yüeh-yang Tower was built over the western city gate of
Yüeh-yang (in modern Hunan) and commanded a fine view of the
famous Tung-t'ing lake.

COMMENTARY

Chang Ts'ai-t'ien connects the poem with a particular event
in the poet's life, but it seems sufficient, for the purpose of appreciation,
to read it as a general expression of the poet's feeling of frustration,
which affected him through most of his life.

POEM 67

Evening Clearing

My secluded dwelling overlooks the imperial viaduct;
Spring is gone, but the summer air is still fresh.
Heaven seems to pity the sequestered blade of grass;
In the human world, we must treasure this evening clearing.
New distance has been added to the view from the tall pavilion;
A little light streaming in brightens the small window.
After the nest of the bird of Yüeh has dried,
It flies home, lighter than ever before.

Notes

Line 1   Imperial viaduct. *Chia-ch'eng*, literally, "flanking city wall," an elevated road first built in 832 along the eastern city wall of Ch'ang-an, leading from the Ta-ming Palace in the north to the Lotus Garden near the Meandering Stream in the south, for exclusive use by the Emperors.

Line 7   Bird of Yüeh. The swallow.

Commentary

The poem describes the refreshing atmosphere of the evening when the weather has cleared after rain. As the poet looks down from his house situated above the imperial viaduct, he observes a solitary blade of grass that seems to enjoy the last glimpse of sunshine after being drenched by the rain all day, and he imagines that heaven has taken pity on the blade of grass and has cleared the sky for its sake. He then reminds us that we humans too should treasure such brief moments of fair weather that follow a long period of rain and will soon be overtaken by the night. As he gazes afar, the newly cleared air affords him a more distant view than before, and the small window is brightened by a little light streaming in. The swallow happily returns, now that its nest has dried. Some commentators think that the blade of grass is an allegorical representation of the poet himself, who hopes that fortune may yet smile on him. Whether this is true or not, the poem remains a wonderful expression of the feeling of relief that we experience when the weather clears after rain and everything acquires a fresh look.

POEM 68

View

The green of the cassia in the garden disturbs the heart;
The red of the lotus in the pond gluts the eye.
In this life we are really distant travelers;
After a few partings you find yourself an old man.
Wind and vapor enter the small curtain;
Mist and rain come in through the tall window.
I recall the days of newly-married happiness:
By the vermilion casement her ornamented zither used to lie.

NOTES

Line 8   Ornamented zither. See Poem 1, and Poem 79, line 12.

COMMENTARY

Some commentators think that this poem was written in memory of the poet's wife; others take it as an expression of homesickness written when she was still alive. Be that as it may, the poem reveals the poet's nostalgia by showing his inability to enjoy the view before him. The opening couplet creates a slight shock with the two unexpected and strong verbs "disturb" (*hsüan*, literally "suspend") and "glut" (*wo*): the green cassia leaves disturb the heart instead of pleasing it and the red lotus flowers glut the eye instead of delighting it. We wonder why, until we read on and realize that the poet is in a sad mood and finds these bright colors too much for him. In the second half of the poem he contrasts the present with the past: as he now watches the mist and rain through the window, he recalls the happy days when he was first married and his wife used to play the zither by the vermilion-painted window.

POEM **69**

Night Thoughts

A hanging screen, a half-rolled-up curtain;
The pillows are cold, the quilts still fragrant.
Why does my soul, for the sake of remembrance,
Fly in a dream across the Hsiao and the Hsiang?

NOTES

Line 1   "Screen" refers to the screen hanging over the door, "curtain" to the bed curtain.

Line 4   Hsiao and Hsiang. Two rivers. Cf. Poem 42, lines 7–8.

COMMENTARY

The poem is probably an expression of the poet's longing for his wife while away from home.

POEM **70**

North Tower

How can the things of spring be my concern?
In human life there is only forced gaiety.
The flowers look as if they had folded for the night;
The wine is cold, but I have not even noticed it.
In this alien land the east wind is moist;
In the Central Realm the wide view must be fine!
From this tower one can gaze northward:
Risking my life, I lean on the dangerous railings.

COMMENTARY

The poem was probably written in 847 in Kweilin (see Part I, 2), which is in South China and which Li Shang-yin clearly regarded as a barbarous and foreign place. The poet can hardly take an interest in the spring scenery around him, and can only force himself to be gay. Even the flowers look tired, and he has left his wine cold and has not even noticed it. (As I pointed out before, in China wine is usually served warm.) This alien land is so humid that even the wind is moist: how different from China proper, where the view now must be magnificent! Desperately longing for home, the poet risks his life by leaning on the dangerous railings of a high tower, which he imagines will afford him a glimpse of his home in the north.

POEM 71

Home Thoughts

Though there is a tower with railings to lean on,
How can I do without wine to pour?
Dank clouds hang over the mountain range in spring;
The river moon shines clear and bright at night.
The fish are disturbed—to whom can letters be entrusted?
The apes cry sadly—my dreams are easily startled.
My old home adjoined the Imperial Park:
It was the time when the oriole moved to the tall tree.

NOTES

Line 5   The line alludes to an ancient poem about receiving a letter put inside a carp. Hence, "fish" and "carp" are common poetic synonyms for "letter" or "messenger."

Line 8   The expression "moving oriole" was used by T'ang writers to refer to passing the examinations or receiving official promotions, alluding to a poem in the *Book of Poetry* about a bird that moved from a dark valley to a tall tree.

COMMENTARY

This poem seems to be a continuation of the preceding one, "North Tower." The poet reiterates his homesickness and recalls the happy time when he lived in the capital and had just passed the Literary Examination.

POEM 72

Written while Traveling on the Kweilin Road

In this warm country, there is no autumn hue;
Over the clear river, a bright sunset.
Buzz, buzz—a few remaining cicadas,
Still reluctant to bid the traveler farewell.
In the small village a dog guards me;
On the flat sand, a monk alone returns.
I wish to gaze toward the northwest,
But all I see are partridges flying again!

NOTES

Line 8   Partridges are supposed always to fly southward.

COMMENTARY

Written about 847, the poem again expresses homesickness. The poet misses the familiar autumn scenery of North China, now that he is in the warm south, and when he tries to gaze towards his home in the northwest, he can only see partridges flying southward.

POEM 73

Lines to Be Sent Home Written on a Rainy Night

You ask me the date of my return—no date has been set.

The night rain over the Pa Mountains swells the autumn pond.

O when shall we together trim the candle by the west window,

And talk about the time when the night rain fell on the Pa Mountains?

NOTES

Title   Some editions have "to be sent to the North," and other editions have "to be sent to my wife." Since there is some doubt whether the poem was addressed to the poet's wife, and since his home was in the North, I have used the word "home," which could apply to either. See also Additional Note 14.

COMMENTARY

This is not only one of Li Shang-yin's best-known poems but also one of the best-known Quatrains in Chinese. Its popularity is probably due to the psychological subtlety that underlies the simplicity of the language: the poet anticipates a happy reunion in the future when the present separation has become a thing of the past, but when we realize that this happy reunion may never take place at all, the present separation becomes more unbearable. Yet the poet is trying to convince his correspondent and himself that it *will* happen, by painting a picture of the future reunion with such intimate details as the candle and the particular window on the west wall.

POEM **74**

Living a Quiet Life

Distant letters and home-going dreams are both few and far between;
Only the empty bed valiantly faces the pale autumn.
Under the steps, nothing but green moss and red leaves.
In rain, there is solitude; in moonlight, grief.

POEM **75**

Written while Feasting with the Chao Brothers at Ho-ch'ing, in the Style of Tu Fu

The splendid view differs from that west of the Yangtze,
The town with the fine name stands near the Wei.
A rainbow closes the rain over the green peaks;
A bird vanishes into the sunset sky.
Years and months go by just like this,
While we sit and watch the distant gray waves.
Here we have truly found a good place:
Let us float and drift about in a fishing boat!

NOTES

Title   The Chao brothers were probably followers of Ling-hu Ch'u, though they cannot be identified with certainty. Ho-Ch'ing is situated in Honan, on the Yellow River.

Line 2   The name Ho-ch'ing means "(Yellow) River Clear," alluding to the traditional wish that the muddy Yellow River would miraculously turn clear. The Wei river is famous for its clarity.

POEM 76

Self-congratulation

I congratulate myself on my snail-cottage,
Which also accommodates a swallow's nest.
The green bamboos shed their powdery leaves;
The red peonies burst their fragrant buds.
A tiger passes: aware of the distant trap;
A fish comes: let it enrich my meal!
Walking slowly, I gradually get drunk;
My next-door neighbor has a pine brew.

NOTES

Line 8   Pine brew. Pine leaves and resin were used in making wine and were believed to be medicinal.

COMMENTARY

This poem involves some ambiguity in attitude. Taken at its face value, it is a description of the poet's simple and modest pleasures: his small but cosy cottage like a snail's shell, the pleasant surroundings with their flora and fauna, the casual walk, the friendly drink with a neighbor. Yet, as Chu Ho-ling suggested, the poem may be ironic: perhaps it is really not self-congratulation but self-lament. The "snail-cottage" in the first line suggests the humble conditions in which the poet is living. The swallow's nest in the second line may contain further irony: since, in Chinese poetry, swallows' nests are often associated with noble mansions, the presence of one here could mean either that the poet is comparing himself to the bird forced to live in modest circumstances, or that he is contrasting his own hospitality toward the swallow with the refusal of some high official to shelter him. The note of irony is to some extent corroborated by a letter Li wrote to Lu Hung-chih before joining the latter's staff in 849 (see Part I, 2), in which the poet speaks of "being confined to a snail-cottage and living insecurely as if in a swallow's nest." (Incidentally, this suggests that the poem, like the letter, was also written in 849 and not in 845, the date assigned to it by Feng Hao and Chang Ts'ai-t'ien.) The next two lines can be taken simply as descriptions of the actual scenery, but they may also indicate the passing of spring, which symbolizes the passing of youth. Line 5 in the original contains a grammatical ambiguity which leads to an ambiguity in imagery: the subject of the verb "to be aware" (*chih*) is not stated, so that it can be identified with the tiger or with the poet. If it is the tiger that is aware of the distant trap, it would seem that the poet is comparing himself to the tiger to show that he is aware of the dangers of political life and is glad to be out of it. If it is the poet who is aware of the trap lying in wait for the tiger, he would seem to be expressing concern over some high official who may be in danger. The remaining lines could be regarded either as an expression of self-content or as self-mockery at the cold comfort he has as compensation for lack of official honor and position. We are left in some doubt whether the poet is congratulating himself for being able to lead a simple but pleasant life, or voicing his discontent in an ironic manner. Should we then condemn the poem as a failure in communication? No, on the contrary, its very ambiguity seems to reflect accurately a complex state of mind, for is it not possible that the poet is feeling two opposite urges at the same time? On the one hand, he wishes to be free from the disadvantages of high office and to enjoy the simple pleasures of life; on the other hand, he cannot quite reconcile himself to a life of obscurity. This mental conflict is conveyed by the ambiguity of the poem.

POEM 77

Amusing Myself on a Spring Night

The place is beautiful, far from the dusty world;
Full of leisure, I think of the passing glory of the year.
The evening has cleared; a wind blows through the bamboos.
Deep in the night, the moon shines upon the flowers.
Among random rocks, I know, the fountain is choked;
Overgrown with moss, the footpath is left to run aslant.
Happily relying on music and wine for comfort,
I forget that I am living in a house among the hills.

COMMENTARY

    The mood of this poem is similar to that of "Self-congratulation." The poet is enjoying his simple and leisurely existence "far from the madding crowd," yet he cannot quite forget the "dusty world," which he affects to despise. The passing glory of the year reminds him of the passing of his own youth, and the fact that he mentions that he is living "among the hills," though pretending to forget it, betrays his concern for the world of officialdom.

POEM 78

Boasting of My Son

Kun-shih, my pride, my son,
Is handsome and bright without a match.
In swaddling clothes, less than a year old,
He already could tell six from seven.
In his fourth year he knew his name,
And never cast his eyes on pears and chestnuts.
My friends and acquaintances often look at him
And say, "This child is a young phoenix!
Even in a previous age when looks were esteemed,
[10] *He would have been placed in the first class!"*
Or else, "He has the air of an immortal!"
Or, "He has the bone structure of a swallow or a crane!"
How could they have said such things?
Just to comfort me in my declining years!
In a beautiful and mild month of spring,
He joins my nephews and nieces at play,
Rushing round the hall and through the woods,
Bubbling with noise like a golden cauldron boiling!
When a worthy guest comes to the door,
[20] *He will rashly ask to go out first;*
When the guest asks what he wants,

He will hedge and not tell the truth.
Then he'll come back to mimic the guest,
Breaking through the door and holding Father's tablet.
He'll ridicule the guest for being dark like Chang Fei,
Or laugh at him for stuttering like Teng Ai.
One moment he is a heroic eagle with bristling feathers;
Next moment he is a brave horse in high spirits.
Having cut a thick bamboo pole,
[30]　He rides on it and runs with wild abandon.
Suddenly he starts to play the stage bully,
Calling the servant in a measured voice.
Then, at night, by the gauze lantern,
He bows his head and worships the Buddha's image.
He raises his whip to catch a spider's web,
Or bends his head to suck the honey from a flower.
He vies with the butterflies in agility,
And does not yield to the floating catkins for speed.
Before the steps he meets his elder sister,
[40]　And loses heavily in a game of draughts.
So he runs away to play with her dressing case,
And pulls off all its golden knobs!
Held by her, he struggles and stumbles,
But his angry pride cannot be subdued.
He bends down and pulls open the carved window;
Then spits on the zither to wipe its lacquered surface!
Sometimes he watches me practicing calligraphy,
Standing upright, without moving his knees.
The ancient brocade he wants for a coat;
[50]　The jade roller, too, he begs to have.
He asks Father to write on a "spring banner";
The "spring banner" is suitable for a spring day.
The slanting banana leaves roll up the paper;
The magnolia flowers hang lower than the brush.
My son, your father was formerly fond of studying;
He worked earnestly and hard at his writings.

Now, haggard and wan, and nearly forty,

He has no flesh left and fears fleas and lice.

My son, don't follow your father's example

[60]　*In studying hard and seeking A's and B's!*

Look at Jang-chü with his Art of War,

Or Chang Liang with what he learnt from the Yellow Stone:

They became teachers of kings overnight,

And no longer had to bother about trifling things!

Moreover, now in the West and in the North,

The Ch'iang and Jung tribes rampage unchecked;

The Court can neither kill nor pardon them,

But allows them to grow like an incurable disease.

You, my son, should quickly grow up,

[70]　*And go to the tiger's den to look for cubs!*

You should become a marquis of ten thousand households;

Don't stick to a bag of Classical books!

NOTES

Lines 4–6　These lines allude to the following lines from a humorous poem called "Reproaching My Sons" by T'ao Ch'ien (365–427):

> Yung and Tuan are both thirteen,
> But cannot tell six from seven;
> T'ung-tzu is nearly nine,
> But only looks for pears and chestnuts.

By saying the opposite, Li Shang-yin shows the superiority of his own son. For the Chinese way of counting age, see Part I, 2.

Line 8　Young phoenix. The original has *tan hsüeh*, literally "vermilion cave," alluding to the legend that phoenixes live on the Vermilion Cave Mountain. The phoenix is, of course, one of the noblest and most auspicious creatures in Chinese mythology and symbolism.

Line 12　Swallow and crane. According to Chinese physiognomy, a "swallow's chin" and a "crane's bone structure" betokened a noble destiny.

Line 24　Tablet. The *hu*, a long and narrow tablet held by officials, originally for writing on, but later a purely ceremonial ornament.

Line 25　Chang Fei (*ob.* 221). A famous general, a household name even now among Chinese children.

Line 26　Teng Ai (197–264). A witty and able official and general, who suffered from stuttering.

Line 31　Stage bully. *Ts'an-chün*, literally "military counselor," the protagonist in a kind of comic skit known as *ts'an-chün-hsi* or "military counselor play," in which the protagonist, dressed like an official, would bully the deuteragonist, dressed as a servant (referred to in the next line).

Line 40   A game of draughts. *Lu-chia*, identified with the *shuang-lu*, a kind of draughts played with six black and six white pieces.

Line 50   Roller. *Chou*, the roller for a scroll of painting or calligraphy.

Line 51   Spring banner. *Ch'un-sheng*, a banner with auspicious words on it hung up to welcome the spring.

Line 54   Magnolia. *Hsin-yi*, also called *mu-pi* or "tree-brush," since its budding flowers are pointed like Chinese writing brushes. The poet here contrasts the brush-like flowers with the real brush.

Line 58   Nearly forty. It was not uncommon for Chinese poets to moan about getting old at such an early age, and one should remember that the general expectancy of life was low. Shakespeare did the same thing.

Line 60   A's and B's. *Chia-yi*, referring to the classification of successful candidates at the examinations.

Line 61   Jang Chü. A general of the fourth century B.C., after whom a book on the art of war was named.

Line 62   Chang Liang (*ob.* 189 B.C.). A military strategist, said to have received a book on the art of war from an old man who said he was the spirit of a yellow stone. Chang was one of the main supporters of the first Emperor of Han and was enfeoffed Marquis of Liu.

Line 66   Ch'iang and Jung tribes. Ancient names for certain Central Asian tribes, used here to refer to the disturbances caused by the Tang-hsiang (one of the Ch'iang tribes) and the Uighurs in 849 and 850.

Line 70   The line alludes to a famous remark by Pan Ch'ao (A.D. 33–103), conqueror of Central Asia, "If you do not enter the tiger's den, how can you get the tiger's cubs?"—a saying that has remained proverbial to the present day. The allusion is particularly appropriate since the poet is exhorting his son to grow up and go to fight the Central Asian tribes.

COMMENTARY

Written about 850, the poem is for the most part a realistic description of a lively and spoilt child, by a doting father, but it also contains an expression of the poet's disillusionment with life. The mood changes from line 55 onwards, from gaiety to seriousness, from happiness to gloom. The boy's request for his father's writing reminds the poet that years of hard work at studying and writing have brought him no success in life. He therefore warns his son not to repeat his mistake but to seek honors by military deeds. This advice, coming from a Chinese literary man, is perhaps not to be taken seriously but should be understood as an ironic expression of bitterness.

POEM **79**

Chamber Music

The roses shed tears on their delicate white petals;
The emerald belts carry small flower-coins.
The spoiled boy is silly like a cloud
Hugging the sun by the west curtain in the morning.
The pillow is made of a stone from the dragon palace:
It has reaped the color of your eyes, clear as autumn waves.
The jade mattress has lost your tender flesh;
Only the green silk coverlet remains.
I remember the spring of the year before last—
[10] You said nothing but were full of sadness.
Now I have returned but you are gone!
The ornamented zither has lasted longer than you.
To-day, a pine at the bottom of the valley;
To-morrow, a po tree on top of the hill!
I shall grieve till heaven and earth turn round,
Till we no longer recognize each other face to face!

NOTES

Title   There was a kind of ancient Court music called "Chamber Music," but the poet is borrowing the name to suggest the intimacy of the bedchamber, since the poem is a lament for his wife.

Line 14   Po tree. Also called "yellow *po*" (*phelodendron amurense*), a tree whose bark and fruit have a bitter taste and are used for medicinal purposes.

COMMENTARY

Written, probably, soon after the death of the poet's wife in 851, the poem expresses his deep grief. The first line, by comparing the dew drops on the roses to tears, at once sets the mood of the poem. (The fact that this image is derived from an earlier writer, as pointed out by

Mr. Takahashi, does not make it less effective.) In the next line, the "emerald belts" probably stand for the twigs and the "flower-coins" for the seeds. (The seeds of the elm tree are commonly called "elm coins," an analogous usage.) The significance of the whole line, as one commentator suggested, seems to be that the poet's wife has left behind young children like the young seeds of the flowers. Lines 3–4 are somewhat ambiguous. The "spoiled boy" has been taken to refer to the poet himself, which is absurd. This must surely refer to his son, who is called "silly" because he is too young to understand that his mother is dead. But some ambiguity still remains, for it is not clear whether the two lines mean that the boy hugs his father like a cloud hugging the sun, or that he is hugging the sunshine in his sleep. On the whole, I think the first interpretation is better, but I have left the ambiguity of the two lines by not using a comma either after the word "silly" or after the word "cloud." (In the original there is, of course, no punctuation.) In lines 5–8, the poet describes how the deserted pillow and the empty bed remind him of his wife: the color of the pillow reminds him of her eyes, and the hard mattress, which used to be a foil to her tender flesh, now bears nothing but a coverlet. The comparison of a beautiful woman's eyes to "autumn waves" is a hackneyed image in Chinese poetry, but it is enriched here by associations aroused by the imagery of the preceding line: the dragon palace evokes the splendors of a rich mansion under water, and the water image then blends with the picture of the beautiful eyes. Moreover, the mention of the dragon palace may suggest that she is a dragon king's daughter and no common mortal. (There is a story about a dragon king's daughter who married a man called Liu Yi.) Lines 9–10 allude to the poet's departure for Hsü-chou in 849 (see Part I, 2), and lines 11–12 refer to his wife's death. In the next two lines the poet laments his sad lot. The pine at the bottom of the valley seems to represent his humble position, and the *po* tree, which has a bitter taste, suggests the bitterness in his heart. As the commentator Ch'ü Fu pointed out, there is an anonymous ancient song containing the lines, "The yellow *po* has been growing since spring, / Its bitter heart growing day by day," where "bitter heart" (*k'u hsin*) is an obvious pun. Further, the sudden change of position from the valley to the hill may indicate that the poet will soon have to leave home again. The last two lines dramatically declare the poet's refusal to cease mourning as long as heaven and earth remain and as long as he himself retains his consciousness. One commentator explained these lines as meaning, "Even if my grief could turn heaven and earth around, how could we ever see each other again?" This does not quite fit the last line, which literally says, "Look at each other but not recognize each other." I prefer to paraphrase the last two lines thus: "I will go on mourning your death, until heaven and earth have turned around and you and I would no longer recognize each other even if we met again."

POEM **80**

Lo-yu Heights

Toward evening I feel disconsolate;
So I drive my carriage up the ancient heights.
The setting sun has infinite beauty—
Only, the time is approaching nightfall!

NOTE

Title   Lo-yu Heights. Famous resort situated to the south of Ch'ang-an overlooking the capital city.

COMMENTARY

This Quatrain has been greatly admired. Some critics think the poet is grieving over the decline of the T'ang dynasty, while others regard the poem as a self-lament. Neither interpretation is really necessary. Rather, we might say that the poet has captured, in a flash of perception, a moment in the natural world, which is the perfect symbol of an emotional mood, no matter what induced the mood. Further, the poem may be taken as an illustration of the common Chinese notion that the extreme of joy leads to its opposite. Realization of the truth of this makes one appreciate even more what is precious and beautiful.

POEM 81

Visiting the Meandering Stream Alone Late in Autumn

When the lotus leaves grew, my spring sadness grew.
Now that the lotus leaves have withered, my autumn sadness is full.
I well know that as long as life remains, emotions remain;
Gazing ahead wistfully by the river, I hear the river's flow.

COMMENTARY

Feng Hao thought the poem was a lament for a girl called Lotus. This may or may not be true. But in any case the poem is an illustration of the truism contained in the third line, and paints a picture of the ever-suffering, sensitive poet.

POEM 82

To Yang Pen-sheng, Who Said He Had Seen My Son Ah-kun in Ch'ang-an

I hear you have come from under the sun,
And there saw my most spoiled child.
Growing older, he should cry often;
Always poor, I fear his schooling is delayed.
Sojourning with strangers, the young dragon grows thin;
Motherless, the phoenix chick turns silly.
As we finish talking, the frontier horn blows;
In the pale lamplight, my hair is streaked with gray silk.

NOTES

Title   Yang Pen-sheng is the courtesy name of Yang Ch'ou, a friend of Li's, who came to Tzu-chou from Ch'ang-an in 853 and brought news of the poet's son. "Ah-kun" is a diminutive for "Kun-shih." (Cf. Poem 78.)

Line 1   Under the sun. The imperial capital.

Line 3   The line may seem paradoxical: a boy growing older should stop crying rather than cry more, but, as one commentator suggested, the poet probably means that now that the boy is older, he should realize his father is away and his mother is dead, and therefore cry more. At the time this was written, the boy was probably six or seven.

Line 5   Young dragon. This is a reference to Li's claim that he was descended from the same ancestors as the imperial family. The dragon is, of course, an imperial symbol.

Line 6   Phoenix. Cf. Poem 78, line 8.

POEM **83**

Second Day of the Second Month

On the second day of the Second Month I walk by the river;

The east wind in the warm sun wafts the sound of pipes.

The flowers' whiskers and the willows' eyes are listless in different ways;

The purple butterfly and the yellow bee both seem to have feelings.

My thoughts return to Yüan-liang's well ten thousand miles away;

For three years I have been following General Ya-fu's camp.

The new rapids do not understand the exile's feelings,

But make a noise like wind and rain on the eaves at night.

NOTES

Title   The "Treading on the Green" festival, held in Ch'ang-an on the third day of the Third Month (see Poem 11, line 3) was held on the second day of the Second Month in Szechwan, where the poet lived from 851 to 855.

Line 5   Yüan–liang's well. Yüan–liang is the courtesy name of T'ao Ch'ien (372–430), also called T'ao Yüan–ming, the poet-recluse *par excellence* in China. "Well" is a synecdoche for "farm."

Line 6   General Ya-fu. Chou Ya-fu (*ob.* 143 B.C.), famous general of the Han dynasty, who encamped at Hsi–liu ("Slender Willows"). The mention of his name here implies a pun on the surname of the poet's current patron Liu Chung-ying, since this name Liu is written with the same character as that for "willow."

COMMENTARY

This poem expresses homesickness. The festive day and the fine scenery described in the first half of the poem only make the poet long for home more acutely. In line 5, he shows his wish to emulate T'ao Ch'ien, who relinquished his official post and returned to live on the farm; in line 6, the poet observes with scant satisfaction that he has been on the staff of Military Governor Liu for three years. The last couplet may be paraphrased: "The new rapids of the river, not knowing how I, an exile, feel, make a noise that sounds like the wind and rain which keep me awake at night."

POEM 84

Expressing My Feelings

A junior official, and often ill to boot,

Following an appreciative patron, I have wandered far.

In friendly talks I am honored as a guest;

On holidays I grope in the dark.

Under the fine trees, I often move my couch;

Watching the strange clouds, I remain upstairs.

Not that there is no beautiful scenery,

Only that I am overcome with homesickness!

NOTES

Line 4   Holidays. *Hsiu-huan*, literally "rest and wash." In T'ang times, officials were given a free day to "rest and wash" every ten days. Grope in the dark. *Ming-sou*, that is, search for the hidden meaning of life.

COMMENTARY

This poem again expresses homesickness. The poet laments his misfortunes: lack of success in his official career, frequent illness, exile far from home. His patron treats him with courtesy, so that he cannot complain; yet on holidays, when he is alone, he feels homesick and meditates on the dark secrets of life. It is not that there is no beautiful scenery around: the fine trees afford shades under which he can lie comfortably on his couch, and the strange-looking clouds provide enough entertainment to while away many an idle hour without his having to leave his room upstairs; it is only that his homesickness returns in spite of all his efforts to forget it.

POEM **85**

Everyday

Everyday the light of spring competes with the light of the sun.

In the hilly town, by a slanting road, the apricot flowers are sweet.

When will my train of thought be free from all cares

And follow the floating gossamer a hundred feet long?

NOTE

As Mr. Ch'ien Chung-shu pointed out, the original involves a play on words in lines 3–4: what I have translated as "train of thought" is *hsin-hsü*, which means literally "heart's silk-thread-ends" and therefore forms a parallel to "floating gossamer" (*yu-ssu*, literally "wandering silk-thread"). But since *hsin-hsü* is a common idiom, I have not translated it as "heart's threads" as A. C. Graham has done, but rendered it as "train of thought," in the hope of retaining something of the verbal play without using unidiomatic English.

POEM **86**

On the Shore of the World

A spring day on the shore of the world—
On the shore of the world the sun is slanting again.
If the oriole's cry had tears,
They should wet the highest flower for me!

NOTE

Title   The original title, *T'ien-ya*, literally means "heaven's shore," and may be translated as "the end of the earth." However, I have borrowed Keats's phrase, since it involves a similar image.

COMMENTARY

Even this simple poem has been interpreted allegorically by Feng Hao and Chang Ts'ai-t'ien, who took the phrase "highest flower" as an allusion to Ling-hu T'ao, since he occupied the highest position in government. A more sensible and perceptive comment is that made by Yao P'ei-ch'ien: that the highest flower is on the top branch and is the one to blossom last. This suggests that the poet feels he has reached the end of his life, and the last ray of hope is fading—an impression already created by the first two lines.

There is some ambiguity in the third line. The word that I have translated as "if" (*ju*) could be taken to mean "as if," in which case the line would mean, "The oriole's cry sounds as if it had tears." This is how Takahashi and Graham understood it in their respective translations. However, this interpretation ignores the word *wei* ("for [me]") in the next line. I have therefore chosen to take *ju* to mean "if" instead of "as if."

Again, as Ch'ien Chung-shu pointed out, the word *t'i* ("cry") is a pun here: it means both "loud utterance" and "weeping." Luckily, the English word "cry" also has these two meanings!

POEM 87

Remembering Plum Blossoms

Settled, settled: I dwell on the shore of the world.
Longingly, longingly, I gaze toward the view.
The winter plum is most hateful,
For it always blossoms with last year's flowers.

COMMENTARY

The poet contrasts his own unhappy fate—having to dwell far from home, as if settled at the end of the earth—with the apparently eternal life of the plum blossoms. As he sees them, he remembers last year, but he is one year older and no nearer home than he was, whereas the flowers seem as fresh as the ones that blossomed last year.

POEM **88**

Living in Seclusion in Late Winter

The day when feathered wings are damaged,
The time when the country garden is quiet—
The cock at dawn disturbs the snow on the tree;
The duck in the cold guards the icy pond.
Time passes quickly; the year is ending.
Worn with age, I am gradually declining.
Why has it never been my lot to fulfil
My lifelong wish to assist the State?

COMMENTARY

Feng Hao dated the poem about 843, when the poet was living in retirement and mourning his mother's death. This does not fit the feelings expressed in the poem; in 843 Li was only thirty, at which age it seems too early even for a Chinese poet to moan about his declining years. Chang Ts'ai-t'ien's suggestion, based on an earlier commentator's, that the poem was written toward the end of Li's life, is more reasonable, although there is no evidence that, as Chang believed, this was the last poem Li ever wrote. The mood of the poem is one of despair and resignation, and it does give the impression of having been written by a man who felt the end was near.

POEMS **89–90**

Two Poems Written When Moved by a Certain Event

Poet's note: The event which moved me to write these poems occurred in the year *yi-mao* and the poems were completed in the year *ping-ch'en*.

89   *The Nine Domains should submit to the King's virtue,*
     The Three Spiritual Lights accord with his sagacious plan.
     How did it happen that men like Pen-ch'u
     Brought death upon themselves like Ch'ü-li?
     There was more than "weeping before the imperial carriage";
     Therefore some were made to "rush from the hall."
     Was this "reporting to the throne on the color of clouds"?
     It was more like destroying the bandits of Reedy Marsh!
     Arrests were made on the evidence of secret letters;
[10] *Lives were lost for guilt by association.*
     All this because the premier of Han was esteemed,
     But the Barbarian Lad was not discovered in time!
     The register of ghosts reduced the ranks of Court officials;
     The beacons of war shone in the noble capital.
     Dare one say this deserves loud lament?
     Still, one cannot help blaming the Huge Furnace!

NOTES

Title   As the poet's note indicates, the poems were written in 836 and they refer to the notorious Sweet Dew Incident, which took place in 835. Details of this incident, to which I have already referred several times, may now be given. The Emperor Wen-tsung, realizing that the eunuchs had usurped too much power and had gained control of the Divine Strategy Armies, secretly consulted Li Hsün, one of the chief ministers, on how to eliminate them. Li, together with Cheng Chu and some other officials, hatched a plot, which backfired. On the 21st day of the Eleventh Month (December 14, 835), an official reported that sweet dew from heaven (an auspicious omen) had fallen on the trees in the quarters of the Chin-wu Guards of the Left. (The Chin-wu Guards were so called because originally the captain of the guards carried a staff carved with the fabulous bird *chin-wu*. They are not to be confused with the other guards known as the Divine Strategy Armies. The former fought against the eunuchs in this incident; the latter were controlled by them.) The Emperor ordered the chief eunuchs to go and investigate. This was a trap, for soldiers were lying in ambush there. When the eunuchs arrived there, the wind, by chance, lifted the curtains and revealed the armed men. The eunuchs hastily withdrew, and a confused skirmish followed. Eventually, the eunuchs succeeded in forcibly escorting the Emperor back to the inner palace, and then summoned five hundred men of the Divine Strategy Armies, who killed all they encountered. Li Hsün himself escaped but was caught and killed two days later. Another chief minister, Wang Ya, who did not take part in the plot, was so tortured by the eunuchs that he "confessed" and was executed together with his whole clan. Altogether the clans of eleven high officials were massacred.

Line 1   Nine Domains. *Chiu-fu*, an ancient term referring to the royal metropolis and to the various fiefs and dependencies.

Line 2   Three Spiritual Lights. *San-ling*, the sun, the moon and the stars.

Line 3   Pen-ch'u. Courtesy name of Yüan Shao (*ob.* 202) of the Han dynasty, who eliminated the eunuchs.

Line 4   Ch'ü-li. Liu Ch'ü-li (*ob.* 90 B.C.), son of Emperor Wu's half-brother. He served as prime minister but was executed because of slander by the eunuchs.

Line 5   This line alludes to the following incident: Emperor Wen of Han (reigned 179–157 B.C.) once shared his carriage with the eunuch Chao T'an. Yüan Yang, an official, protested, whereupon the Emperor ordered the eunuch to leave the carriage. Chao wept in anger and shame.

Line 6   Rush from the hall. The eunuch Chang Fang, who was powerful under Emperor Shun of Later Han (reigned A.D. 126–144), was forced to rush away from the throne hall when being accused by other eunuchs.

Line 7   Reporting on the color of clouds. Officials were supposed to report to the throne astrological omens such as the color of clouds near the sun.

Line 8   Reedy Marsh. Huan-fu, a notorious haunt of bandits in the state of Cheng. In 521 B.C. they were destroyed by government forces.

Line 11   Premier of Han. Wang Shang (*ob.* 25 B.C.), prime minister of Han, had an imposing appearance and was highly esteemed by the Emperor. Here he stands for Li Hsün, who also had an imposing appearance.

Line 12   Barbarian Lad. *Hu-ch'u* (literally, "Barbarian Chick"), an allusion to Shih Le (274–?), who was of Turkish origin. When he was a boy, Wang Yen saw him and heard him whistle. Later Wang said to someone else, "That barbarian lad I saw looks like one with strange ambitions, and I am afraid he will disturb the empire in the future." Wang then sent someone to catch him, but it was too late. When he grew up, Shih became the founder of the Later Chao Dynasty. The poet seems to have Cheng Chu in mind.

Line 14   Beacons. Perhaps this should read "blades." See Additional Note 15.

Line 16   Huge Furnace. *Hung-lu.* The philosopher Chuang Tzu compared the universe to a huge furnace wherein nature fashioned everything.

PARAPHRASE

    The Emperor should rule over all the Nine Domains by his virtue and be protected by the celestial lights. Why should he trust men like Li Hsün, men who failed to emulate Yüan Shao in eliminating the eunuchs but who brought death upon themselves like Liu Ch'ü-li? They tried to inflict even greater punishment on the eunuchs than that which Chao T'an suffered, the humiliation of having to descend from the imperial carriage, and they forced the eunuchs to leave the hall in haste, like Chang Fang. What began as the reporting to the throne of an auspicious omen (the sweet dew), following the custom in ancient times when the color of clouds would be reported, developed into a general slaughter, like the destruction of the bandits of Reedy Marsh recorded in history. People were arrested on the evidence of secret letters, and killed for their guilt by association. All this happened because Chief Minister Li Hsün (who, like Wang Shang of the Han dynasty, had an imposing appearance) was esteemed and trusted by the Emperor, whereas the dangerous opportunist Cheng Chu, who is comparable to Shih Le, the "Barbarian Lad," was not exposed for what he was. Many courtiers entered the register of ghosts, and beacons of war (or perhaps glittering blades) shone in the capital. I dare not openly lament, yet I cannot help complaining against heaven, the great artificer who fashions all things as if in a huge furnace.

90   *Memorials were still being presented to the vermilion steps,*
        When suddenly a battle began within the scarlet court.
        Faced with danger, the Emperor summoned Lu Chih,
        And regretted, too late, employing P'ang Meng.
        The imperial guards withdrew from the front throne hall,
        While the vicious scoundrels fought with their backs to the wall.
        In hurried confusion came the Five-colored Clubs;
        The growth of the unique spirit of yang *was checked and choked.*
        In ancient times rogues were purged from the sovereign's side;
[10]   *Even now there is no lack of elder statesmen.*
        Though the heart did not change its former intent,
        This act is really too dishonorable!
        Who is to close the eyes of those wrongfully killed?
        Should one gulp down heartbreaking sobs?

Recently I heard that at the royal birthday banquet
They did not fail to play the tunes Hsien *and* Ying.

NOTES

Line 1   Vermilion steps. In Han times the steps of the throne hall were
          painted with vermilion lacquer. Later the expression became merely
          conventional.

Line 2   Scarlet court. The central court of the palace was painted red in Han
          times.

Line 3   Lu Chih (159–192). A minister who helped Yüan Shao (see note on
          line 3 of Poem 89) to destroy the eunuchs. Here, according to a
          note by the poet himself, the name stands for Ling-hu Ch'u, who
          had been a chief minister and was summoned by the Emperor to
          the palace after the incident.

Line 4   P'ang Meng (*ob.* 30). A general who was at first trusted by Emperor
          Kuang-wu of Later Han but later rebelled. Here the poet means
          Li Hsün, who proved unworthy of the Emperor's trust.

Line 7   Five-colored Clubs. When Ts'ao Ts'ao (155–220) was in charge of
          the imperial guards, he had five-colored clubs made, with which all
          offenders against the law were punished. Here the phrase refers to
          the Chin-wu Guards.

Line 8   Spirit of *yang*. The incident occurred at the time of the winter
          solstice, which was supposed to mark the return of the spirit of *yang*
          (the active or masculine principle of life).

Line 9   Rogues purged from the sovereign's side. The expression originated
          with Chao Yang of the state of Chin (sixth century B.C.).

Line 13   Close the eyes. People with grievances at the time of death are said
          to have died without closing their eyes.

Line 16   Hsien *and* Ying. Abbreviations for *Hsien-ch'ih* and *Lu-ying*, music of
          the legendary sages the Yellow Emperor and Emperor K'u res-
          pectively. Here the two names not only represent Court music in
          general but also hint at the tragic irony that one of the wrongfully
          killed chief ministers, Wang Ya, had himself supervised the revision
          of Court music.

PARAPHRASE

While officials were still reporting to the throne, a battle
suddenly began in the palace. Faced with danger, the Emperor summoned Ling-Hu Ch'u, who might have been able to deal with the
eunuchs as Lu Chih did in Han times, but it was too late, and the
Emperor began to regret having used Li Hsün, who proved unworthy
of his trust (like P'ang Meng, who betrayed the trust of an earlier
emperor). The Emperor and his guards withdrew from the throne hall
to the inner palace, while the vicious eunuchs fought with their backs to
the wall. The Chin-wu Guards came in hurried confusion with their
weapons, as if these had been the five-colored clubs with which Ts'ao

Ts'ao chastised all offenders. The fighting smothered the growth of the spirit of *yang*, which normally would have begun at this time of year, the winter solstice. In ancient times, Chao Yang purged wicked men from the side of his sovereign, and even now there is no lack of elder statemen (such as Ling-hu Ch'u) who might have been entrusted with the task of eliminating the eunuchs, instead of men like Li Hsün. Though Li Hsün did not change his intent, which was good, the means he adopted was really too dishonorable. Now, who can console the spirits of those wrongfully killed so that they might close their eyes and rest in peace? And should one suppress one's heartbreaking sobs? Recently I heard that at the royal birthday banquet they played solemn music as usual, the same music that the murdered chief minister Wang Ya had himself helped to revise!

COMMENTARY

Li Shang-yin shows great moral courage in writing these poems to lament the victims of the Sweet Dew massacre and to express his indignation against the eunuchs. Naturally he could not mention the real names of those concerned but had to use allusions as substitutes. Besides, the substitution of ancient names for contemporary ones was an accepted poetic convention, comparable to Milton's use of "Lycidas" for Edward King or Shelley's use of "Adonais" for Keats. Although these poems may lose all their poetic qualities in translation, in the original they are highly successful. They express the poet's feelings in a succinct and oblique manner, and to those who can understand the points of the allusions they are moving elegies, not merely skillful exercises in allusive writing.

POEM **91**

Written while Traveling through the Western Suburbs

In the year of the Snake, the Twelfth Moon,
I return from the land of Liang to the land of Ch'in,
Descending the southern slope of the Ta-san,
Crossing the Wei to reach its northern bank.
The grass and trees are half open and cracked,
Not as they should be on an icy and snowy morning,

But rather as if suffering from the heat of summer,
Parched and curled, without fragrant moisture.
In the upper fields grow oak trees;
[10]   In the lower fields grow brambles and thorns.
Farming tools are discarded by the road;
Hungry oxen die on the empty mounds.
With lingering steps I walk through the village;
Out of ten houses, not one survives.
The survivors all avert their faces and weep,
Without clothes in which to welcome a guest.
At first they seem afraid to be questioned,
But reaching the door, they speak to me fully:
"The land to the right of the capital is poor and thin,
[20]   And the people here are often in hardships and poverty.
Formerly it was known as a happy land,
Thanks to the benign rule of good governors.
The officials were as pure as ice or jade,
The clerks as dear as one's six relatives.
The boys did not go to distant wars;
The girls were married into neighbors' families.
Coarse liquor filled the earthen pots:
Stored rice was left to rot in the granaries.
Strong lads kept concubines;
[30]   Old men pampered their grandchildren.
Moreover, since the Chen-kuan reign,
High officials had mostly been scholars,
And it had been a custom for virtuous governors
To be summoned to Court to control the Potter's Wheel.
But by the time of the K'ai-yüan reign,
A wicked man had obstructed the administration:
The Duke of Chin, jealous of scholarly governors,
Often praised the merits of frontier commanders,
And appointed those who were brave and strong
[40]   To govern the people who had lived in peace.
Then trouble arose on the Central Plain:

Appointments and dismissals no longer came from the throne,
But either from the Emperor's favorite courtiers
Or from the imperial relatives by marriage.
The people of the Central Plain were butchered and dissected,
While flunkeys were glutted with fat pigs.
A royal baby was abandoned without milk,
While an imperial consort 'adopted' a barbarian.
Heavy gifts exhausted the Middle Kingdom;
[50]   Strong soldiers reached the northern frontier—
Two hundred thousand with bows and arrows,
All with arms as long as those of apes.
Over a distance of three thousand li,
To and from the capital traveled the Vulture:
Every five li he changed his horse;
Every ten li he had a feast.
A stir of his finger or a glance moved the sun;
His moods changed spring and autumn round.
Ministers and courtiers were shamefully scolded, scorned,
[60]   Spat on, and thrown away like balls of dung!
At the Court, where envoys from all nations assembled,
The Son of Heaven sat behind the porch;
Where colorful banners turned in the rising sun,
And an auspicious haze surrounded the jade throne,
Not only was a golden screen specially set up,
But the curtain of pearls was lifted high.
Stroking his beard and looking proudly ahead,
The traitor sat before the imperial couch.
Those who offended him died at his heels;
[70]   Those who fawned on him were raised to the top.
He showed off one luxury after another,
And encroached on the lands of other powerful men.
Because of the mistake of treating him with favor,
His demands gradually grew more and more.
The barbarian traitors came from the northeast,
So quickly that the sky seemed overturned.

At the time the people had forgotten how to fight,

And heavy troops were mostly on the frontier;

In rows of towns by the long river,

[80]   At daybreak the rebel's banners were raised.

One only heard the barbarian horsemen coming,

But did not see imperial troops stationed.

Wives with children in their arms cried;

Concubines held onto the carriage awnings.

Having been born and reared in years of peace,

They didn't know doors should be closed at night!

The young and strong were drafted into the army;

The weak and old guarded the empty village.

Parting alive, they vowed to fight to the death;

[90]   Their wiped-off tears joined the autumn clouds.

The courtiers were scared like timid roebucks;

The generals fled as if they had been sick.

For the rebel they cleaned the Shang-yang Palace,

And caught people to send to the T'ung Gate.

The jade carriage headed for the Southern Dipper,

Not knowing when it would ever return.

Truly one knows that after long peace

Such thunderstorms would be encountered!

Messengers asked about the tripods' sizes;

[100]   Sycophants sought high offices.

They scrambled for gains and spied on one another;

Who could tell the owl from the phoenix?

A thousand horses left—not one returned,

Nor any of the ten thousand carriages.

The city empty: sparrows and mice died.

The people gone: jackals and wolves howled.

In the south, the riches of Wu and Yüeh were exhausted;

In the West, the River's source was lost to the barbarians.

Therefore the Imperial Treasury of the Right

[110]   Fell to ruins, leaving empty walls.

It was just as if a man's body

Had only its left side but not its right:
The muscles of the body were half paralyzed,
And rank odor grew under the arms.
The successive sacred Emperors suffered this shame;
They felt it in their hearts but could not speak.
The counselors stood there with their hands folded,
Warning one another not to be forward.
The empire was so poor that looms were empty,
[120]   And the Imperial Treasury had no gold or coins.
Brave soldiers stood in frost and snow,
Their stomachs empty and their clothes thin.
Most of the time their pay was overdue,
While the value of copper and lead rose.
Shan-tung looked toward Ho-pei:
They were still linked by cooking smoke.
The Court hardly had time to supply itself;
Hardships lasted more than half a year.
Travelers were charged levies on their goods;
[130]   Residents were taxed on their houses by the room.
Then some began to create obstacles;
In wild confusion spears and lances were used.
Imperial envoys came with staff and banner
To bestow noble ranks of the heavenly Court.
Of those defeated, whole families died;
Those who survived proved enduring:
Treated with honors a king should not bestow,
Appeased as if they had been barbarian tribes.
Was this to court the loss of Red Town?
[140]   No, only in the hope of saving the whole.
High and mighty stands the council chamber,
Where the premier is glutted with eight delicacies.
May one presume to ask the subordinate official:
Who is wielding this power now?
Sores and ulcers have grown for several decades,
But no one dares to pluck them by the root!

The country is poor; taxes grow heavier.
People are few; military duties increase.
In recent years, the son of a cow-doctor
[150]   Climbed up the city wall and the altar.
With blind eyes he held the great banner
And dwelled in this western suburb of the capital.
Enjoying others' misfortunes, he forgot his enemies;
Forming a faction, he was aggressive and conceited.
In life he was feared by other people;
In death he was pitied by no one.
A sharp knife cut off his head,
Which was hung up like a pig's or cow's.
At Feng-hsiang, three hundred li from the capital,
[160]   Soldiers and horses roamed like the Yellow Turbans.
At midnight came a military order:
Fifteen thousand men to be stationed here.
The villagers, scared that they had to support so many,
Fled, old and young holding each other.
Sons and grandsons not yet reaching childhood
Were abandoned without even a sad look.
People no longer discussed where to go,
But simply wished to die among the hills.
Since then, it has been another three years,
[170]   And no sweet rain has fallen in spring.
Thieves and bandits rise at midday:
Who are they but mostly the poor people!
The military governor killed the local constable;
This, we fear, is no way to catch the thieves.
We can hardly see one another at a foot's distance;
There's so much dust after long drought!
The government soldiers carry bows at their waists,
Claiming they are on official patrol,
But we fear, when they come to a desolate place,
[180]   These men will shoot at the common people!
We are ashamed to tell you the whole story,

And we want you, traveler, not to tarry:

Go to Mei-wu from Ch'en-ts'ang,

For in this place one should avoid nightfall!"

As I finish listening to this talk,

I feel as if burned by indignation.

I've heard that when one man, Hui, was raised,

All the bandits fled for fear of him.

I've also heard that order or disorder

[190]   *All depends on man and not on heaven!*

I would, for the sake of this affair,

Rip my heart out before the sovereign;

Knock my head on the ground until fresh blood

Gushes out and defiles the Purple Palace!

But the ninefold gates darkly debar me;

In vain do my tears wet my lips!

Junior clerks are now high ministers;

Servants and stable boys are now generals.

Be careful not to utter these words again,

[200]   *For these words are unbearable for one to hear!*

NOTES

Title   The original title contains the words "a hundred rhymes," which I have omitted. The poem was written when Li Shang-yin was on his way back to the capital from Hsing-yüan, situated to the southwest of Ch'ang-an.

Line 1   Year of the Snake. The year *ting-ssu* (A.D. 837–38), the sign *ssu* being supposed to correspond to the snake.
Twelfth Moon. The original has "the month of *ch'ou*," which was the twelfth month that year and corresponded to January, 838, in the Julian calendar.

Line 2   Liang and Ch'in. Hsing-yüan had been called Liang, one of the nine provinces of China in antiquity, and Ch'ang-an was situated in the land formerly called Ch'in. Chinese poets often call a place by its ancient name, like using "Albion" for England.

Lines 3–4   The geographical details in these lines are puzzling. The Ta-san Mountain is to the *north* of Hsing-yüan, so that it is hard to see how the poet could have descended its *southern* slope. Moreover, since Ch'ang-an was on the southern bank of the Wei river, the poet had no need to cross to its northern bank. Perhaps he is more concerned with verbal antithesis than geographical accuracy.

Line 31   Chen-kuan. Reign title of Emperor T'ai-tsung, 626–49.

Line 34   Potter's Wheel. Traditional metaphor for the premiership, since the premier controls the working of the State as a potter uses his wheel to mold his vessels.

Line 35   K'ai-yüan. First reign title of Emperor Hsüan-tsung, 713–41.

Lines 36–40   These lines refer to Li Lin-fu, Duke of Chin, who was held responsible for the policy of appointing foreign generals to provincial governorships.

Line 41   Central Plain. Chung-yüan, used for that part of North China which was considered the center of the civilized world, roughly covering the lower Yellow River valley.

Line 47   Royal baby. Not identified. One commentator suggested that this might refer to the execution of several of Emperor Hsüan-tsung's sons, but none of them was a baby.

Line 48   This line alludes to the story that Hsüan-tsung's favorite concubine, the Honorable Consort Yang, in jest "adopted" the "barbarian" general An Lu-shan.

Line 49   Gifts. Euphemism for bribes paid by the Court to foreign tribes to appease them.

Line 54   Vulture. An Lu-shan.

Lines 55–74   He. An Lu-shan.

Line 55   Changed his horse. This refers to An's obesity.

Line 75   Northeast. The original has "northwest," which is an obvious mistake, since An Lu-shan launched his rebellion from northeast China and moved westward. I have therefore adopted Chu Ho-ling's emendation. Geography is obviously not Li Shang-yin's strong point!

Line 86   "Not closing the doors at night" is a conventional description of a Utopian society. Hence, the line means that people were so spoiled by peace that they did not even know how to guard their houses at night, let alone how to fight.

Line 93   Shang-yang Palace. A palace in the eastern capital Lo-yang, in which city An Lu-shan proclaimed himself Emperor.

Line 94   The line refers to the fact that officials who surrendered to An forced courtiers, Court ladies, etc., to go to Lo-yang via the T'ung Gate.

Line 95   The line alludes to Hsüan-tsung's flight to Szechwan in the southwest.

Line 99   In 605 B.C., the Viscount of Ch'u asked the messenger from the King of Chou about the sizes and weights of the royal tripods, thus revealing his aspirations to royal status. Hence, the expression "asking about the tripods" means wishing to usurp the royal prerogative.

Line 100   Sycophants. The original has *ts'un-che*, which could mean "those who remained" or "those who enquired after (the rebels)." I have adopted the latter explanation.

Line 108   The line refers to the occupation of the upper Yellow River valley by the Tibetans after the An Lu-shan rebellion broke out.

Line 109   Treasury of the Right. Some editions have "Treasury of the Left." Since the former contained revenue from the provinces, and the latter contained rare objects sent to the Court as tribute to the

Emperor, the reading "Right" seems preferable, meaning that provinces and dependencies had ceased to send in their revenue.

Line 114 Rank odor under the arms. A sly reference to An Lu-shan's "barbarian" origin, since only "barbarians" were supposed to have body odor.

Line 119 Looms were empty. A conventional description of poverty, derived from the *Book of Poetry*.

Line 124 Copper and lead. During the reign of Te-tsung (779–805), owing to inflation, coins were sometimes minted from lead and tin, covered with copper outside.

Line 125 Shan-tung and Ho-pei. Not the two modern provinces called by these names. The former refers loosely to the land east of the Han-ku Gate, which included the capital Ch'ang-an; the latter in T'ang times meant a region comprising the modern Hopei, Shantung, and part of Honan north of the Yellow River.

Line 126 Linked by cooking smoke. Meaning that the metropolitan area and the northeast occupied by rebellious governors were so close that people could see the cooking smoke from each other's houses.

Lines 131–38 These lines refer to the various warlords who fought among themselves and were appeased by the Court like foreign tribes.

Line 139 Red Town. Ch'ih-ch'eng, a town in Inner Mongolia, used here to represent border regions.

Lines 145–46 The mixed metaphor is the poet's own!

Lines 149–59 These lines refer to Cheng Chu, one of the most influential officials under Wen-tsung. He participated in the plot against the eunuchs and was killed by them when the plot failed. See note on title of Poem 89.

Line 149 Son of a cow-doctor. The expression was first applied to Huang Hsien of the Later Han period, whose father was a veterinarian. It is borrowed here as a contemptuous reference to the fact that Cheng Chu was at first a physician. (In traditional Chinese society, physicians were classified with fortune-tellers, astrologers, etc.)

Line 150 City wall and altar. Allusion to the expression "city wall foxes and altar rats," that is, petty men who rely on the influence of others to bully those below themselves.

Line 151 Blind eyes. Cheng Chu had bad eyesight.

Line 152 Western suburb. Cheng was appointed military governor of Feng-hsiang, to the west of Ch'ang-an.

Line 154 Aggressive and conceited. *K'uang-chüan*, first used by Confucius to describe "those who are forward" (*k'uang*) and "those who would not do certain things" (*chüan*), but here, I think, used in a more general sense.

Lines 157–58 These lines refer to Cheng's execution after he was caught by the eunuchs.

Line 160 Yellow Turbans. Huang-chin, a group of rebels who rose in 184.

Line 183 To Mei-wu from Ch'en-ts'ang. Geographically this does not make sense, for if the poet followed this advice he would be traveling backward! The reverse should be the direction.

Line 187   Hui. Shih-hui, on whose appointment as commander-in-chief of Chin in 592 B.C., all bandits in the state fled.

Line 194   Purple Palace. Tzu-ch'en, a conventional phrase, though there was a palace so called in T'ang times.

Line 195   Ninefold gates. See Poem 12, line 6.

COMMENTARY

In this long poem, the poet paints a moving picture of the miseries of the people, bitterly denounces the government for its failure to cope with the situation, surveys recent history to trace the sources of trouble, and cries in anguish at his own powerlessness to remedy the conditions in the country. Written by Li Shang-yin as a young man who had recently passed the Literary Examination, the poem shows his altruistic concern for the people, and belies the charge of indifference to social problems made against him by some Chinese critics. Structurally, the poem may be analyzed as follows. After a brief introduction (lines 1–4), the poet describes the appalling scene of desolation and poverty that meets the eye as one enters the village (5–16), and then lets the villagers tell their own sad story. In the long monologue put in the mouth of the villagers, he first paints a nostalgic picture of a happy past (21–30), and then blames Li Lin-fu for having advocated the policy of appointing foreign generals as provincial governors—a policy which the poet believes to be ultimately responsible for the rebellion of An Lu-shan (31–40). Next, the poet describes the corruption and chaos at Court (41–52), launches a personal diatribe against An Lu-shan (53–74), and shows the disastrous effects of the rebellion (75–114). He goes on to write of the economic aftermaths of the rebellion (115–30); the disturbances wrought by provincial warlords (131–40); the selfishness, cowardice, and inefficiency of government officials (141–48); and the misdeeds of Cheng Chu (149–58). Finally he depicts the villagers' sufferings inflicted by government troops as well as by a natural disaster (159–68). The long list of woes comes to a conclusion at the end of the monologue (181–84). The remaining lines of the poem (185–200) contain an outburst of indignation, which shows that the poet is unwilling to take a fatalistic attitude and accept everything as the will of heaven. The violence of his language betrays the intensity of his feelings and recalls the passionate poetry of Ch'ü Yüan.

POEM **92**

The Young Marquis of Fu-p'ing

The seven states and the three frontiers have caused him no worry;

At thirteen he inherited the title of Marquis of Fu-p'ing.

He does not pick up the golden pellets lost beyond the woods,

But begrudges the silver pulley-frame above the well.

Among the decorated trees, lanterns glisten like scattered pearls;

Round the sandalwood pillow are elaborate carvings like jade.

The attendants on duty will not announce an early morning caller;

His lordship has newly acquired a beauty named Sans Souci.

NOTES

Title   Emperor Ch'eng of Han (reigned 32 B.C.–7 B.C.) often said he was a member of the household of the Marquis of Fu-p'ing when he went out incognito in search of pleasure.

Line 1   Seven states. Either the seven major powers of the Warring States period (403–221 B.C.) or the seven princedoms that rebelled against Emperor Ching of Han in 154 B.C.
Three frontiers. The three states Yen, Chao, and Ch'in of the Warring States, which all had frontiers with the land of the Hsiung-nu, or the three border prefectures of Yu, Ping, and Liang.

Line 3   Golden pellets. Han Yen, a favorite of Emperor Wu of Han, was fond of shooting birds with golden pellets, and every day he lost ten or more, which children picked up. There was a rhyme going round among the people of the capital, "If you suffer from hunger and cold, / Go and chase the pellets of gold!"

Line 8   Sans Souci. See note on Poem 8, line 3.

COMMENTARY

I am inclined to agree with Feng Hao that this poem is a satire upon the boy emperor Ching-tsung (reigned 824–27), as suggested by the allusion in the title. As mentioned before in Part I, 1, Ching-tsung came to the throne at fourteen and indulged in sensual pleasures, until he was killed by the eunuchs three years later. Thus he fits the description in the poem quite well. Line 1 means that he is not worried about rebellious warlords or frontier troubles. Line 2 shows his youth.

Lines 3–4 illustrate his being "penny wise and pound foolish." (However, the word here translated as "but," *ch'üeh*, could be taken to mean "how," in which case line 4 would mean, "How should he begrudge, etc.," and simple further emphasize his extravagance.) Lines 5–6 describe his indulgence in luxury, with a possible reference to Ching-tsung's particular fondness of carved objects. The last two lines probably refer to the fact that the Emperor often held his morning audience late because of his dalliance with ladies. Feng thought the last line referred to the two Court entertainers Fei-luan and Ch'ing-feng, who were presented to Ching-tsung, and Miss Su Hsüeh-lin believes that the poet was in love with them both. She also thinks that these were two sisters whose surname was Lu, since in the song by Emperor Wu of Liang (quoted in the note on Poem 8, line 3), the girl Sans Souci (Mo-ch'ou) married into the Lu family. All this is fascinating but hardly proved. Besides, there is no reason to think that the name Mo-ch'ou stands for two women instead of one. Finally, it would be too cynical and hypocritical on the part of Li Shang-yin to criticize the boy Emperor for his infatuation for the two girls with whom Li himself was in love. I think the poet is using the name because of its literal sense ("Don't Worry"), to show that the Emperor is leading a carefree life. In any case, the poem is a successful portrait of a young dandy.

POEM 93

The Dragon Pool

At the Imperial banquet by the Dragon Pool, the cloud-screens opened.

The barbarian drum sounded loud; all other music stopped.

At midnight, returning from the feast as the palace waterclock dripped away,

Prince Hsüeh was heavily drunk, but Prince Shou was sober.

NOTES

Title   Emperor Hsüan-tsung's former residence was said to have had a "dragon pool," which augured his future accession to the throne.

Line 1   Cloud-screens. See Poem 9, line 3.

Line 2   Barbarian drum. *Chieh-ku*, a kind of drum probably named after the Chieh (a Turkish tribe). The name can also be taken to mean "weather drum." See Edward Schafer, *The Golden Peaches of Samarkand*, p. 52. Hsüan-tsung was particularly fond of the sound of this drum.

Line 4   Prince Hsüeh. One of Emperor Hsüan-tsung's grandsons.
Prince Shou. Hsüan-tsung's eighteenth son, whose wife Yang became the Emperor's favorite concubine.

COMMENTARY

This poem is a satire upon Emperor Hsüan-tsung for his incestuous relation with the Honorable Consort Yang. Some scholars tried to whitewash the Emperor's reputation by arguing that Yang had not really been married, only engaged, to Prince Shou when she became the Emperor's concubine, but Professor Ch'en Yin-k'e has demonstrated that the dates of certain official documents prove clearly that she was Prince Shou's wife when the Emperor first set eyes on her. The relevant dates are as follows: On February 10, 736 (I have converted the Chinese dates into their equivalents in the Julian Calendar), a lady from the Yang family was proclaimed the consort of Prince Shou. In November, 740, the Emperor visited the hot spring on Mount Li, where apparently he saw her for the first time and fell in love with her. He was then fifty-six and she twenty-one. After their encounter, she became nominally a Taoist nun in the palace but actually entered the Emperor's harem. On August 28, 745, a new wife for Prince Shou was officially proclaimed, and the formal elevation of Yang to the status of Honorable Consort (*kuei-fei*, the highest rank for an imperial concubine) followed soon afterwards, on September 17. Traditional Chinese historians blamed the Emperor's infatuation for Yang as the cause of the An Lu-shan rebellion in 755. The real causes were, of course, far more complicated (see E. G. Pulleyblank, *Background of the Rebellion of An Lu-shan*), but they do not concern us here, since Li Shang-yin naturally took the traditional attitude. In fact, Li is far more censorious about Hsüan-tsung than Po Chü-yi, whose famous *Song of Eternal Grievance* (*Ch'ang-hen ko*) is a highly idealized and romanticized version of what was in truth a sordid story.

The poem is an effective piece of satire. The first three lines sound innocuous enough; the sting comes out only in the last line, which depicts a gloomy Prince Shou, who alone remained sober at the banquet since his wife had been taken away from him by his own father.

POEMS **94-95**

Ma-wei Slope

94   *The horses of Chi and the armors of Yen came shaking the earth;*
Alone the beautiful lady was buried, and alone she turned to ashes.
If the king had known that she could overthrow the State,
Would the jade carriage have passed the Ma-wei Slope?

NOTES

Title   When An Lu-shan's rebel forces approached Ch'ang-an in 756, the Emperor fled with his court. When they reached Ma-wei Slope, the Imperial guards refused to proceed unless the Honorable Consort Yang was killed, since they believed her responsible, together with her cousin, the chief minister Yang Kuo-chung, for the conditions which brought about the rebellion. The Emperor allowed her to be led away to a Buddhist temple, where she was strangled.

Line 1   Chi and Yen. Ancient names for the region near modern Peking, whence An Lu-shan launched his rebellion.

Line 3   Overthrow the state. A woman who can "overthrow the State" is the Chinese equivalent of a *femme fatale*. The expression is derived from a song by Li Yen-nien, whose sister was a favorite of Emperor Wu of Han:

> In the north there is a beauty:
> Surpassing the world, she stands alone.
> A glance from her will overthrow a city;
> A second glance will overthrow the State.
> Don't I know she can overthrow the city and the State?
> But such a beauty cannot be found again!

Li's song is in turn based on the lines from the *Book of Poetry:*

> Wise men build cities;
> Wise women overthrow them!

COMMENTARY

This poem again blames Emperor Hsüan-tsung for his infatuation for the Honorable Consort Yang, but it also shows some pity for her fate. It ends by saying that if the Emperor had realized what dire consequences his infatuation would bring, he might have spared himself the flight from the capital, and his concubine her tragic death.

95   *"What is the good of learning that nine other continents lie beyond the seas?*

One cannot prophesy about the next life, but this one is all over!

In vain does one hear the tiger-like nightwatches beat their wooden bells;

No more will the palace-crier announce the arrival of dawn!

On this day, the Six Armies together stopped their horses;

Formerly, on Seventh Night, we laughed at the Cowherd!"

Why was it that a Son of Heaven who had reigned four dozen years

Could not emulate the man from the Lu family with his Sans Souci?

NOTES

Line 1   Nine other continents. The philosopher Ts'ou Yen (third century B.C.) speculated that there were nine continents beyond the seas in addition to the one occupied by China.

Line 4   Palace-crier. *Chi-jen*, literally "cock-man." Such an officer was supposed to have existed in Chou times (twelfth to third centuries B.C.), whose function was to wake up the Court officials at dawn before important sacrificial ceremonies. In later ages, palace guards, when they heard the cock crow, were sometimes supposed to pass on the message, since no cock was allowed to be kept inside the palace.

Line 5   Six Armies. See Additional Note 16.

Line 6   Seventh Night. See Poems 38–41.

Line 7   Four dozen years. *Ssu-chi*, each *chi* being twelve years. This is not very accurate; Hsüan-tsung actually reigned for 43 years.

Line 8   This line alludes to the song about the girl called Sans Souci (Mo-ch'ou or "Don't Worry"), who married into the Lu family. See Poem 8, line 3; Poem 18, line 1; Poem 92, line 8.

COMMENTARY

This poem is more sympathetic toward the Emperor than the preceding two, but still ends on a moralizing note. The first six lines are written from the Emperor's point of view (that is why I have put them in quotation marks). The first line possibly contains an allusion to the story, told in Po Chü-yi's *Song of Eternal Grievance* and in the accompanying prose romance by Ch'en Hung, that after Lady Yang's death the Emperor sent a Taoist magician to search for her soul, and that the magician finally found her as an immortal on a fairy mountain beyond the seas. Whether this allusion is intended or not, the first two lines may be paraphrased thus: "What is the good of knowing that there might be other worlds than ours, since I cannot be reunited with my love? I cannot foretell what my next reincarnation will be like and whether I shall be reunited with her, as we vowed we would be, but as far as this life is concerned, all is over with me!" Line 3 means that the Emperor has in vain assembled brave soldiers as guards, for not only did they fail to protect his beloved but they even demanded her death. Line 4 could mean, as Feng Hao suggested, "Now that she is dead and gone to sleep for ever, she will no longer hear the palace-crier announcing the dawn," but it could also mean that the Emperor wishes never to see another morning again. The couplet formed by lines 5 and 6, much admired for its ingenious and exact verbal antithesis, contrasts the present plight of the Emperor with his former happiness: "On this day, the guards refused to proceed and forced me to let her die; formerly, on the seventh night of the Seventh Month, when the stellar lovers —the Cowherd and the Weaving Maid—had their annual reunion, we even laughed at them, thinking that we were for ever united and would never part!" In the final couplet, the poet speaks in his own person and ridicules the Emperor for his inability to protect the woman he loved— he is less fortunate than a commoner who can keep his beautiful wife.

POEMS 96-97

The Northern Ch'i Dynasty

96   *The moment a single smile bewitches its victim, a kingdom is lost.*
Need one wait till thorns grow in the palace to feel sad?
The night Little Lovely's jade-like body lay flat
Already augured the Chou army's entry to Chin-yang!

NOTES

Title   Kao Wei, Ruler of Northern Ch'i (reigned 565-76) had a favorite concubine called Hsiao-lien ("Little Lovely;" sometimes the second syllable of the name is written with the character meaning "lotus"), who was a skillful musician and dancer as well as a great beauty. The ruler was infatuated with her and neglected his duties. When the army of Chou besieged Chin-yang (in modern Shansi), he abandoned the city and fled. Subsequently he was forced to abdicate.

Line 1 This line alludes to the famous story about Pao-ssu, the favorite of King Yu of Chou (reigned 781–71 B.C.). Pao-ssu was a woman who rarely smiled, and in order to amuse her, the King ordered beacons lit. When the feudal lords arrived in answer to the call and found it to be a false alarm, their chagrin induced the beauty to smile. Later, when a real invasion came, the King again ordered the beacons lit, but none of his vassals came to his rescue, so that he was killed, and his favorite captured by the Jung tribe. This story is the Chinese equivalent of the story of the boy who cried "wolf."

COMMENTARY

The poem moralizes on the dangers of a ruler's infatuation for a beautiful woman: as soon as he is bewitched, his kingdom is doomed, and one need not wait until the palace is destroyed to lament the vanquished country. The lesson is brought home by the shocking contrast in the last two lines, between the ruler's first night with the seductive woman and the conquest of the city by his enemy, between the erotic picture evoked by line 3, and the terrible fate suggested by line 4.

---

97   *A skillful smile, we know, can rival ten thousand plans.*

       Beauty that can overthrow a city is most fatal in war.

       Chin-yang is already fallen: do not look back,

       But request His Majesty to hunt yet another round!

NOTE

Line 2 See note on Poem 94, line 3.

COMMENTARY

The second poem strikes a note as ironic as the first. The poet addresses the dead beauty: "The city of Chin-yang is fallen: what of it? Don't look back, but ask the King to continue the hunt!" There is a slight difficulty here: historically, Little Lovely asked the Ruler of Northern Ch'i to continue the hunt when the Chou army besieged P'ing-yang, not Chin-yang. The poet may have confused the two cities, or, as one commentator suggested, he may have intended the last two lines to mean, "Chin-yang is fallen; do not look back to the time when you [Little Lovely] could still ask the King to go on hunting!"

POEM 98

Master Chia

To the audience hall the worthy banished minister was recalled;
Master Chia's talents were matchless in the world.
Alas, in vain did the Emperor move his seat forward at midnight—
Instead of asking about the people, he asked about the gods!

NOTES

Title   Master Chia. Chia Yi (201–169 B.C.), famous scholar and statesman, who was banished from the court of Emperor Wen of Han, but later recalled. The Emperor asked him about the gods, and Chia embarked on a discourse on the subject, which went on until midnight and which so interested the Emperor that he moved his sitting mat forward.

Line 1   Audience hall. Hsüan-shih, the main hall of the Wei-yang Palace in Han times, where the Emperor summoned Chia Yi.

COMMENTARY

The poem is a satire upon the superstitions of the T'ang emperors, many of whom believed in Buddhism and Taoism and tried to obtain the elixir of life (see Part I, 1). The poet shows his disapproval of such superstitious beliefs by deploring the fact that when Emperor Wen of Han recalled the banished Chia Yi to Court, all His Majesty wanted to learn from the latter was about the nature of spirits and gods instead of the conditions in which the people lived.

POEM **99**

Drooping Willow

A thing of beauty in the little park,
Fair and lovely, east of the Meandering Stream.
Its Court-dress pendants all droop to the ground;
Its light garments, like fairies', are full of wind.
Why did the Seven Worthies prefer the bamboo?
Let the pine enjoy the Third Rank!
It breaks its heart before the Ling-ho Hall
To see the late Emperor's jade throne empty.

NOTES

Line 5   Seven literary men of the third century are known as the Seven Worthies of the Bamboo Grove.

Line 6   Empress Wu (reigned 690–705) bestowed on a pine tree the Third Rank. See also Poem 48, line 40.

Lines 7–8   These two lines allude to Chang Hsü, a scholar-official famous for his nobility of character and personal elegance. Emperor Wu of Southern Ch'i (reigned 483–93) admired him so much that when another official presented willows from Szechwan, the Emperor had them planted before the Ling-ho Hall and remarked that their grace reminded him of Chang.

COMMENTARY

The poem appears to express sympathy for some Court official or lady who enjoyed high favor under a previous Emperor. The former favorite, now neglected, is compared to the fragile willow.

POEM **100**

The Memorial Inscription by Han Yü

The Yüan-ho Emperor was endowed with martial mien:

What was he but another Charioteer or Tamer of Beasts?

He vowed to wash away the shames of his holy predecessors,

To uphold the law at Court, and make the barbarians pay homage.

In the land west of the Huai there had been rebels for fifty years:

Big wolves begot wild cats; wild cats begot bears.

They did not occupy mountains or rivers but occupied the flat plain;

Long spears and sharp lances were marshaled every day.

The Emperor obtained a sage premier; the premier was called Tu;

[10]   He had survived an assassin's knife, for the gods protected him.

Carrying the premier's seal, he was made commander-in-chief,

As the gloomy wind coldly blew on the heavenly king's banners.

Su, Wu, Ku, and T'ung became his teeth and claws;

The secretary from the Ministry of Rites followed with his writing brush.

The military adviser was not only wise but brave;

The forty hundred thousand soldiers were like tigers and leopards.

They entered Ts'ai, captured the rebel, and offered him to the Ancestral Temple;

Their merits were duly rewarded, and imperial favors were not stinted.

The Emperor spoke: "You, Tu, are first and foremost in merit,

[20]   And it is meet that your counselor Yü should indite a record."

Yü bowed his head to the ground and performed the ceremonial dance:

"To write an inscription for bronze or stone is what your servant can do.

In olden days, such a piece was called magnum opus:

This affair does not depend on those normally in charge.

[25]   *Since ancient times, there have been tasks too noble to decline!"*

When he finished speaking, the Emperor nodded again and again.

The Master withdrew, fasted, and sat in a small chamber,

And dipped his brush in ink—how richly did it flow!

He adapted words from the Document of Yao *and the* Document of Shun;

[30]   *He altered lines from the* Pure Temple *and the* Birth of Our People.

When he finished composing, he wrote it down in an original hand:

Early next morning, bowing twice, he spread it on the vermilion steps,

And spoke: "Your servant Yü, risking death, presents this."

This eulogy of the Emperor's divine success was carved on stone;

The stone was thirty feet high, with words as big as bushels,

Carried by a sacred tortoise, with a hornless dragon coiling on top.

The lines were striking, the words solemn; those who understood, few.

Then slander reached the Son of Heaven that it was biased.

A hundred-foot rope pulled the tablet down;

[40]   *With rough gravel the words on the big stone were rubbed off.*

But the Master's writing, like the vital force of nature,

Had already penetrated into people's hearts:

As with the mottoes on T'ang's Basin and K'ung's Tripod,

The objects are no longer there, but the words remain still.

Oh, the sage Emperor and the sage premier

Shone together in glory and left pure light behind!

If the Master's writing is not preserved for future ages,

How can their deeds be known, following The Three and The Five?

I wish to write ten thousand copies of it, recite it as many times,

[50]   *Till saliva drips from the corners of my mouth, my right hand callous!*

May it be handed down for seventy-two ages,

To be used as the Jade Label to sacrifice to Mount T'ai, the foundation of the Hall of Light!

NOTES

Title The original title simply says "Han's Memorial Tablet," but I have expanded it to make it clear that this does not refer to a memorial tablet in honor of Han, but to a memorial inscription written by him. The inscription in question concerns the victorious campaign against the rebel Wu Yüan-chi, and the whole story may be told as follows. In the ninth year of the Yüan-ho period (A.D. 814), military governor Wu Shao-yang of Huai-hsi ("West of the Huai," an area comprising several prefectures) died, and his son Wu Yüan-chi made himself his father's successor. The Court refused to recognize him, and open rebellion ensued. Fighting between the imperial and rebel forces dragged on for more than two years, until in August, 817, the chief minister P'ei Tu (765–839) was appointed Commissioner for the Pacification and Management of Huai-hsi and took charge of operations against the rebels. The government forces won several battles, and in November of that year a general under P'ei's command, Li Su, led a surprise attack by night on the rebel headquarters at the prefectural city Ts'ai-chou and captured Wu Yüan-chi alive. The captive was presented to the Emperor and to the Imperial Ancestral Temple and then beheaded, on December 12. The famous writer Han Yü (768–824) who had followed P'ei Tu in the campaign as military adviser (*hsing-chün-ssu-ma*) and returned with the latter to the capital in January, 818, was ordered by the Emperor to write an account to commemorate the victory. This was duly done, and Han's writing was inscribed on a stone tablet. In his memorial inscription, Han Yü dwelt largely on the merits of Chief Minister P'ei Tu, rather than those of General Li Su, who was directly responsible for the capture of the rebel. Li's wife, who had access to the palace, complained to the throne that Han was biased. Consequently the Emperor ordered Han's inscription rubbed off and a new one written by Tuan Wen-ch'ang, a member of the Academy of Letters. This episode provided the setting of the poem.

Line 1 Yüan-ho. Reign title of Emperor Hsien-tsung, 806–20.

Line 2 Charioteer and Tamer of Beasts. Hsüan-yüan, also called the Yellow Emperor (Huang-ti), and Fu-hsi, two mythical sage-kings.

Line 3 Shames of his predecessors. The Emperor's predecessors had suffered humiliations at the hands of insubordinate military governors.

Line 9 Tu. P'ei Tu.

Line 10 Assassin's knife. On July 13, 815, an assassin killed the chief minister Wu Yüan-heng (no relation to the rebel Wu Yüan-chi, the two surnames being written differently in Chinese). Another assassin attacked P'ei Tu, who was then assistant chief censor (*yü-shih chung-ch'eng*). P'ei was stabbed three times and left for dead, but miraculously survived. Within a month he was appointed chief minister.

Line 13 Su, Wu, Ku and T'ung. Abbreviated reference to Li Su (who captured the rebel), Han Kung-wu, Li Tao-ku, and Li Wen-t'ung. Teeth and claws. Aides or supporters.

Line 14 Secretary from the Ministry of Rites. Li Tsung-min. (See above, Part I, 1.)

Line 15 Military adviser. Han Yü. The line alludes to his offer to lead five thousand men in a surprise attack on the rebels, an offer which P'ei declined, but which showed Han's bravery and his anticipation of Li Su's action.

Line 23   Magnum opus. *Ta-shou-pi*, literally "big hand brush," a term applied to writings on State occasions. The expression originated with Wang Hsün (350–401), who dreamed of someone giving him a writing brush as big as a rafter and took it as an omen that he would soon be called upon to write on an important event.

Line 24   Those normally in charge. Members of the Academy of Letters. The line ironically foreshadows later development: when Han's inscription was erased, it was a member of the Academy who was ordered to write a new one.

Line 27   The Master. The word thus translated is *kung*, which is used here as
et seq.   a respectful way of referring to Han Yü, not in the sense of "duke."

Line 29   *Document of Yao* and *Document of Shun*. Two chapters of the *Book of History* (*Shu-ching*), purporting to record the words of the legendary sage-kings Yao and Shun.

Line 30   *Pure Temple* and *Birth of Our People*. Two hymns of the Chou dynasty preserved in the *Book of Poetry* (*Shih-ching*). For translations, see Bernhard Karlgren, *The Book of Odes*, pp. 239, 200; Arthur Waley, *The Book of Songs*, pp. 226, 241.

Line 32   Vermilion steps. See Poem 90, line 1.

Line 42   People's hearts. Literally, "people's liver and spleen."

Line 43   T'ang's Basin. King T'ang, founder of the Shang dynasty, was said to have had a motto inscribed on his washing basin to exhort himself. See James Legge, *The Chinese Classics*, Vol. I, p. 361.
K'ung's Tripod. Cheng-k'ao-fu, an ancestor of Confucius (K'ung Tzu), had a tripod bearing an inscription which showed his great humility. Cf. Legge, vol. V, pp. 618–19.

Line 48   The Three and The Five. The Three Kings and The Five Emperors (San-huang Wu-ti), legendary sage-kings.

Line 51   Seventy-two ages. According to the *Records of the Historiographer* (*Shih-chi*), seventy-two ancient kings sacrificed to Mount T'ai. Some editions of Li Shang-yin have "seventy-three ages." If the poet really wrote "seventy-three ages," he presumably included the T'ang emperor eulogized in this poem.

Line 52   Jade Label. A jade label inlaid with gold was used in sacrificing to Mount T'ai.
Hall of Light. Ming-t'ang, supposed audience hall of ancient kings. See Arthur Waley, *The Poetry and Career of Li Po*, pp. 1–2. The line alludes in particular to the Hall of Light at the foot of Mount T'ai, where the kings of Chou were said to have received their vassals. Cf. Legge, vol. II, p. 161. Han Yü's inscription ends with the words:

> Now that Huai-Ts'ai is pacified,
> The barbarians from four sides come to Court;
> The Emperor opens the Hall of Light
> And sits there to rule over them.

COMMENTARY

The poem is not only a personal tribute to Han Yü but also a vindication of the power of literature. The poet is concerned not so much with recounting the historical events which led to the writing of the memorial inscription as with tracing the fate of the inscription itself.

It is only when we realize this that we can understand the structure of the poem.

The opening four lines form an introduction, which at once sets the tone of the whole poem—solemn and dignified. The use of such epithets as "divine" and "holy" is conventional in Chinese and should not be taken as a sign of obsequiousness. Lines 5–8 describe the rebels, and lines 9–18 eulogize the chief minister P'ei Tu and his followers, including Han Yü. All these lines, however, merely serve to set the scene for the true drama—the composition of the memorial inscription and its subsequent history. Lines 19–26 describe the solemn occasion, 27–33 the act of writing, 34–37 the momentary glory, with a touch of irony in line 37 ("those who understood, few"), and 38–40 the ignominy, which forms a sharp contrast to the glory described in the preceding lines. Finally, lines 41–52 constitute a paean to Han Yü's greatness and to the everlasting power of words.

The style of the poem is lofty and rugged, in imitation of Han's own style. The deliberately loose syntax and the repetition of words (in lines 9 and 34–35, for example) add to the impression of archaism and clumsiness. Nevertheless, there are some striking images and hyperboles.

The poem is regarded as one of Li Shang-yin's major works and is placed by Feng Hao at the beginning of Li's collected poems. It transcends its immediate historical context and becomes a poet's tribute to the art he serves.

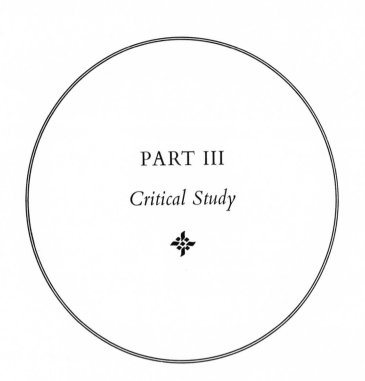

PART III

Critical Study

I

Toward a Chinese Theory of Poetry

In *The Art of Chinese Poetry*, I attempted to evolve a view of poetry from various schools of traditional Chinese criticism as well as from my own reflections, the latter having been influenced to some extent by certain contemporary Western critical theories and methods. I now wish to develop this view further, elaborating and clarifying some points and adding a few others, in the hope of taking a further step toward a more adequate theory of poetry, which, though conceived primarily with Chinese poetry in mind, may bear some relevance to poetry in other languages as well.

To recapitulate briefly what I wrote in my earlier book: I suggested a view of poetry as an exploration of worlds and of language. By a "world," in poetry, I meant a fusion of external objects, scenes, and events with inner experiences such as thought, feeling, and memory.[1] In other words, a poem is at once a reflection of external reality and an expression of the poet's total consciousness, through the medium of language. This conception of poetry as a double exploration does not involve the old dichotomy of "content" and "form." In fact, I explicitly denied this when I said, "A poet does not take an experience as the 'content' of his poem and pour it into a 'form'."[2] What I call the "world" of a poem is not the same thing as what is sometimes called the "content": it is not something preconceived, something given, which can be extracted from the actual poem, but the particular state of being that emerges from the verbal structure of the poem. Nor does the "world" mean the same thing as the "theme" of a poem. The theme of a poem is only what it is about, not what it is. The world of a poem often transcends its theme and cannot be reduced to a simple formula. Furthermore, the theme of a poem, though relevant to our understanding of and response to it, cannot form a basis for evaluation, just as the "subject" of a painting, be it a Madonna by Fra Angelico or a "petite danseuse" by Degas, may influence our response to it but cannot determine whether it is a good painting. On the other hand, whether a poem embodies a coherent world of its own, and what kind of world

This chapter is substantially the same as my article bearing the same title, which appeared in *Yearbook of Comparative and General Literature* (Bloomington, 1966).

[1] Cf. *The Art of Chinese Poetry*, p. 96.
[2] *Ibid.*

that is, are questions about the value of the poem, which cannot be avoided in a critical evaluation.

As for the "language" of poetry, of course this refers not merely to the sum of technical devices but to the poet's total mode of expression in language. Specifically, what I call the "verbal structure" of a poem does not refer to the prescribed "verse form" (whether it is a Chinese Quatrain, or an Italian sonnet), but the way in which various elements of language—sound, meaning, and imagery—are brought together to form a whole. The verse form is merely a set of rules which provide a guiding line and put a limit to the poet's choice of words; the structure of a poem is not prescribed or preconceived but can only be discerned from an analysis of the words after the poem has been written.

There is another reason why I wish to eschew the word "form" (apart from the possibility of confusing the structure of a poem with the verse form in which it is written), and that is to avoid the false analogy sometimes made between poems and physical artifacts. I believe that poetry belongs to the category of things "created" rather than things "made," and the distinctions between the two are not hard to see. In the first place, as R. G. Collingwood pointed out,[3] "making" means imposing a new form on preexisting matter, whereas "creating" does not involve such a process. To illustrate: we can make an indefinite number of tables having the same form, and use the same material or different materials, but we cannot write even two poems having the same structure made up by the same words. When we have made a table, we have a little less material; but when we have written a poem, we have not lost any words. Thus it can be seen that we do not use words as the "material" of poetry in the same way that we use wood or metal to make tables. The same argument can be used to show that we do not use "experiences" as the "material" of poetry either.[4] Moreover, things created, whether by nature or by the human mind, cannot be said to have any other purpose or function than being themselves, while things made have purposes that constitute their very nature. For example, though we may cut down a tree and use its timber, it cannot be said that a tree exists in order to be cut down for timber. In fact, when we cut it down, we destroy its arboreal nature. On the other hand, a chair is by definition something to sit on, and if it fails to fulfill this purpose, it loses its nature of being a chair. Since a poem is created and not made, it cannot properly be said to have any other purpose than being itself. Of course a poem can be used to serve certain purposes, such as moral instruction, political propaganda, social criticism, or personal satire, but none of these constitutes the nature or raison d'être of poetry, just as we may use a cat to catch mice, but this does not constitute feline nature or the raison d'être of cats. In view of what has

---

[3] *The Principles of Art*, p. 129. See also René Wellek and Austin Warren, *Theory of Literature*, pp. 140–41.

[4] I have expressed similar ideas in an article in Chinese on theories of poetry of the Ch'ing period. (See bibliography.)

just been said, it seems best not to speak of the "form" or the "material" of poetry at all.

In short, the world of a poem emerges from the language, and the language embodies the world. The two are not separate or separable entities but two aspects of the same thing. I am in sympathy with the currently prevailing "holistic" view of poetry, which sees each poem as an integral whole,[5] and if my terminology savors of dualism, this dualism seems to be inherent in the nature of poetry itself. After all, no one can deny that poetry is written with words, so that we cannot avoid discussing the language of poetry; on the other hand, unless we are content with extreme formalism or aestheticism, and declare that poetry is nothing more than "beautiful language" or "pure sound" with no meaning and no relevance to actual life or to objective reality, we have to use some term to refer to what is conveyed by a poem. Thus some kind of dualistic terminology seems hardly avoidable. For instance, Collingwood, after exposing the false analogy between art and craft that lies behind the use of the terms "form" and "content," nevertheless states, "There is always in art a distinction between what is expressed and that which expresses it."[6] Similarly, Wellek and Warren, after repudiating the distinction between "form" and "content," draw a distinction between "materials" and "structure" of poetry.[7] It seems to me the term "world," in its inclusiveness and its relative freedom from implied false analogies, may be less misleading than certain other terms like "content" or "material." Moreover, by using the term "world," I wish to suggest that what a poem conveys to us is not an abstract idea, or a simple emotion, or a purely sensuous experience or intuitive apprehension, but an imaginative synthesis of all these. And to speak of the "world" and the "language" of a poem does not imply a belief in the two as separate entities, any more than to speak of the "mind" and the "body" of a person implies a belief that these are separable.

My use of the word "exploration" also seems to require some clarification. By saying that poetry is an exploration I intended to suggest the dynamic and creative nature of poetry. That is why I wrote, "A poem is not a dead record of a past experience but a living process of blending a past experience with the present experience of writing or reading the poem."[8] But apparently some readers thought that I regarded poetry as a search for novel experiences and absolutely original expressions. This is not what I meant. I did not say that only those poems which explore new worlds are great poems; what I did say was, "great poetry either makes us experience new worlds or makes us experience old worlds in a new way."[9] In other words, poetry embo-

---

5 See Wellek and Warren, *Theory of Literature*, pp. 140–41; Wellek, *Concepts of Criticism*, pp. 54–68, 294; W. K. Wimsatt, Jr., *The Verbal Icon*, p. 52.

6 Collingwood, *Principles of Art*, pp. 22–24.

7 Wellek and Warren, *Theory of Literature*, pp. 140–41.

8 *Art of Chinese Poetry*, p. 96.

9 *Ibid.*, p. 99.

dies a process of probing into reality and experience, and, at the same time, a process of searching for the right words. Thus the word "exploration" is meant to emphasize that poetry is neither a physical object nor a kind of code which communicates a "message,"[10] but a verbal symbol which embodies a mental process of creation on the part of the poet and evokes a similar process of re-creation on the part of the reader. The poet explores the potentialities of language as he seeks to embody a world in the poem, and the reader, by following the development of the verbal structure of the poem, repeats the process and re-creates the world.

This concept of poetry as the embodiment of a mental process of exploration is not commensurate with metaphysical idealism. I do not deny the existence of all objective reality, only the *actual* existence of poetry (which is, after all, a product of the human mind) apart from the poet's experience of creating it and the reader's of re-creating it. It seems to me that a poem, once created, has only a *potential* existence until someone reads it and actualizes it, to a greater or lesser extent according to that reader's ability to re-create the poem. Further, it may be pointed out that the concept of world as a fusion of the external and internal aspects of life implies the existence of objective reality, without which there would be nothing for the poet's mind to be fused with.

From the concept of exploration we may derive some further ideas concerning the temporal and timeless aspects of poetry. Since poetry embodies and evokes a process of exploration, this process naturally takes time and takes place in time, so that a poem has a temporal existence rather than a spatial one (unless we are so naïve as to take the physical printed words on the page as the "poem"). Even in silent reading, and even with regard to Chinese poems, where the written forms of the characters may add to the visual appeal, the words of a poem have to be read in the right order, and this must extend over a period of time, however brief. Professor G. Wilson Knight's advice that we should read a poem "at once in a single glance, like a patterned carpet"[11] seems to be contrary to common experience, and to take this advice literally would be as absurd as to have all the notes of a symphony played at once. As a matter of fact, poetry is by nature more analogous to music than to the visual arts, and the basic difference between poetry and music is that the former is not merely a sequence of sounds but also involves meaning on several levels. (This is not to say that music is "meaningless," but only that it has no immediately recognizable verbal meaning.) Therefore, I would prefer to describe the structure of poetry metaphorically as "polyphonic" rather than "stratified", as has been suggested.[12] This polyphonic structure refers to the

[10] See I. A. Richards, "The Future of Poetry", printed with *The Screens and Other Poems*, pp. 105–27.

[11] *The Starlit Dome*, p. xii. The words are from W. F. Jackson Knight's introduction but refer to G. Wilson Knight's spatial approach to poetry.

[12] Wellek and Warren, *Theory of Literature*, pp. 141, 152; Wellek, *Concepts of Criticism*, pp. 68, 294, 364.

simultaneous development of the patterns of sound, meaning, and imagery in a poem, and it is the interaction among these that produces the total effect of the poem. By reacting to this effect, the reader re-creates the poem as conceived by the poet.

Herein lies one of the paradoxes about poetry: when the reader re-creates the poem, that moment in the poet's life when he created it is revived and stands outside time, so that we may say that poetry is both temporal and timeless, or that it is the intersecting point of time and timelessness. This idea of the timeless nature of poetry is not the same as the common boast of poets that their works will make themselves or their subjects immortal, for it is not the poet's name or what he writes about that is immortalized, but the creative moment. Even if a poem is anonymous, this still holds good. As long as someone reads the poem, so long that moment embodied in it will stand beyond time. Nor is this idea quite the same as the Romantic notion that poetry reveals eternity to us, as Shelley claims.[13] I make no such claim for poetry, but only assert that it sets apart the moments of creation from the poet's lifetime and turns them into timeless mental objects to be revived indefinitely. Nor do I suggest that all poetry is a *recherche du temps perdu* in the Proustian sense, for it is not so much the poet's personal experience as the creative process of exploration that is revived and made timeless.

The same paradox about poetry per se also applies to the individual words that make up a poem. Every word has a life history, often as long as that of the language itself. From the moment the word is first invented, it passes through countless mouths and is written down by countless hands, with ever shifting meanings, implications, and associations. It is part of the evolutionary process of the language and is therefore subject to time. Even words of a "dead" language must have had a life history during the time when that language was spoken and written, and as long as there are people who can read a language, it is never completely dead, for the words of that language are temporarily revived as one reads them and recaptures their shifting meanings.[14] But once a word is used in a poem, its meaning is modified by all the words that precede it and those that follow, while it in turn enriches and modifies its context, bringing to bear the weight of its whole life history. Now its position in the unique verbal sequence of the poem is fixed once and for all, and it achieves a kind of permanency, a timelessness. Of course this does not mean that the word will never be used again; on the contrary, it joins the common march of all the other words of that language in their historical evolution, but it sheds a self which is for ever transfixed in that particular position in the poem. In the

---

[13] Shelley, *A Defense of Poetry.* See also Georges Poulet, "Timelessness and Romanticism," *Journal of the History of Ideas,* 15, no. 1: 3–23.

[14] This is true even of Classical Chinese, which has been used for centuries purely as a written means of expression, not identical with, though by no means unrelated to, the spoken language of any period.

famous Chinese romance known to Western readers as *Monkey*, the magic Monkey can transform a hair from his body into a replica of himself, thus creating innumerable Monkeys if necessary. A word performs a similar magic trick when one self becomes fixed and timeless in a poem while another self marches on, shedding more selves on the way in more poems. Thus the words in poetry too have a paradoxical nature: they have a temporal existence as words of a language but achieve timelessness as constituent elements of poems.

Since poetry has no other purpose than being itself, the only proper criterion for judging a poem is how far it succeeds in being a poem. This seemingly tautological question can be rephrased and divided into two questions: How far does the poem coherently explore and embody a world of its own? How far does it realize the potentialities of the language in which it is written? This is a modified version of the main critical standards which I previously suggested in the form of these questions: "Does this poem explore a world of its own, and if so, what kind of world is it?" and "Does it break new grounds in the use of language?"[15] The question how far a poem embodies a world is closely related to the idea that poetry is both temporal and timeless, for the more a poet has succeeded in integrating the external and internal elements of life into a coherent world by means of language, the more fully can the reader re-create that world and revive the creative process of exploration, thereby making it timeless. Bad poetry will disintegrate on analysis—the images will not coalesce into a consistent pattern, the external details described will not be in keeping with the implied emotion—and will naturally fail to enable the reader to re-create any world or to revive the moment of creation. As for the question, "What kind of world is it?," strictly speaking this is not an aesthetic question. However, in practice it would be very difficult to exclude this question completely from our considerations. The fact is, in literary criticism we constantly use words implying extra-aesthetic values. As soon as we say that one poem is "great" and another one is merely "good," or say this poem is "profound" and that one "trivial," we are introducing value judgments of an extra-aesthetic kind. Even such modern favorites as "maturity" and "irony" are not purely aesthetic terms but imply certain attitudes toward life. I see no way of escaping from such terms entirely, nor do I even think it desirable to do so, for if we did, we might be left with only vague emotive terms like "beauty" and might lapse into the kind of impressionistic "appreciation" that used to pass for literary criticism. All we need to do is to guard against the danger of confusing extra-aesthetic values with aesthetic ones. And when we come to appraise a poet's works as a whole, it becomes even more necessary to consider the kinds of worlds embodied in his poetry and the relative depth of thought, intensity of emotion, sensitivity of feeling, breadth of vision, and fecundity of imagination revealed in these worlds.

[15] *The Art of Chinese Poetry*, p. 98.

With regard to the second major criterion for poetry, to ask whether a poem breaks new grounds in the use of language, as I formerly suggested, may seem to put undue emphasis on originality. That is why I have rephrased the question by asking how far a poem realizes the potentialities of language. This involves originality not of an absolute kind (which is impossible anyway, as T. S. Eliot pointed out) but of a relative kind, a kind of originality which may be described as kaleidoscopic in the sense that the words, images, and the like in a poem may be conventional but the way they are brought together results in a new pattern, just as the same pieces of colored glass in a kaleidoscope present a different pattern every time we shake it. This second question to ask about poetry is also intimately connected with the temporal and timeless aspects of poetry. The better the poet, the more fully does he render words timeless in their poetic contexts and at the same time modify and enrich their meanings, implications, and associations, thus adding to their future potentialities. Therefore, to ask how far a poet has succeeded in realizing the potentialities of a language, both in individual poems and in his poetry as a whole, is to ask how far he has changed the language as he found it.

The answers to the two main questions set forth above are, of course, interrelated. A poet's degree of success in embodying a world in a verbal structure depends on the extent of his successful search for the right words, and the extent of his contribution to the evolution of language is often proportionate to that of his exploration of worlds. To answer these questions we have to carry out careful analyses of various elements of poetic language. It is from such analyses that we come to discern the structure of each poem as a whole, and it is from the total structure that we perceive, in turn, the world embodied in the poem. At the same time, analyses of the effects of poetic language on us may enable us to become more aware of the nature of our response to poetry. This response is at once sensuous, emotional, intellectual, and imaginative, since the polyphonic structure of poetry affects us on several levels of consciousness and in several ways simultaneously. I suppose it would be possible, in theory, to describe in neurological terms the precise nature of our response to poetry, but I doubt if such a description would enhance our enjoyment of poetry, just as I doubt if a detailed knowledge of the digestive system would increase one's appetite. On the other hand, a nonscientific description of our response to poetry may enhance our enjoyment, just as reading a recipe or even a menu can sometimes make one's mouth water!

In the following pages I shall discuss various worlds that emerge from Li Shang-yin's poems, and also various aspects of language which he explored and exploited in his poetry. I shall adopt a qualitative rather than quantitative method: each aspect of his poetry will be examined and illustrated by examples, but no attempt will be made to give exhaustive lists of poetic devices or statistics of his linguistic habits. I believe with Professor W. K. Wimsatt, Jr. that a discussion on such themes as metaphor or symbol is likely to be very interesting and useful but "an interpretation or appreciation of a specific poem by the means mainly of an appeal to categories expressed by such terms is another sort of thing," and likely to be less interesting.[16] To put it more bluntly: a catalogue of the technical devices or linguistic features of a poem does not amount to an interpretation or an evaluation, but it is precisely these two things—interpretation and evaluation—that constitute the proper business of literary criticism.

[16] *Hateful Contraries*, p. 218.

2

The Worlds of Li Shang-yin's Poetry

Although the world and the language of a poem are two aspects of the same thing, we may still describe each aspect in turn, just as we may first describe a person's physical appearance and then his character, or vice versa. Of course, no discussion on either aspect of poetry can do it full justice, just as no description of a man's physical features or mental traits can adequately sum up his whole personality. But such discussions and descriptions still have their uses. Or, to draw another analogy, in a film the camera constantly shifts its focus, and the director, by means of close-ups, fade-outs, flashbacks, montage, and other devices, seeks to create a coherent picture and evoke a total response from the audience. In a similar fashion, we may discuss a poet's works from different angles, focusing attention now on a whole poem, now on some details of a poem, and now on features common to a group of poems or to all his poems. Such discussions will naturally involve overlappings, cross references, and recurrent motifs, and will not allow rigid and arbitrary divisions of topics.

In this chapter I shall consider how far Li Shang-yin's poems succeed in embodying different worlds, and what kinds of worlds these are. Naturally, more attention will be paid to poems which successfully embody complex worlds. These will be analyzed in some detail to show how each world emerges from the structure of the poem and how the structure is inherent in the coalescence and interaction of various elements of language. Less complex and less successful poems will be briefly commented on or passed over in silence.

Some of Li Shang-yin's poems (and these are among his best) explore highly complex worlds representing several levels of reality. The most notable is the very first poem in this volume, *The Ornamented Zither*. The fact that there is so much controversy about this poem shows that most readers have felt the impact of its language and become aware of a world embodied in it, though they may differ widely in their descriptions of that world and of their responses to it. Some critics may have been mistaken about the nature of the world of this poem and about the reason for their responses, but this does not mean that their responses are not genuine. In fact, there may be more in common among different critics' responses to the poem than they realize, and the divergence of their expressed opinions on the poem does not mean that it is a failure. On the contrary, it is just because the world embodied in this poem is so complex and many-faceted that it allows so many different interpretations, for each critic may have perceived only one aspect of this complex world and described it to the exclusion of the other aspects.

The world that emerges from this poem is one that transcends the limits of space and time. Things that cannot coexist are brought together here: moonlight and sunshine, sea and land, present sensations and emotions and past experiences, what actually happened and what is imagined. The present is mingled not only with the poet's personal past but also with historical past and mythical past (through the allusions to the philosopher Chuang Tzu, who dreamed of being a butterfly, and to the mythical Emperor Wang, whose soul was transformed into the cuckoo). The human world is fused with the natural and the supernatural, and the boundary between the poet's mind and the external world is broken down. This poetic world involves several levels of reality. On the physical level, there is the zither as an actual object, possibly the one that the poet's wife used to play in life. On the imaginary level, we see the pearls under moonlight and the jade lying in the sun. The butterfly in the philosopher's dream and the cuckoo in the myth about the emperor represent reality one stage further removed from actuality. And, of course, the poem also reveals reality on the emotional level (the poet's sadness, regret, and so forth) and on the intellectual level (his meditation on the meaning of life and love). Thus, the poem appeals to our senses, emotions, imagination, and intellect at the same time. On the sensuous level alone, the poem appeals to several senses. The ornamented zither has obvious musical implications as well as visual appeal; further auditory associations are aroused by the cuckoo which adds to the rich visual suggestions made by the butterfly, the sea, the moonlight, the pearls, the mountain, the sun, the jade, and the smoke. We may notice, incidentally, the contrast between the clear picture of pearls in moonlight and the vague impression of jade in smoke. The implication of wetness in "sea" and "tears," of hardness in "pearls" and of smoothness in "jade," all appeal to the tactile sense; while the warmth of the sun appeals to the thermal sense. Emotionally, the poem makes us share the poet's feelings of sadness, regret, disappointment, and bewilderment. Imaginatively, it enables us to experience in concrete terms the worlds of dream and fantasy as well as those of actuality and memory. Intellectually, it makes us wonder about the meaning of life and the nature of reality, although ultimately its greatness does not lie in expressing a new or necessarily true philosophy of life but in embodying a mode of being aware of human existence which has been experienced by many but has never before been so embodied.

That this poem is able to reveal such a complex world to us and affect us so strongly and in so many different ways is, of course, due to its unique verbal structure, as I hope to show below.

With regard to the structure of meaning (not the total complex meaning of the poem but its more obvious intellectual meaning), we may trace the development of the poet's thought as follows. He begins by questioning the raison d'être of the zither, and hence that of human life. He then raises the question about the relative nature of dream and reality, as exemplified by the butterfly and the cuckoo—and the cuckoo also arouses associations with unhappy love. Next he presents a tragic vision of life, illustrated by pearls shedding tears and inaccessible jade lying in smoke. Finally he confesses his sense of puzzlement.

Described thus, the meaning of the poem appears thin; in fact, however, it is not so baldly expressed but is embodied in the rich and complex language of the poem. A few points about the diction may be noted. The word "ornamented" (*chin*, literally "brocade"), not only has visual appeal but suggests richness and splendor, and therefore the "ornamented zither" represents the happy, youthful years of one's life. The expression "for no reason" in the first line at once raises doubt about the meaning of life, and the repetition "each string, each bridge" (in the original, "one string, one bridge") makes us visualize the zither in greater detail and at the same time stresses the idea of past years being recalled one by one. Line 3 contains the words "dream" (*meng*) and "confuse" (*mi*), both of which emphasize the feeling of bewilderment; line 4 arouses erotic associations by the word "spring." In the next couplet, the word "tears" naturally adds to the sad mood, and "smoke" reinforces the impression of bewilderment. In the final couplet, "might have become" again indicates uncertainty; "only" suggests regret; and "bewildered and lost" epitomizes the dominant feeling.

The images in the poem are extremely effective. We have already noted their sensuous appeal, but may further consider their nature. On the literal level, the zither may be regarded as a simple image, one that describes an actual object without involving a comparison of two things. This literal significance of the zither need not be excluded, though of course it has symbolic significance as well. The cuckoo and the butterfly may also be considered simple images, though they exist on an imaginary level. The same may be said of the sea, the moonlight, and the sunshine. The tears of pearls form a compound image. The jade in the sun may be taken as a compound image representing an unattainable woman or poetic excellence.

These images, apart from their functions of description and comparison, also possess symbolic significance. The zither, the key symbol of the poem, may represent life in general as well as marriage and poetry; the butterfly symbolizes the transient and seemingly unreal nature of human existence; the cuckoo is a symbol of tragic, illicit love; the pearls may represent parted lovers or unappreciated talent, or both; the jade, as we have seen, probably symbolizes unattainable objects or ideals.

Some of these images and symbols involve definite allusions—to the philosopher's dream and to the emperor's metamorphosis. Others suggest associations with possible allusions, such as the stories about the mermaid and about the daughter of the King of Wu. All these allusions, whether they refer to historical events and persons or to legends and myths, and whether or not they are consciously intended by the poet, enrich the poetic context by further layers of meaning.

The various elements of poetic language discussed above all develop simultaneously to form one integral structure. As we follow the patterns of words, imagery, and symbolism, we become aware of their underlying significance, while reacting to their sensuous appeal. We become emotionally involved and intellectually alerted; we enter imaginatively into a special world, which is rich in its sensuous allure, intense in its emotional impact, and profound in its intellectual implications. This world is revealed to us through a complex and subtle verbal structure, which shows an extraordinarily fine and sophisticated sensibility and a consummate mastery of language. Both as an exploration of life and as an exploration of language *The Ornamented Zither* (in the original, of course) is a great poem.

The two poems entitled *Peonies Damaged by Rain at Hui-chung* (Poems 2–3) form a closely-knit unit and may be said to embody a unified world, which again transcends the boundaries of space and time and blends the physical with the metaphysical, the actual with the imaginary, and human life with the life of nature.

On the factual level, the poet's past experience in the capital ("the bygone years at the Lower Park") is juxtaposed with the present scene ("to-day, in the western county") thousands of miles away (allowing for a little rhetorical exaggeration). On the imaginary level, the damaged peonies, likened to dancing girls, are juxtaposed with the willows in the streets of Ch'ang-an, which are compared to Court ladies with slender waists. Further, the poet anticipates the future, when the peonies have completely withered away, like beautiful women who have grown old or talented men whose lives have been wasted. Thus, present, past and future all mingle in one constant flow. The poet's sensitivity to time is also shown by his regret that the bygone years are irrevocably lost, that the pomegranate blossoms too late for spring, and that the peonies are falling before their time. The passage of time is finally symbolized by the image of the drifting dust. At the same time, the external world and the poet's inner experience are unified. The raindrops on the flowers are the same as his tears as well as the remembered tears of some woman and the imagined tears shed by the mermaid in the story; the sound of the rain is the same as that of the zither strings plucked by him or by his wife, or imaginary music played by the sad goddess of the River Hsiang. Thus, feelings, memories, and fantasies are identified with physical reality.

Intellectually, the world that emerges from these two poems symbolizes ravaged beauty (both natural and human), wasted youth, and frustrated genius. Emotionally, it enables us to feel pity, regret, and apprehension. And like *The Ornamented Zither*, these two poems also appeal to several senses. The visual appeal of the imagery is obvious and needs no comment. We may note, using I. A. Richards' terms, the olfactory appeal of "fragrance," "pollen," and "sweet"; the auditory implications of "strings" and "zither"; the tactile suggestions of "silk mat," "jade plate," and "powdery beauty"; and the thermal ones of "chill" and "warmth unknown." Once more, we see how the poetic world emerges from the structure, which integrates the words, images, symbols, and allusions.

Two outstanding poems, both of considerable length, embody complex worlds in which aesthetic and intellectual elements predominate. These are *Painting of Pine Trees, A Gift from Li Hung* (Poem 48) and *The Memorial Inscription by Han Yü* (Poem 100). Both have been structurally analyzed in the commentaries accompanying them and need only be briefly commented on here. In the former poem, the poetic world synthesizes an aesthetic experience with a philosophic meditation on life and a transcendental vision of the Taoist paradise. The description of the painting involves imagery and allusions suggesting physical beauty (fine fox fur, thick tufts of hair on a child's head, dense, dark eyebrows of a beautiful lady, green coverlet like the vault of heaven, famous beauties making up their faces in the morning) as well as spiritual power (primeval air of nature, upright gentlemen, brave knights, dragons, works of the gods, phoenixes, immortals). The vicissitudes of human life, illustrated by the fate of the previous owner of the picture, are contrasted implicitly with the immortality of art, and the poet's wish to transcend such human vicissitudes is embodied in his vision of the Taoist heaven. In the latter poem, historical consciousness is united with moral conviction and aesthetic appreciation. Here, too, the fickleness of fortune (exemplified not only by the fate of Han Yü's memorial inscription but also by the political and military events which led to its writing) is contrasted with the everlasting power and value of art. The human passions and struggles, be they political, moral, or merely personal, pale in significance beside the timelessness of great literature.

The untitled poem beginning "At eight, she stole a look at herself in the mirror" (Poem 11), *High Noon* (Poem 12), and *The Sun Shoots Its Beams* (Poem 13) reveal less complex worlds but also succeed in unifying diverse kinds of experience and different levels of reality. As suggested before, the girl in Poem 11 may represent lost youth, beauty, and talent, with possible references to some particular girl and to the poet himself; the desire for the unapproachable lady in Poem 12 can be taken as a symbol of universal aspirations for the impossible; the solitude of the woman in Poem 13 may at the same time express the poet's own loneliness.

Many of Li Shang-yin's poems are concerned with love. These are generally not simple, straightforward love poems addressed to the beloved, but explorations of different worlds of love, or, at least, of the world of love seen in different lights. First of all, there are poems which explore a world of passionate love, often mixed with doubt and despair, a kind of love which is so intense and all-consuming that it becomes self-destructive and often arouses thoughts of death. This world of passion is clearly seen in such lines as these:

> Do not let the amorous heart vie with the flowers in
>   burgeoning:
> One inch of longing, one inch of ashes!
>
>   [Poem 5]

> The spring silkworm's thread will only end when death
>   comes;
> The candle will not dry its tears until it turns to ashes.
>
>   [Poem 6]

> She grinds vermilion and breaks stones but heaven is
>   unaware:
> Would that she had a Heavenly Jail to lock up her wronged
>   soul!
>
>   [Poem 7]

> The fragrant root is broken in the middle; the incense-heart
>   dies.
>
>   [Poem 10]

> What hope is there for one who takes life lightly?
> The white moth dies stiff upon the folding screen.
>
>   [Poem 12]

Sometimes this passionate world is seen from the man's point of view (for example, in Poems 4, 5, 6, 8, 12), sometimes from the woman's point of view (Poems 7, 17, 18, 43), and sometimes from both (Poems 9, 10). In each instance, we are enabled to enter sympathetically into this world of hopeless passion and to taste its bitter-sweetness, its *plaisir d'amour* as well as *chagrin d'amour*.

Then there are poems (for example, Poems 19–20) in which we perceive a world of love less intense, less compounded with anguish, and more light-hearted, as suggested by lines like:

> As she passed the hook from another seat, the spring wine
>   was warm;
> Divided into teams, we guessed at riddles under the red
>   candle's light.
>
>   [Poem 19]

The group of poems written for the girl Willow Branch (Poems 60–64), though wistful, are also less intense than the first group.

So far we have considered poems in which the world of love is seen in a sympathetic light. But there are some other poems of Li Shang-yin's, where love is viewed with irony if not sarcasm, such as in Poems 14, 15, 16 and 27. The tone of sarcasm is unmistakable in such lines as:

> Amid the spring flowers, the birds will certainly nestle in
>   pairs.
> After the drinking party, do not walk with a red candle!
>   [Poem 16]

Next, the poems involving Taoist nuns (Poems 21–23, 24–26, 28–33,
35), whether they are ostensibly concerned with the Green Jade City in
heaven, or the Holy Lady's Temple, or the Goddess of the Moon, all
seem to reveal an ambiguous attitude toward love. For instance, do the
lines

> If the morning pearl were not only bright but fixed,
> One would always face the crystal plate all one's life
>   [Poem 21]

express a fond wish or are they a satirical comment on another's
infatuation? Or take the lines

> The *Life of Emperor Wu* is plain for all to see:
> Do not say that no one in the whole world knows!
>   [Poem 23]

To whom are these words addressed? And do they express self-mockery
or moral disapproval of others? It seems to me, this ambiguous attitude
is possibly a result of an unresolved conflict in Li Shang-yin's own
mind: on the one hand, his conscious convictions oblige him to dis-
approve the secret and licentious love of Taoist nuns; on the other
hand, his subconscious desire for them cannot be suppressed, whether
he actually had affairs with them or not. The tension between moral
disapproval and physical desire is discernible in many of these poems.
For example, in the couplet from one of the *Holy Lady's Temple* poems,

> Throughout the spring, a dream-rain often flooded the
>   tiles;
> All day long, the spiritual wind has not filled the banners
>   [Poem 25]

the first line, which contains associations with the amorous Goddess of
Mount Wu, suggests the flood of erotic passion, whereas the second
line appears to condemn the nun for her spiritual failings. Again, does
the famous couplet

> Ch'ang-o should regret having stolen the elixir:
> The green sea—the blue sky—her heart every night!
>   [Poem 28]

express pity for the goddess (that is, nun) or ridicule for her inability to
keep her vows of chastity? Even in the poem addressed explicitly to the
Sung sisters of Hua-yang Temple (Poem 35), the tone is still ambiguous.
Because of this ambiguity, the world of love in these poems is not seen
from one angle but several.

At times Li Shang-yin rises above personal emotions and views the
world of love from an impersonal angle. Instead of expressing the
sufferings of one lover, some of his poems show a compassionate, tragic

vision of the fate of all lovers. For instance, in Poem 34, he wishes the world would come to an end so that lovers could be freed from their agonies:

> O when will the seas all be turned into mulberry fields,
> So that the Yi River can no longer flow to the east?

And in Poem 41, he exclaims:

> Would that one could exchange endless separation in this world
> For the reunion that comes once a year!

However, in spite of the pains that love brings, the poet is unwilling to forego the human capacity for love and suffering:

> No need to follow recklessly the immortal on Mount K'ou—
> The zither of Hsiang and the flute of Ch'in have enough feelings of their own.
>
> [Poem 37]

Or, more explicitly:

> I well know that as long as life remains, emotions remain;
> Gazing ahead wistfully by the river, I hear the river's flow.
>
> [Poem 81]

In brief, Li Shang-yin's love poetry, taken as a whole, displays various facets of the world of love and reveals its paradoxical nature—its attractions and its penalties, the latter more often than the former. And it is the poems which emphasize the anguish of hopeless yet unrepenting love that are the most successful and the most famous, as they deserve to be.

In the *Green Jade City* and the *Holy Lady's Temple* poems, not only do we see a complex world of love, but also a world of fantasy. The imaginary world of the goddesses is described in vividly concrete terms: green jade city walls with winding rails, rhinoceros' horns, jades, phoenixes perching on trees, pines and bamboos, moss-grown gates, and the like. These images blend the actual world with the supernatural, thus making the latter more credible. Sometimes the unreal, supernatural world impinges on the actual with startling force. This is made possible by such fantastic imagery as

> Stars sinking to the bottom of the sea can be seen at the window;
> The rain over the river's source, viewed from another seat
>
> [Poem 21]

where the supernatural world, represented by the stars that sink to the bottom of the sea and the river's source high on the mountains, is brought into contact with the world of everyday life, exemplified by "window" and "seat," in a flash of imagination. Similarly, in the couplet

> Pines and bamboos grow by the hall with an orchid-
> fragrant curtain;
> A dragon protects the jasper window; a phoenix closes the
> door
>
> [Poem 24]

the actual world, in which the pines and bamboos grow by the hall,
becomes imperceptibly merged in the unreal world inhabited by dragons and phoenixes.

Of all Li Shang-yin's poems, the one that most completely embodies
the world of dream and fantasy is Poem 42, which, apart from its
possible psychological implications, is a convincing presentation of the
experience of dreaming or daydreaming. The world of the poem is
irrational, yet the various elements that constitute this world do cohere,
not in a logical fashion, to be sure, but with the persistency of images
seen in a dream.

The poems with unambiguous references and explicit themes naturally embody more easily perceptible and describable worlds, yet even
here one can distinguish between poems which perfectly achieve a
fusion of the external and the internal and those which fail to do so.
One can, of course, also distinguish various kinds of worlds, though it
is hardly necessary to label each one of them. I shall discuss some of the
more interesting ones.

Not many of Li Shang-yin's poems reveal a happy world, but a few
do. The early poem *Spring Outing* (Poem 46) is a good example. In this
poem, the external scene is in perfect harmony with the inner mood.
The galloping horse, the soaring birds, the fresh willow leaves moist
with mist, the spring wind, which is "wild" but not fierce, the tower
that affords a distant view, the precious sword—all these answer to the
poet's feelings of youthful gaiety, ambition, and self-confidence. The
allusion to Yü Yi, who won literary fame as well as military successes
as a young man, gives further expression to these feelings, and the
conceit in the last line completes the identification of the external
environment with the poet's consciousness.

The Quatrain *Early Rising* (Poem 55) likewise embodies a world in
which light-heartedness is mingled with spring scenery.

Evening Clearing (Poem 67) is another successful example of a poem
which unifies a happy state of mind with the natural setting. Less
successful are *Being Intoxicated among the Flowers* (Poem 58) and
Written While Feasting with the Chao Brothers (Poem 75), in both of
which the natural scene remains somewhat distinct from the emotions
expressed, although each poem contains a few particularly effective
touches.

Far more often, Li Shang-yin's poems explore various worlds of un-
happiness, from gentle melancholy to overwhelming grief. Among
poems expressing gentle melancholy and ennui may be mentioned
Sunset Tower (Poem 47) and *Fallen Flowers* (Poem 57). In the former,

the lonely wild goose becomes a perfect symbol of the poet's own destiny:

> I wish to ask the lonely wild goose whither it is flying,
> Not knowing that my own destiny is just as vague as his!

In the latter, the poet's heart becomes one with the flowers:

> Their fragrant heart, following spring, dies;
> What they have earned are tears that wet one's clothes.

A similar world is revealed in *Drinking Alone in a Small Garden* (Poem 59), although here the identification of the self with nature is less complete, and one feels the presence of the poet distinct from the natural environment.

The world of nostalgia is seen in many of Li's poems (for example, Poems 68–74, 83–84). Although this is a familiar world in Chinese poetry, it is revealed by our poet in different ways and with various degrees of emotional intensity. Sometimes nostalgia is suggested by the bleakness and solitude of the present surroundings, such as in *Night Thoughts* (Poem 69):

> A hanging screen, a half-rolled-up curtain;
> The pillows are cold, the quilts still fragrant.

This is immediately followed by the outburst:

> Why does my soul, for the sake of remembrance,
> Fly in a dream across the Hsiao and the Hsiang?

Similarly, in *Living a Quiet Life* (Poem 74), the nostalgic world emerges from descriptions of the lonely surroundings combined with direct expression of emotion:

> Distant letters and home-going dreams are both few and far
>   between;
> Only the empty bed valiantly faces the pale autumn.
> Under the steps, nothing but green moss and red leaves.
> In rain, there is solitude; in moonlight, grief.

At other times, homesickness is induced by the very splendor of the natural environment, which sharply contrasts with the poet's state of mind. This is clearly brought out by the opening lines of *View* (Poem 68):

> The green of the cassia in the garden disturbs the heart;
> The red of the lotus in the pond gluts the eye.

Nostalgia is sometimes felt acutely, as in *North Tower* (Poem 70):

> From this tower one can gaze northward:
> Risking my life, I lean on the dangerous railings.

Or in *Second Day of the Second Month* (Poem 83):

> The new rapids do not understand the exile's feelings,
> But make a noise like wind and rain on the eaves at night.

And sometimes it is felt less strongly and expressed in a more conventional manner, such as in *Written While Traveling on the Kweilin Road* (Poem 72):

> I wish to gaze toward the northwest,
> But all I see are partridges flying again!

The difference between this couplet and the one from *North Tower* quoted above is obvious.

In several of these poems (Poems 68, 69, 73), nostalgia is mingled with longing for the poet's wife, although it is not always clear whether she was already dead at the time he wrote the poem. A more moving expression of his grief over her death is given in *Chamber Music* (Poem 79), which has been analyzed in the commentary following the translation. The analysis has shown, I hope, how this world of bereavement is revealed through the imagery, associations, and other verbal elements which form the structure of the poem.

Frustrated ambition, which is present in some of the poems mainly concerned with nostalgia (Poems 71, 83, 84, for example), is the dominant element in the worlds explored by Poems 50, 51, and 66. Of these, the best one is *The Tower on the City Wall of An-ting* (Poem 50), where the natural surroundings are blended with the poet's feelings and thoughts. The actual river with its banks and islets (line 2) flows into the metaphorical rivers and lakes to which the poet wishes to return in his old age after having set the world right (lines 5–6). It is, the frustration of this ambition that makes the poet feel sad and compare himself to the tearful Chia Yi and the wandering Wang Ts'an (lines 3–4).

In *Boasting of My Son* (Poem 78), disappointed ambition enters a world dominated by paternal love. As we have seen, the poem at first leads us into the world of childhood as seen by the doting father, but it changes its mood and becomes an expression of disillusionment. The contrast between the two parts of the poem adds to the complexity of its world.

A number of poems (Poems 80–81, 85–88), probably written towards the end of Li Shang-yin's life, explore deeper springs of sadness, instead of the gentle melancholy discussed above. In *Lo-yu Heights* (Poem 80), a feeling of impending darkness, of having come to the end of one's life, is embodied in the image of the setting sun:

> The setting sun has infinite beauty—
> Only, the time is approaching nightfall.

This famous couplet, with its suggestions of infinite sadness and regret, also strikes a note of fatalism. A similar note is heard in *Living in Seclusion in Late Winter* (Poem 88):

> Why has it never been my lot to fulfil
> My lifelong wish to assist the State?

And this mood of forlorn hope verging on despair is interwoven with the chilly scenery:

The day when feathered wings are damaged,
The time when the country garden is quiet—
The cock at dawn disturbs the snow on the tree;
The duck in the cold guards the icy pond.

When we turn to Li Shang-yin's poems on historical or contemporary events, we find, instead of the private worlds of love, melancholy, fantasy, and so forth, the public worlds of political and social realities. Of course, these public worlds are not isolated from the private ones. For instance, the poems lamenting the death of Liu Fen (Poems 52–53) mix personal grief with moral indignation and political passion. Since most Chinese readers may be presumed to know that Liu was exiled because of his brave denunciation of the eunuchs, their sympathy for his lot and their outraged sense of justice can be readily aroused by the references to the Emperor's palace, as remote as the palace of heaven, and the implicit comparison of Liu Fen to the great Ch'ü Yüan who, according to tradition, also suffered unjust exile. At the same time, the poet's feeling of personal loss is vividly brought out by such touching concrete details as the lees left in his friend's wine jar and the cold rue leaves on his books. Finally, the poet's deep sorrow and helpless anger are unified with his friend's soul carrying its burden of grievance and wandering alone by the image of the wind-blown wild goose, whose cry is unheeded by heaven.

Even in the poems satirizing Emperor Hsüan-tsung's infatuation for the Honorable Consort Yang (Poems 93–95), the poet enables us to enter imaginatively into the feelings of the historical characters involved. Thus, in *The Dragon Pool* (Poem 93), the Emperor's gaiety is contrasted with his son Prince Shou's sullen sobriety (it was the latter's wife who had become the Emperor's favorite); and in the second of the *Ma-wei Slope* poems (Poem 95), the poet recalls the favorite concubine's death from the Emperor's point of view, while condemning him for his infatuation.

Among Li Shang-yin's poems on public themes, the most remarkable ones are *Written While Traveling through the Western Suburbs* (Poem 91) and *Two Poems Written When Moved by a Certain Event* (Poems 89–90). The former gives a panoramic view of late T'ang society—the poverty of the peasants, the inefficiency and tyranny of the government, the ravages of war, the havoc made by warlords, the economic chaos, the afflictions caused by natural disasters—as seen through the eyes of the suffering villagers. The poet combines description with narrative and dramatic monologue, and integrates his own feelings of sympathy for the villagers, indignation against the government, and hatred for the rebels and warlords with the external facts he observes. Contemporary and recent political and social events are informed with the emotions of the people and those of the poet himself. In the latter two poems, the poet uses a more oblique mode of expression—historical analogy. The outrage of the "Sweet Dew" massacre and the poet's reaction to it—his futile rage and moral indignation, his compassion for the victims, his concern for the Emperor, and his appraisal of the officials involved—are revealed through historical allusions. Apart from obvious practical reasons, this indirect way of expression also adds the authority of historical lessons to the poet's own opinions and sentiments. The Chinese have always regarded history as a "mirror," and by referring to historical experience the poet implies that this massacre is not an isolated incident but a recurrent phenomenon in Chinese history, with awful warnings for the future. The significance of these poems, therefore, extends far beyond the events which occasioned their writing.

In short, although some of Li's poems are concerned with political and social issues and have a didactic purpose, they are not social documents, or political pamphlets, or moralistic tracts, but genuine poetry, and what makes them poetry is the way in which external events are integrated imaginatively with thought and emotion. We may not share all Li Shang-yin's views, and his analyses of T'ang society may not be right, but this does not prevent us from appreciating his poetry, just as we need not share Milton's puritanism or Dante's Thomism to appreciate their works.

To conclude: most of Li's poems succeed, to a greater or lesser degree, in exploring and embodying various worlds. When the external environment, whether natural or human, forms a perfect "objective correlative" of the inner experience, and when different kinds of experience—intellectual, emotional, sensory, and intuitive—are perfectly balanced and blended, the poem is most satisfactory. When the external scene or event remains unassimilated by the poet's consciousness, or when his consciousness is dominated by one kind of experience to the exclusion of other kinds, the poem is less rewarding. Some poems embody complex worlds involving several levels of reality and various kinds of experience, while others reveal simple worlds, each binding together a natural scene or human event and a particular emotion or mood.

The worlds of Li Shang-yin's poetry present considerable variety. Some, such as those of nostalgia or melancholy, are familiar to all readers of Chinese poetry; others are less common, such as those of desperate love or fantasy. But all are explored with unusual intensity of emotion, sensitivity of perception, and boldness of imagination. And these are matched by the richness, complexity, and subtlety of Li's language.

3

His Exploration of Language

The variety of worlds explored in Li Shang-yin's poetry naturally involves a corresponding variety of styles. The more complex the world embodied in a poem, the more complex is its verbal structure. Even in relatively simple poems, the kind of world embodied depends on the kind of language used, and vice versa. Of course, the variety of styles is inevitably lost to a great extent in the translations, for to reflect accurately the various styles used by Li Shang-yin one would have to write like Shakespeare in one poem, Milton in another, and Wordsworth in a third—a feat of versatility which a great English poet might have been able to bring off but which it would be presumptuous for me even to contemplate. Nevertheless, I have tried to give some inkling of the different styles of Li's poetry, such as the colloquial style of

> My son, don't follow your father's example
> In studying hard and seeking A's and B's!
>
> [Poem 78, lines 59–60]

in contrast to the formal style of

> The Nine Domains should submit to the King's virtue,
> The Three Spiritual Lights accord with his sagacious plan
>
> [Poem 89, lines 1–2]

or the exuberance of

> The candle's light half encircles the golden kingfishers;
> The musk perfume subtly permeates the embroidered lotus
> flowers
>
> [Poem 4, lines 5–6]

as compared with the austerity of

> A bird vanishes into the sunset sky
>
> [Poem 74, line 4]

or the compactness of

> Tears sprinkled on jade plates repeatedly hurt one's heart;
> Startled strings on the ornamented zither frequently break
> one's dreams
>
> [Poem 3, lines 3–4]

in contrast to the expansiveness of

> Their offshoots give forth tiny leaves
> As soft as a fine fox fur coat,
> Or the thick tuft of hair on top of a child's head,
> Or the dense dark eyebrows of a beautiful lady.
>
> [Poem 48, lines 13–16]

Again, Li's style may change from the easy flow of

> At eight, she stole a look at herself in the mirror,
> Already able to paint her eyebrows long.
> At ten, she went out to tread on the green,
> Her skirt made of lotus flowers.
> At twelve, she learnt to play the small zither:
> The silver plectrums she never took off
>
> [Poem 11, lines 1–6]

to the ruggedness and archaic quaintness of

> The Emperor spoke: "You, Tu, are first and foremost in
> merit,
> And it is meet that your counselor Yü should indite a
> record."
>
> [Poem 100, lines 19–20]

Li Shang-yin's various styles can be analyzed from the point of view of different elements: diction, syntax, versification, imagery, symbolism, and allusions. These are the main elements which form the verbal structure of each poem and decide its distinctive style. Naturally, these have all been touched upon before, but it may be interesting to concentrate our attention on each one in turn. In reading the following pages, the reader is asked to bear in mind that my analyses are inevitably handicapped by the fact that I am writing in English for readers who may not know Chinese.

DICTION

As indicated above, the diction of Li Shang-yin's poetry can be formal or colloquial, elaborate or simple, straightforward or oblique, in accordance with the kind of world explored. For example, in Poem 6, the world of hopeless passion is partly revealed by such words as "powerless" (*wu-li*), "wither" (*ts'an*), "death" (*ssu*), "end" (*chin*), "ashes" (*hui*), "dry" (*kan*), and "cold" (*han*), all of which suggest exhaustion and despair. In Poems 15–16, which view the world of clandestine love in an ironic light, the poet uses words full of erotic innuendoes: "sleep" (*mien*), "intertwine" (*chiao*, which in Chinese also means sexual intercourse), "mat" (*tien*), "pillow" (*chen*), "hairpin" (*ch'ai*), "spring" (*ch'un*, which often has amorous associations in Chinese), "pair" (*shuang*). To move on to a totally different world, we may turn to Poem 78, *Boasting of My Son*. Here, the poet's love for his young son is expressed in a plain and often colloquial language. In particular, he uses the colloquial forms for "son" and "father," *erh* and *yeh*, instead of the more literary forms *tzu* and *fu*.[1] Similarly, he uses the diminutive prefix *ah* (or *o*) before the word *tzu* ("elder sister"). These familiar forms of address, together with the words for "nephews and nieces" (*sheng, chih*), create an intimate domestic atmosphere, which provides a setting for the poet's paternal love. This atmosphere is further emphasized by words referring to objects and activities of daily life, such as "swaddling clothes" (*wen-pao*), "pears and chestnuts" (*li li*), "lantern" (*teng*), "dressing case" (*hsiang-lien*) and "spring banner" (*ch'un-sheng*). At the same time, references to various games and theatrical characters add details to the world of childhood.

There is no need to go over more poems, but it may be of some interest to observe what Li Shang-yin's favorite words are. These include highly emotive words like "sorrow" (*ch'ou, ch'ou-ch'ang*), "regret" or "grievance" (*hen*), "longing" (*ssu*, or *hsiang-ssu*), "tears" (*lei*), "remember" (*yi*), "heart" (*hsin*), "love" or "emotion" (*ch'ing*), "cry" (*t'i*), "soul" (*hun*), and "death" (*ssu*); words with strong sensuous appeals, such as various color words, "brocade" (*chin*), "embroidered" (*hsiu*), "gold" (*chin*), "jade" (*yü*), "crystal" (*shui-ching*), "coral" (*shan-hu*), "fragrance" (*fang, fang-fei*), "perfume" or "incense" (*hsiang*), "pearl" (*chu*), "silk" (*lo, ssu*), "warmth" (*nuan*), "cold" (*leng, han*); words associated with intimacy, feminine beauty, and amorous atmosphere, such as "bed" (*ch'uang*), "pillow" (*chen*), "quilt" (*pei*), "curtain" (*lien*), "screen" (by the bed, *p'ing-feng*), "dance" (*wu*), "waist" (*yao*), "cloud" (*yün*, associated with erotic love), "rain" (*yü*, when used together with "cloud", meaning sexual love), "girdle" (*tai*); and words associated with fantasy and the supernatural, like "dream" (*meng*), "dragon" (*lung*), "phoenix" (*feng*), various goddesses and immortals, and the fairy mountain P'eng. This is not an exhaustive list, but it may help to show the worlds most frequently explored in Li Shang-yin's poetry. Some of these involve the use of imagery or allusions, which will be discussed later.

SYNTAX

The syntax of Chinese poetry, especially Regulated Verse,[2] differs from that of Classical Chinese prose in several ways. First, although in Chinese prose words already enjoy a high degree of fluidity as parts of speech, this fluidity becomes even greater in poetry. Second, the word order of poetic language often differs from that of prose, involving inversions which are not found or seldom found in the latter. For example, in prose a verb normally precedes its object (except in negative and interrogative sentences), an adjective normally precedes the noun it modifies, and an adverb usually precedes the verb. In poetry,

---

[1] The words *erh* and *yeh* were colloquial in T'ang times and rarely used by poets. The former is still the common word for "son," but the latter is no longer the common word for "father". I have therefore resisted the temptation to translate *yeh* as "Daddy."

[2] For a description of this kind of verse, see Liu, *The Art of Chinese Poetry*, pp. 26–27.

the order is often reversed. Third, although in Chinese prose there are no inflections, there are particles indicating completion or anticipation of action, interrogation, exclamation, and so forth, as well as connective particles corresponding to English prepositions, conjunctions, and relative pronouns. Such particles, which are normally, though not always, used in prose, and even pronouns and verbs, are often omitted in poetry.[3]

These syntactic differences between poetry and prose are partly due to the demands of metrical rules, which set strict limits to the number of syllables and sometimes also prescribe the tone patterns and rhymes, and partly due to the efforts of poets to overcome such limitations and to exploit the possibilities of verbal structure that they afford, so as to avoid monotony and introduce variations on the standard patterns. Since the number of syllables in each line is limited, and since there are only a limited number of available words with the requisite tones and rhymes as well as the desired meanings and relevant associations, the poet has to have greater freedom in his use of words as different parts of speech, and in word order. Otherwise, poetry would be intolerably dull. Imagine what Chinese poetry would be like if all lines were simple sentences consisting of a subject, a verb, and an object! In fact, although the lines are generally five- or seven-syllabic, grammatically they present a great variety of syntactic patterns, many of which are not found in prose. At the same time, the limited number of syllables necessitates the frequent omission of subjects, verbs, connective particles, final particles, and the like. As a result, the language of poetry is more concise, more concrete, and more ambiguous than prose. However, a poet may sometimes consciously adopt the syntax of prose for special reasons. In Li Shang-yin's poetry, we find both tendencies—the tendency to depart as far as possible from prose syntax, and the opposite one of writing poetry with the syntax of prose. This syntactic variation in style is not merely a display of technical virtuosity but a reflection of the variety of poetic worlds explored. On the whole, the more exotic and the further removed from daily life the world of a poem is, the more its language differs grammatically from prose.

I shall now illustrate the syntactic variations of Li Shang-yin's poetry. In doing so, I shall not attempt to emulate Professor Wang Li, who, in his book *Prosody in Chinese*,[4] provides comprehensive and thorough analyses of syntax in Chinese poetry, but seldom discusses the aesthetic reasons for, and effects of, syntactic changes. On the contrary, I shall direct attention chiefly to the poetic effects of syntactic variations in Li Shang-yin's poetry. Once more I wish to remind the reader that some of the features I describe may not appear in the translations, owing to the demands of English grammar and idiom, but if I were to confine myself to those features which I have been able to preserve in translation, I would be doing less than justice to Li's poetry.

[3] *Ibid.*, pp. 39–47.
[4] *Han-yü Shih-lü Hsüeh*, 1958.

Let us begin with unusual uses of words as parts of speech. In Poem 4, which embodies a world of hopeless love, the word *lung*, normally a noun meaning "cage," is used as a verb meaning "to encircle."[5] In the second of the *Terrace of Yen* poems (Poem 8), which are also concerned with unhappy love, line 4, which I translated as

> At midnight, the roaming youth in vain carries a crossbow of thorny wood

actually does not contain the word "carries" in the original, but uses "crossbow of thorny wood" (*che-tan*) verbally:

> yeh-pan   hsing-lang   k'ung   che-tan
> midnight   roaming   youth   vainly   thorny-wood-crossbow

The effect of using nouns as verbs is to render the action more concrete, although the poet may have been primarily concerned with the demands of meter.

Two examples may be given of adjectives used as verbs. In *Seventh Night of the Year "Jen-shen"* (Poem 40), which describes the Weaving Maid waiting to be reunited with her lover, line 4 reads:

> yüeh   po   pu   yen   hua
> moon   thin   not   charming   flowers

Here the word *yen*, normally used as an adjective, "charming," or stative verb, "to be charming," is used as a transitive verb. I therefore translated the line as:

> The moonlight is pale, not lending charm to the flowers.

By using the word *yen* as a transitive verb, the poet has shown the causal relation between the pale moonlight and the flowers hardly visible in the dark: it is because the moon is so pale that it fails to add charm to the flowers. If he had written

> yüeh   po   hua   pu   yen
> moon   thin   flowers   not   charming

then the relation between the two would not be so close, apart from considerations of tone and rhyme.

In the first of the five poems written for the girl called Willow Branch (Poem 60), Li Shang-yin writes:

> feng   hsiung   chia-tieh   tz'u
> bee [is] male   butterfly [is] female

using the words for "male" and "female", *hsiung* and *tz'u* verbally. This, together with the fact that these two syllables are placed in the two key positions in the line (the second and the fifth, the former preceding the caesura, the latter at the end of the line), emphasizes the contrast in sex between the bee and the butterfly. If the poet had used

---

[5] See Part I, 4.

hsiung and *tz'u* as adjectives, and had followed the normal word order, the line would have read

> *hsiung   feng   tz'u   chia-tieh*
> male   bee   female   butterfly

which would have been less effective. Unfortunately one cannot use "male" and "female" as verbs in English, and to add the weak cupola and write

> The bee is male and the butterfly is female

seems even less satisfactory than not to use any verb at all but simply to write

> A male bee and a female butterfly.

Examples of nouns used adverbially have been given before[6] and need not be repeated.

Some of the examples given above already involved inversions. We may look at a few more examples. These inversions, too, are partly due to the necessity of observing tone patterns and rhymes and partly due to a desire to create an effect of novelty or to put emphasis on certain words.

Inversions of verbs and their objects occur in various poems. In *North Tower* (Poem 70), the object "wine" (*chiu*) is placed at the beginning of line 4:

> *chiu   ching   pu   chih   han*
> wine   even   not   know   cold

The prose word order would have been:

> *ching pu   chih   chiu han*
> even   not   know   wine   cold

The inversion is needed mainly, no doubt, to make the line contrast with the preceding line,

> *hua   yu   ts'eng   lien   hsi*
> flowers   seem   already   folded   evening

since metrical rules demand that these two lines should form an antithetical couplet. But the inversion also calls attention to the wine, before anything is said about it. It is as if one were to say, "The wine? Why, I didn't even notice it was cold," instead of "I didn't notice the wine was cold."

Similarly, in *Home Thoughts* (Poem 71), in line 6, the object, "dreams" (*meng*), is placed before the verb, "startle" (*ching*):

> *yüan   ai   meng   yi   ching*
> apes   sad,   dreams   easily   startle

I have tried to preserve the inversion by using the passive voice in English:

> The apes cry sadly—my dreams are easily startled.

[6] See Part I, 4.

Sometimes adverbs are placed after the verbs instead of before them. For instance, in the poem entitled *To Yang Pen-sheng, Who Said He Had Seen My Son Ah-kun in Ch'ang-an* (Poem 82), adverbs and verbs are put in reversed order in the second halves of lines 3 and 4:

> *chien ta   t'i   ying   shuo*
> gradually big,   cry   should   repeatedly
> *ch'ang p'in hsüeh k'ung ch'ih*
> always   poor,   study   fear   late

where the prose word order would be *ying shuo t'i* ("should repeatedly cry") and *k'ung ch'ih hsüeh* or *k'ung hsüeh ch'ih* ("[I] fear [he will] study [too] late"). The inversions emphasize the words "cry" and "study" and render the lines more complex in structure than they would otherwise be.

Many of Li Shang-yin's lines involve inversions as well as omissions of various grammatical particles. Such lines are often so far removed from prose and so condensed in structure that they defy paraphrase into prose. If we changed the word order and added necessary particles, such lines would lose their poetic qualities and still not make good prose. For example, the lines from Poem 3,

> *yü-p'an ping lei shang hsin shuo*
> jade   plates   sprinkled   tears   hurt   heart   repeatedly
> *chin-se ching hsüan p'o meng p'in*
> ornamented-zither startled strings break dreams frequently

would require rearrangement as well as additional words to be turned into tolerable prose:

> *ping yü yü-p'an chih lei shuo shang jen hsin*
> sprinkled-on-jade-plates-tears repeatedly hurt one's heart
> *chin-se pei-ching chih hsüan p'in p'o jen meng*
> ornamented-zither's startled strings frequently break one's
> dreams

The compact syntax of lines like these can often lead to ambiguity, and I shall discuss this more fully later.

As for grammatical particles, since they are commonly omitted in poetry, it is their presence rather than their absence that calls for comment. We may, however, note the omission of verbs in a few cases. In *Ch'ang-o* (Poem 28), the goddess of the moon is imagined to feel lonely at night:

> Ch'ang-o should regret having stolen the elixir:
> The green sea—the blue sky—her heart every night!

The last line contains no verb but indirectly suggests her loneliness by contrasting her heart with the sea and the sky. Had the poet used a verb and written something like

> *pi hai ch'ing t'ien yeh-yeh ai*
> green sea blue sky every-night saddens

instead of

> pi   hai   ch'ing   t'ien   yeh-yeh   hsin
> green sea   blue   sky   every-night heart

the line would have been too obvious and left nothing for the reader to
imagine, apart from the question of rhyme.

Verbs also can be dispensed with when the poet intends to paint a
scene, particularly a quiet one, through a succession of images, such
as in

> The autumn insects under the grass, the frost on the leaves—
> > [Poem 29, line 1]

or in

> The day when feathered wings are damaged,
> The time when the country garden is quiet—
> > [Poem 88, lines 1-2]

In short, the omissions of verbs and particles, together with inversions, result in a style markedly different from that of prose. In contrast,
some of Li Shang-yin's poems have a deliberately loose, prosaic syntax,
and make abundant use of grammatical particles normally found in
prose. For instance, in the long poem *Written While Traveling through
the Western Suburbs* (Poem 91), we find no inversions but many pronouns and particles. To be precise, the first person pronoun *wo* is used
three times, the pronoun *che* ("one who", "those who") seven times,
so ("that which") four times, the possessive adjective *ch'i* ("his") once,
and the objective pronoun *chih* ("him," "it") four times. We also find
the possessive particle *chih* used once. As for connective particles, we
find *k'uang* ("moreover"), *chi* ("by the time of"), *yin* ("therefore")
twice, *sui* ("then"), *huo* ("either . . . or . . ."), *yi* ("with," "by," "in
order to," etc.) three times, *yü* ("and"), and *tsai* ("in," "at," etc.) twice.
We may also note that the verbs *lei, ju,* and *jo*, all meaning "resemble,"
"seem," or "be like," which are often omitted in poems with a concise
style, are used frequently in this poem. The word *lei* occurs six times,
jo three times, and *ju* no less than ten times.[7] Consequently, the style of
the poem is straightforward and relatively plain, well suited to the
narrative and monologue it contains and the world of social reality
it explores.

Another notable example is *The Memorial Inscription by Han Yü*
(Poem 100). Here too we encounter numerous pronouns and particles.
Specifically, the pronoun *pi* ("he") occurs once, *ju* ("you," "your")
twice, *ch'en* ("your servant"[8]) twice, *kung* ("his excellency,"[9] translated
as "the Master" in my translation) three times, *che* ("those who") once,
chih ("him," "it") three times, *ch'i* ("his") twice, and *tz'u* ("this") once.
We also find the exclamatory particles *tsai* and *wu-hu;* the possessive
particle *chih;* the connective particles *yü* ("and"), *ch'ieh* ("also," "not
only . . . but . . .") twice, *chi* ("as well as"), *yü* ("in," "at"), and *yi*

---

[7] This of course also involves the use of similes. Cf. below.

[8, 9] These are of course not pronouns in English, but they function as such in Chinese.

("with," "by") twice. In addition, the poet uses the verbs *yu*, *ju*, and *jo*, meaning "seem," "be like"; and the verb *yüeh*, "speak" or "say," introducing direct quotations. All these add to the prosaic style of the poem. As for word order, we find no inversions but many repetitions, which further loosen the syntactic structure and produce a halting rhythm.[10] The style of the whole poem is deliberately prosaic and quaint, not only because the theme is lofty and serious but also because this is the typical style of Han Yü himself, to whom Li Shang-yin is paying the compliment of imitation.

Syntactic changes naturally affect the rhythm and sometimes also the type of imagery used. The interrelation among these will be discussed below, in connection with versification and imagery respectively.

VERSIFICATION

It is obvious that discussions on technical details of Chinese versification would be meaningless to readers who have no knowledge of Chinese. However, I think it is possible to describe, in terms comprehensible to such readers, the verse forms used by Li Shang-yin and how these are related on the one hand to the poetic worlds explored, and on the other to the verbal structures and styles. Further, we may consider the relation between sense and sound, between syntax and rhythm, as well as specifically auditory devices like alliteration and rhyme, and structural features like repetition, parallelism, and antithesis, which affect both syntax and rhythm. An important auditory feature of Chinese verse which will not be discussed is the tone pattern, since it has no counterpart in English.

Like all Chinese poets of the T'ang and subsequent periods, Li Shang-yin writes in the two major verse forms of classical poetry, Ancient Verse (*Ku-shih*) and Regulated Verse (*Lü-shih*), also known as Ancient Style and Modern Style.[11] In both forms, the lines are either five-syllabic or seven-syllabic, though some liberty is allowed in Ancient Verse. Ancient Verse has no fixed length or tone pattern, and permits different rhymes in one poem; Regulated Verse confines each poem to eight lines, has a prescribed tone pattern, and requires the same rhyme throughout the poem and two antithetical couplets in the middle. Two other verse forms are regarded as subdivisions of Regulated Verse: the Quatrain (*Chüeh-chü*), which metrically corresponds to half of an eight-line Regulated Verse, and Multiple Regulated Verse, (*P'ai-lü*), an extended form of Regulated Verse, having an indefinite number of antithetical couplets, instead of the mandatory two, sandwiched between the opening and concluding couplets. Among Li's extant poems (excluding a few wrongly attributed to him), there are twenty-nine in five-syllabic Ancient Verse, eighteen in seven-syllabic Ancient Verse, 146 in five-syllabic Regulated Verse, 120 in seven-syllabic Regulated

---

[10] See below.
[11] See Liu, *The Art of Chinese Poetry*, pp. 24–29.

Verse, thirty-two five-syllabic Quatrains, 201 seven-syllabic Quatrains, and fifty-two poems in five-syllabic Multiple Regulated Verse. This statistic shows his preference for Regulated Verse over Ancient Verse, and for the seven-syllabic Quatrain over the five-syllabic variety. The reasons for this should become clear later.

The poems translated in this volume include twelve in five-syllabic Ancient Verse (Poems 11, 48, 56, 60–64, 78, 79, 81, 91), seven in seven-syllabic Ancient Verse (Poems 7–10, 12, 42, 100), twenty-one in five-syllabic Regulated Verse (Poems 31, 38, 40, 43, 46, 53, 57, 59, 65, 67, 68, 70, 71, 72, 75, 76, 77, 82, 84, 88, 99), twenty-two in seven-syllabic Regulated Verse (Poems 1, 2–3, 4–5, 6, 17–18, 19, 21–23, 24, 25, 37, 39, 45, 50, 52, 83, 92, 95), seven five-syllabic Quatrains (Poems 32, 33, 54, 55, 80, 86, 87), twenty-eight seven-syllabic Quatrains (Poems 13, 14, 15–16, 20, 27, 28, 29, 30, 34, 35, 36, 41, 44, 47, 49, 51, 58, 66, 69, 73, 74, 85, 93, 94, 96–97, 98), and three poems in five-syllabic Multiple Regulated Verse (Poems 26, 89–90). Based on these poems, a rough correlation between the kind of world embodied in a poem and its verse form may be discerned, though of course we cannot draw simple equations between the two. Generally speaking, Ancient Verse, with its indefinite length and greater freedom in tone and rhyme, is more suited to narrative, elaborate description, and unrestrained expression of emotion. Hence we find poems exploring external worlds of event and action (for example, Poems 91, 100) or giving vent to strong feelings (Poem 79) written in this verse form. Regulated Verse, with its exact rules, is both more restricting and more challenging, for although it imposes many restrictions, it also affords opportunities for subtle and ingenious verbal constructions not possible in Ancient Verse. The necessity for conciseness in this verse form often leads to highly compact, complex, and ambiguous structures which are well suited to the complex, elusive, and ambiguous worlds explored by many of Li Shang-yin's poems. Thus we find that most of his poems concerned with esoteric worlds and complicated emotions (for example, Poems 1–6) are in Regulated Verse, particularly the seven-syllabic variety (the seven-syllabic line naturally gives more scope for expression than the five-syllabic). At the same time, poems exploring more familiar worlds and expressing more conventional sentiments (Poems 46, 57, 59) tend to be in five-syllabic Regulated Verse. As for the Quatrain, whether five- or seven-syllabic, the brevity of the verse form renders it incapable of elaborate descriptions or complex modes of expression, but it is a perfect vehicle for the embodiment of moments of perception, particular feelings, moods, or fancies, such as in Poems 13, 55, 80, and many others. Of the two kinds of Quatrains, the five-syllabic demands greater severity of expression, since it consists of merely twenty syllables. That is perhaps why Li Shang-yin, whose poetic genius inclines to the exuberant, prefers the seven-syllabic kind. As for Multiple Regulated Verse, this is the most artificial, ornate, and restricting verse form, and does not lend itself easily to spontaneous expression. In fact, many of Li Shang-yin's poems in this verse form were addressed to patrons, and one cannot help suspecting that they were mainly intended to impress the recipients with the poet's erudition and literary skill. That is why I have translated only three poems in this form, and these are among the exceptions to the foregoing remark.

Stylistically, Li's poems in Ancient Verse tend to be archaic and lofty (for example, Poem 100) or colloquial and plain (Poems 78, 91), while his poems in Regulated Verse are generally concise and elliptical yet often ornate. This is because the former verse form allows room for a more leisurely pace and for more explicit and expansive expressions, whereas the latter demands concentration and elaboration. It is no accident that the examples of prosaic syntax given above are all from Ancient Verse, and those of inversions are mostly from Regulated Verse. We may also observe that in Ancient Verse we find enjambment, whereas in Regulated Verse a line often corresponds to two clauses or sentences in prose. Examples of enjambment may be given from Poem 91, which contains a dozen instances, but two will suffice:

> *she nien chien ch'ou yüeh*
> Snake year, *ch'ou* [twelfth] month
> *wo tzu Liang huan Ch'in*
> I from Liang return [to] Ch'in
>
> [Lines 1–2]

> *k'uang tzu Chen-kuan hou*
> moreover from Chen-kuan after
> *ming kuan to ju-ch'en*
> appoint officials mostly scholar-ministers
>
> [Lines 31–32]

These examples show how in Ancient Verse it often takes two lines to form one grammatical sentence. Indeed, we even find four lines making up one sentence:

> *wo wen chao-yao-ching*
> I hear reflect-monster-mirror
> *chi-yü shen-chien-feng*
> as-well-as divine sword-blade
> *yü shen hui yu ti*
> entrust selves may have place
> *pu wei fan wu meng*
> not by common object obscured
>
> [Poem 48, lines 57–60]

In contrast, in Regulated Verse, enjambment is impossible in the four middle lines, which have to form antithetical couplets, and even the opening and concluding couplets seldom run on grammatically. Instead, a line may form a complete sentence, or leave the sentence unfinished, or consist of two clauses. Examples of the first kind are innumerable. We need only look at one or two:

> *t'ien yi lien yu ts'ao*
> heaven's feeling pities sequestered grass
>
> *jen-chien chung wan ch'ing*
> human world treasures evening clearing
>
> [Poem 67, lines 3–4]

Unfinished sentences are lines like those quoted before to illustrate the omission of verbs. As for lines having two clauses, the following are examples:

> *ch'iao chün pan-chui chi*
> bridge [is] steep, piebald-horse [is] fast
>
> *ch'uan ch'ang po niao kao*
> river [is] long, white birds [are] high
>
> [Poem 44, lines 1–2]
>
> *Chia-shih k'uei lien Han-yüan shao*
> Lady Chia peeped [at] curtain, Secretary Han [was] young
>
> *Fu-fei liu chen Wei-wang ts'ai*
> Princess Fu left pillow, Prince [of] Wei [was] talented
>
> [Poem 5, lines 5–6]

In short, the presence of enjambment, together with the use of particles and prose word order, results in a loose structure and a relatively straightforward style in Ancient Verse, whereas the compact syntax, involving inversions and omissions of particles, creates a tight structure and a more heightened style in Regulated Verse

Although syntax is to some extent influenced by the verse form, it can, in turn, modify the rhythm imposed by the latter. Indeed, the art of versification does not lie in mechanically observing metrical rules, nor in throwing all rules overboard, but in transcending such rules and even turning them into positive advantages. This art is to be perceived in the tension between the metrical rhythm and the syntactic rhythm, between the abstract pattern prescribed by the verse form and the actual pattern of the finished poem. Let us see some examples of the way Li Shang-yin modifies metrical rhythm with syntactic variations.

Sometimes the poet introduces minor pauses in addition to those inherent in the meter. For instance, in the lines from Poem 3 quoted before:

> *yü-p'an ping lei shang hsin shuo*
> jade plates sprinkled tears hurt heart repeatedly
>
> *chin-se ching hsüan p'o meng p'in*
> ornamented-zither startled strings break dreams frequently

the metrical rhythm (disregarding the tones) is

$$-\,-\,/\,-\,-\,/\,-\,-\,-$$

in each line, but the syntax requires a slight additional pause before the final syllable, so that the rhythm becomes

$$— — / — — / — — / —$$

Or he may shift the positions of pauses, as in the following line from Poem 70:

> chiu   ching   pu   chih   han
> wine   even   not   know   cold.

Here, the standard metrical rhythm is

$$— — / — — —$$

but the syntactic rhythm is:

$$— / — — — / —$$

These examples illustrate how syntactic variations not only affect the sense but also the rhythm.

The above examples are from Regulated Verse. Even in Ancient Verse, where the metrical rules are freer, most poets observe the basic patterns of

$$— — / — — —$$

for five-syllabic lines, and

$$— — / — — / — — —$$

for seven-syllabic lines. However, Li Shang-yin often deviates from these. One poem alone, Poem 100, provides sufficient variations:

(a)   pi   ho-jen   tsai   Hsüan   yü   Hsi
      he   what-man   Oh!   Hsuan   and   Hsi
$$— / — — — / — — —$$

[Line 2]

(b)   Su   Wu   Ku   T'ung   tso   ya-chao
      Su,   Wu,   Ku,   T'ung   became   teeth-claws
$$— / — / — / — / — — —$$

[Line 13]

(c)   hsing-chün-ssu-ma   chih   ch'ieh   yung
      military   adviser   wise   and   brave
$$— — — — / — — —$$

[Line 15]

(d)   ju   ts'ung-shih   Yü   yi   wei   tz'u
      your   counselor   Yü   fit   make   writing
$$— / — — / — / — — —$$

[Line 20]

(e)   Yü   pai   chi-shou   tao   ch'ieh   wu
      Yü   bow   knock-head   leap   and   dance
$$— / — / — — / — — —$$

[Line 21]

(f)   *tz'u-shih   pu   hsi   yü   chih-ssu*
      this affair not depend on officials-in-charge
      — — / — — — / — —
                                                    [Line 24]

These lines sound more like prose than normal verse—which again illustrates the interrelation between sense and sound, syntax and rhythm.

Auditory devices, such as alliterative and rhyming compounds, reduplications, and onomatopoeia,[12] though most of them cannot be preserved in translation, also merit some attention in analyzing Li Shang-yin's style in the original. Examples of alliteration are: *ling-lo* [*lieng-lâk* in Ancient Chinese] ("scatter, fall away," which I translated as "fade and fall") in Poem 3, line 2; *hsiao-hsi* [*siäu-siǝk*] ("news") in Poem 17, line 6, and Poem 26, line 5; Hsiao Hsiang [*Sieu Siang*] (names of two rivers) in Poem 42, line 7 and Poem 79, line 4. As for rhyme, since end rhyme occurs in all Chinese poetry and is not a distinctive feature of Li Shang-yin's verse, it needs no comment. Rhyming compounds are used quite frequently, such as: *lan-kan* [*lân-kân*] ("railing") in Poem 21, line 1, and Poem 29, line 2; *chia kua* [*ka kwa*] ("fine melon") in Poem 62, line 1; and *ts'ang-mang* [*ts'âng-mâng*] ("distant and vague") in Poem 26, line 2. Sometimes an alliterative compound is used in contrast to a rhyming one, such as in the description of the dream in Poem 42:

> *huang-hu* [*xwâng-xuǝt*]   *wu-ni   ming   yu   an*
> vague   no-reason   bright   again   dark
>
> *ti-mi* [*tiei-miei*]   *pu-yi   tuan   huan   lien*
> indistinct   no-stop   break   again   join
>
> Everything was vague and confusing—bright one moment,
>   dark the next;
> The indistinct forms emerged endlessly—broke up, then
>   continued.
>   [Lines 13–14]

Here the alliterative *huang-hu* [*xwâng-xuǝt*] and the rhyming *ti-mi* [*tiei-miei*] both mean "vague" or "indistinct," and the effect of these synonyms is greatly enhanced by the alliteration and rhyme.

Reduplications, as distinct from repetitions (which will be discussed below), are generally used for emphasis, such as *yin-yin* [*.iǝm-.iǝm*] ("dark, dark") in Poem 8, line 2, though sometimes they are merely idioms, like *jan-jan* [*ńźiam-ńźiam*] ("gradually") in Poem 7, line 1.[13] Some reduplicated words involve onomatopoeia, such as *sa-sa* [*sâp-sâp*] (sound of wind, which I translated as "soughs and sighs") in Poem 5, line 1.

All these auditory devices not only enhance the effect of individual words but also enrich the total sound pattern of a poem.

12 Cf. Liu, *The Art of Chinese Poetry*, pp. 34–37.
13 Cf. *Ibid.*, pp. 34–35.

We may now turn to some structural features which affect both meaning and rhythm. First, there are different kinds of repetitions. A word may be repeated in the same line:[14]

> It is *hard* for us to meet, and also *hard* to part.
>
> [Poem 6, line 1]

Or in two successive lines:

> Young Liu already resented the distance of the *P'eng Mountain*;
> Now ten thousand more *P'eng Mountains* rise!
>
> [Poem 4, lines 7–8]

In these instances, the words are obviously repeated for emphasis. In other instances, however, words seem to be repeated not primarily for emphasis but to create a deliberately halting rhythm and a naïve, archaic style, such as in Poem 81:

> When the *lotus leaves grew*, my spring *sadness grew*.
> Now that the *lotus leaves* have withered, my autumn *sadness* is full.
> I well know that as long as life *remains*, emotions *remain*;
> Gazing ahead wistfully by the *river*, I hear the *river's* flow.

Or in Poem 100, where we find the following lines:

> Big wolves *begot wild cats*; *wild cats begot* bears.
>
> [Line 6]
>
> The Emperor obtained a sage *premier*; the *premier* was called Tu.
>
> [Line 9]
>
> This eulogy of the Emperor's divine success was carved on *stone*,
> The *stone* was thirty feet high, with words as big as bushels.
>
> [Lines 35–36]
>
> Oh, the *sage* Emperor and the *sage* premier!
>
> [Line 45]

On the whole, repetitions are more frequently met with in Ancient Verse than in Regulated Verse, since in the former there is no restriction in this respect and a rugged rhythm is more appropriate, while in the latter a word can be repeated in two consecutive lines only if they are the opening or concluding couplet but not in the four middle lines, which, it will be remembered, must form two antithetical couplets. In the examples given above, the first two are from Regulated Verse and the rest from Ancient Verse.

Two similar but not identical structural devices are parallelism and antithesis.[15] The former mainly results from the presence of two or more lines which are syntactically alike and often contain repetitions of

---

[14] Since the words repeated in the originals are also repeated in the translations, I have not thought it necessary to give the original lines in transliteration here.

[15] Cf. Liu, *The Art of Chinese Poetry*, pp. 146–149.

words; the latter is confined to two lines consisting of antonyms placed in corresponding positions, and allows no repetitions.[16] Parallelism generally occurs in Ancient Verse, which gives more scope for extended verse-paragraphs than Regulated Verse, whereas antithesis is obligatory in the two middle couplets of Regulated Verse, and is sometimes also used in the opening couplet. Moreover, such is the natural tendency of Chinese toward antithesis that it appears quite often even in Ancient Verse, though less strictly formulated than in Regulated Verse.

The following are examples of parallelism. In Poem 11, parallelism forms the basis of the structure of the whole poem:

> At eight, she stole a look at herself in the mirror,
> Already able to paint her eyebrows long.
> At ten, she went out to tread on the green,
> Her skirt made of lotus flowers.
> At twelve, she learnt to play the small zither;
> The silver plectrums she never took off.
> At fourteen, she was hid among her relatives,
> And, one imagined, not married yet.
> At fifteen, she weeps in the spring wind,
> Turning her face away from the swing.

The succession of syntactically similar couplets results in fluency of rhythm and simplicity of structure, both of which are in accord with the charming naïveté of the world embodied in this poem.

Parallelism also occurs in Poem 91, such as:

> Every five *li* he changed his horse,
> Every ten *li* he had a feast.
>
> [Lines 55–56]
>
> Of those defeated, whole families died;
> Those who survived proved enduring.
>
> [Lines 135–136]
>
> In life he was feared by other people;
> In death he was pitied by no one.
>
> [Lines 151–52]
>
> I've heard when *one* man Hui was raised,
> All the bandits fled for fear of him.
> I've also heard that order or disorder
> All depends on man and not on heaven!
>
> [Lines 187–90]

These parallel lines help the flow of the narrative and highlight certain points in the development of the poem.

As for antithesis, although this is required in Regulated Verse, it is often more than a mechanical matching of words: it is a means to bring together disparate elements of life, such as in

---

[16] In translation, of course, such strictness is not always possible.

> In the vast sea, under a bright moon, pearls have tears;
> On Indigo Mountain, in the warm sun, jade engenders
>   smoke.
>
> [Poem 1, lines 5–6]

Or in

> The spring silkworm's thread will only end when death
>   comes;
> The candle will not dry its tears until it turns to ashes.
>
> [Poem 6, lines 3–4]

In such lines, antithesis joins together things which have no logical connection with one another, and at the same time serves as a cohesive link between syntactically unconnected lines, in the absence of grammatical particles. It is therefore no mere embellishment but an integral part of the poetic structure.

IMAGERY AND SYMBOLISM

Since imagery is often the primary means by which the world of a poem is revealed to us, it has been necessary to refer to it again and again in the previous pages, and enough has been said, I think, to show how imagery works in individual poems. What remains to be done is to make some general observations on the types and sources of imagery in Li Shang-yin's poetry, before turning our attention to symbolism.

But first of all I should clarify my terminology. I make a distinction between "simple" and "compound" imagery, the former referring to verbal expressions which convey sensuous experiences without involving two terms, and the latter to those which describe one thing in terms of another or translate one kind of experience into another.[17] While I admit that it is not always possible to draw a clear line of demarcation between the two kinds of imagery, I wish to point out that by calling some images "simple" I do not mean that they are simple in significance or effect but in form, as compared with compound images; nor is it my purpose to establish rigid categories. I wish merely to draw attention to two different modes of poetic expression. It should be obvious that in lines like

> Gathering birds fly around the fishing boats;
> A fading rainbow brushes past the horse's saddle
>
> [Poem 65, lines 3–4]

we have a different sort of imagery from, say,

> The winged visitor of the honeycombs is like her fragrant
>   heart,
> Acquainted with all the wanton leaves and seductive twigs.
>
> [Poem 7, lines 3–4]

In the first quotation, the images (the birds, the boats, the rainbow, and

---

[17] Cf. Liu, *The Art of Chinese Poetry*, pp. 102–4.

the horse) do not involve any comparisons, nor do they represent particular objects or emotions. They simply form part of the external aspect of the poetic world, of which the poet's emotions and thought form the internal aspect. In contrast, in the second quotation, the images involve complicated comparisons,[18] and the heroine's emotions are explicitly identified with the external scene. Therefore, I think the distinction between "simple" and "compound" imagery is a valid one.

Further, I distinguish four types of compound imagery: images of juxtaposition, comparison, substitution, and transference.[19] This classification is based on various stages of the mental process of connecting two things, rather than on the formal distinctions (for example, between simile and metaphor) in traditional Western rhetoric. The characteristics of each type should become clear from the examples to be given below.

Simple imagery occurs frequently in Li Shang-yin's poems, without marked preponderance in any particular group of poems. Obvious examples are:

> On the steep bridge the piebald horse gallops;
> Over the long river the white birds soar.
>
> [Poem 46, lines 1–2]
>
> A rainbow closes the rain over the green peaks;
> A bird vanishes into the sunset sky.
>
> [Poem 75, lines 3–4]

Sometimes images can be highly evocative and suggestive but still remain "simple" in form, such as

> The candle's light half encirlces the golden kingfishers;
> The musk perfume subtly permeates the embroidered lotus
> flowers.
>
> [Poem 4, lines 5–6]

In spite of their strong sensuous appeal and emotional associations, these images do not involve comparisons, nor do they embody particular emotions. It would be going too far, I think, to say that the candle represents the speaker's love here. In Poem 6, by contrast, the candle is clearly a compound image and stands for the speaker himself:

> The candle will not dry its tears until it turns to ashes.

Thus the former image, though visually very effective, has less emotional impact than the latter one. The former remains in the realm of sensuous experience, but the latter unifies the world of things with the world of emotion, the physical with the mental. Even the "golden kingfishers" and "embroidered lotus flowers," referring to the quilt and the bed-curtain respectively, though they would be called synecdoches in the terminology of traditional Western rhetoric, do not

---

[18] See below.
[19] Cf. Liu, *The Art of Chinese Poetry*, pp. 106–8.

constitute compound images in my sense of the term, since they do not
compare the quilt and the curtain to kingfishers and lotus flowers, but
only mention the latter two as actual details of the former two.

Compound images of juxtaposition, which place two things side by
side without comparing them to each other, are not often used in Li
Shang-yin's poems, although they are common in earlier Chinese
poetry, especially in *The Book of Poetry*. An example may be found in
Poem 81:

> When the lotus leaves grew, my spring sadness grew.
> Now that the lotus leaves have withered, my autumn
> sadness is full.

Here, any relation between the natural environment and the human
situation is barely suggested by the juxtaposition of the two.

In at least one poem (Poem 64), we find a kind of double juxtaposition:

> Painted screens and embroidered curtains
> Naturally form pairs, like everything else.
> How is it when I gaze on the lake,
> I can only see mandarin ducks?

The screens and curtains are contrasted with the poet's separation from
the girl he loves, and so are the happy pairs of mandarin ducks. At the
same time, these objects are juxtaposed to each other.

The most common type of compound imagery in Li Shang-yin's
poetry is that of comparison, whether explicit or implicit. Explicit
comparison is made when the tenor (the thing which is the object of
attention) and the vehicle (the thing to which it is compared) are joined
by such words as *ju*, *jo*, *ssu*, or *yu*, corresponding to "is like," "resembles," "looks as if," and the like in English. Such images occur more
often in Ancient Verse than in Regulated Verse, because in the latter the
need to be concise and to avoid repetitions in the antithetical couplets
makes it hard to use explicit comparisons except in the opening and
concluding couplets. In Ancient Verse, on the other hand, since there
are no similar restrictions, Li Shang-yin at times indulges in giving
several images of explicit comparison (or similes, if the traditional term
is preferred) in succession, such as in Poem 48:

> Upright as the persons of true gentlemen,
> Erect as brave knights with chests thrust forward.
>
> [Lines 7–8]
>
> Again, they are like dragons running in surprise,
> Silently encountering rushing clouds.
>
> [Lines 11–12]
>
> Then I seem to be in a cool secluded chamber,
> Where a green coverlet spreads like the vault of heaven,
> Or watching the maidens from the Wisteria Hill

Making up their faces early in the morning.

[Lines 21–24]

In life he was like the moon over the blue sea;
In death he was trampled like grass in the frosty countryside.

[Lines 53–54]

In the original poem, these lines contain the words *ju* or *jo* ("is like," "seems," etc.), making the comparison explicit. Even more examples can be found in Poem 91, but they need not be given here. In general, although these images are less concentrated than other kinds of compound imagery, they are well suited to narrative and extended description.

One notable feature of Li Shang-yin's use of similes is that he often uses a strong verb to join the tenor and the vehicle, instead of such weak verbs as *ju, jo, yu,* and *ssu*. For instance, in Poem 4, lines 7–8, the heart is compared to flowers but in the following manner:

Do not let the amorous heart vie with the flowers in burgeoning:
One inch of longing, one inch of ashes!

In Poem 17, lines 3–4, a round fan is likened to the moon, and the sound of a carriage to thunder, but in each case the two things compared are linked by an active verb: "[her] fan, *cutting* the moon's soul" (*shan ts'ai yüeh p'o*) and "[his] carriage, *driving* the thunder's noise" (*ch'e tsou lei sheng*). The use of "cutting" (*ts'ai*) and "driving" (*tsou*) is highly original and daring, and renders the imagery more effective than if the poet had written "[her] fan *is like* the moon's soul" (*shan ju yüeh p'o*) and "[his] carriage *seemed like* thunder's noise" (*ch'e ssu lei sheng*), which would have satisfied metrical requirements equally well. Similarly in Poem 78, lines 37–38, we find:

He *vies* with the butterflies in agility,
And does not *yield* to the floating catkins for speed.

In other compound images of comparison, the tenor and the vehicle are bracketed together without any connecting word, such as "moon('s) waves" (*yüeh-lang*) in Poem 10, line 1; "incense-heart" (*hsiang-hsin*, punning on "fragrant heart") in Poem 11, line 6; "wind-chariot" (*feng-ch'e*) and "rain-horse" (*yü-ma*) in the same poem, line 15; "cloud-leaves" (*yün-yeh*) in Poem 31, line 6; and "flower-coins" (*hua-ch'ien*) in Poem 79, line 2. These images, in which the tenor and the vehicle are, as it were, hyphenated, have an extremely condensed form and a strong, immediate impact, comparable to Dylan Thomas's "heron priested shore" or "sea faiths."

Compound images of substitution are those in which the tenor is understood and only the vehicle is mentioned, such as "silk mat" for "grass" in Poem 2, line 4; "morning pearl" for "sun" in Poem 21, line 7; "whirlpools" for "creases" in Poem 8, line 6; and "jade wheel" for "moon" in Poem 38, line 2.

The situation is reversed in images of transference, such as "fragrant heart" (*fang hsin*); here the tenor is mentioned but the vehicle is un-identified. Although we could identify the vehicle as "flower" or "herb," this is unnecessary, just as in Andrew Marvell's famous "green thought in a green shade," it is surely unnecessary to ask whether "thought" is being compared to green grass, or green leaves, or any-thing else definite. Such images are uncommon, but two other exam-ples may be given from Poem 68:

> The green of the cassia in the garden *disturbs* the heart;
> The red of the lotus in the pond *gluts* the eye.

The effectiveness of "disturbs" and "gluts" would not be increased (indeed, it would be weakened), if we were to think of the cassia as being compared to a man and the lotus flowers as being compared to some kind of food!

Naturally, two or more types of imagery may be used together. For example, in the line from Poem 3,

> Tears sprinkled on jade plates repeatedly hurt one's heart,

the context makes us realize that "tears on jade plates" refers to rain-drops on the peonies, thus forming a compound image of substitution, where the tenor "raindrops" is understood and the vehicle "tears" is mentioned. At the same time, through the allusion to the mermaid whose tears turned into pearls on a jade plate, a compound image of comparison is implicitly involved, where "tears" becomes the tenor and "pearls" is the vehicle. Incidentally, it is interesting to note that in Poem 1, the two terms are reversed, with "pearls" as the tenor and "tears" as the vehicle:

> In the vast sea, under a bright moon, pearls have tears.

Similarly, in Poem 83, line 3,

> The flowers' whiskers and the willows' eyes are listless in different ways,

the use of "whiskers" and "eyes" for "pistils" and "young leaves" respectively constitutes an image of substitution, while the attribution of these to flowers and willows involves transference.

An example of extreme complexity in the form of imagery occurs in Poem 7, lines 3–4:

> The winged visitor of the honeycombs is like her fragrant heart,
> Acquainted with all the wanton leaves and seductive twigs.

The "winged visitor of the honeycombs" is, of course, an image of substitution, whereas the "fragrant heart," as we have seen, is an image of transference. These two are then joined by the verb *lei* ("resembles") to form a compound image of comparison. In the next line, the use of "wanton" and "seductive" involves images of transference or implicit comparison. Furthermore, since this line applies both to the bee and the heart, it suggests at once the bee's flying among the leaves and twigs and the heart's restless search for love. The intensity and complexity of such imagery might be called, with some justification, Shakespearean.

While the types of imagery used affect the verbal structure and style of a poem, the sources from which imagery is drawn reflect the world explored. For example, in poems which explore the world of fantasy, many images are drawn from the supernatural; in those which explore the world of love, imagery is often drawn from indoor life. This should be evident from the discussions on individual poems and we need not go into more details here. However, a few general comments may be made on the sources of Li Shang-yin's imagery.

First, it may be remarked that in Li Shang-yin's poetry, nature imagery is not of paramount importance, as it is in the works of many other Chinese poets, notably T'ao Ch'ien and Wang Wei. In Li's poetry, we seldom enter a world in which nature is seen as an end in itself, but usually find ourselves in one in which the natural environment is seen in the light of some dominating emotion and provides the setting for the human drama.

Even quantitatively, nature imagery is not the most important kind in his poetry, but competes with imagery drawn from human life as well as from the world of the supernatural.[20] In some of his poems, such as Poems 1, 2–3, 7–10, 21–23, we find imagery from all three spheres, since the worlds explored in these poems bring together the natural, the human, and the superhuman. In other, simpler poems, we still encounter nature imagery side by side with imagery drawn from daily life and human activities. This can be proved by a glance at his poems, and no examples need be given here.

Another point that may be worth commenting on is that Li Shang-yin is not afraid to use as images objects not generally considered "poetic" in themselves. When the world embodied in a poem is a harsh one, he often uses images involving objects with unpleasant associations. For instance, in Poem 91, which describes political and social conditions, we find many such images:

> The people of the Central Plain were *butchered* and *dissected*,
> [Lines 45–46]

> Ministers and courtiers were shamefully scolded, scorned,
> *Spat on, and thrown away like balls of dung!*
> [Lines 59–60]

> The city empty: *sparrows and mice died;*
> The people gone: *jackals and wolves howled.*
> [Lines 105–6]

---

[20] This statement is based on a rough estimate; I have not counted every single image in Li Shang-yin's poetry!

It was as if *a man's body*
Had only its left side but not its right:
The muscles of the body were half *paralyzed,*
And *rank odor* grew under the arms.

[Lines 111–14]

Sores and *ulcers* have grown for several decades,
But no one dares to pluck them by the root!

[Lines 145–46]

A sharp knife cut off his head
Which was hung up *like a pig's or cow's*

[Lines 157–58]

I would, for the sake of this affair,
Rip my heart out before the sovereign;
Knock my head on the ground till *fresh blood*
Gushes out and defiles the Purple Palace!

[Lines 191–94]

What a contrast these images form to the pearls, jades, embroidered lotus flowers, and perfumed coverlets of the love poems! But the harshness and unpleasant associations of the former are fully justified by the world of political corruption and social evil that they help to reveal. Moreover, they also show the poet's attitude toward what he is describing, and influence our response to it. In particular, we may compare these lines from Poem 91:

In life he was feared by other people;
In death he was pitied by no one.
A sharp knife cut off his head,
Which was hung up like a pig's or cow's

with the following ones from Poem 48:

In life he was like the moon over the blue sea;
In death he was trampled like grass in the frosty countryside.

The first quotation describes the death of Cheng Chu, who was one of the officials involved in the plot against the eunuchs but was himself generally regarded as a ruthless and wicked man. That Li Shang-yin felt no compassion for his death is clearly shown in the imagery, which evokes horror and disgust but no pity. By contrast, the imagery in the second quotation, which refers to the death of the anonymous owner of the painting of pine trees, makes us feel regret and pity.

Harsh imagery is also used in Poem 100, line 6. Here, the rebels are compared to wild beasts:

Big wolves begot wild cats; wild cats begot bears.

Moreover, the repeated use of the word "begot" (*sheng*) may suggest that these are no common beasts but monstrous hybrid creatures. In the same poem, the poet's admiration and reverence for Han Yü are expressed in hyperbolic imagery:

> I wish to write ten thousand copies of it, recite it as many
>   times,
> Till saliva drips from the corners of my mouth, my right
>   hand callous!

[Lines 49–50]

This may not sound very "poetic," but the strength of the poet's
feelings demands such violent imagery. It seems to me that Li Shang-
yin is deliberately exaggerating to the point of apparent absurdity: the
picture of the poet reciting Han Yü's writing till his mouth drips with
saliva or copying it so many times till his hand grows callous reminds
one of some religious devotee keeping a vow to recite Amitabha
Buddha (or Ave Maria for that matter) or to copy some holy scripture
thousands of times, so that we feel that the poet's reverence for Han Yü
and his dedication to literature approach the intensity of religious
devotion. Thus, what may at first seem absurd becomes touching in a
pathetic sort of way. Had Li Shang-yin used more "poetic" imagery,
and written, let us say,

> Till breath expires from my mouth like perfume, my right
>   hand drooping like a willow twig,

how ridiculous it would have been!

In short, the sources of imagery used and the kind of world explored
in a poem are mutually dependent. Consequently, in poems exhibiting
similar worlds, we find similar and even recurrent images. Such
recurrent images suggest underlying cross references among various
poems, but they should not be taken as indications that these poems
necessarily concern the same actual persons or events.

Some images involve allusions (we can, of course, put it the other
way round and say that some allusions involve imagery), although their
effect does not always depend to the same extent on our recognition of
the allusions. In some instances, such as "Blue Bird" for a messenger
(Poem 6, line 8; Poem 26, line 5) the image would be pointless unless
we recognized the allusion; the sensuous appeal of the image is of minor
importance. In other instances, on the contrary, the sensuous appeal of
the imagery is so strong that an immediate effect is produced even if the
allusion is not recognized, such as in "white elms" for stars (Poem 26,
line 10); or when there is uncertainty about what allusions are involved,
as in the case of the jade in the smoke in Poem 1. Again, the effect of an
image involving an allusion may depend equally on its sensuous character and on our recognition of the allusion, as in the lines about the
philosopher's dream of the butterfly and the Emperor's metamorphosis
into the cuckoo in Poem 1. It is immaterial whether we consider such
verbal expressions primarily as imagery or as allusions, so long as we
realize their functions in their poetic contexts.

Most of Li Shang-yin's imagery has a high degree of originality, in
form and usage if not always in basic conception. Naturally he is not
entirely free from hackneyed imagery, such as "cloudy hair." But

sometimes, even when he is using a hackneyed image, he gives it a new lease of life. For instance, in using the *cliché* "autumn waves" for a woman's eyes, not only does he combine this with another water image, but he uses an unusual verb:

> The pillow is made of a stone from the dragon palace:
> It has *reaped* the color of your eyes, clear as autumn waves.

The image of the precious stone from the dragon palace under water, as I suggested before, merges in the picture of the beautiful eyes as clear as autumn water, and the comparison of the color of the pillow to that of the eyes is effected by the verb "reaped" (*ke*).

Originality is not the sole criterion for judging poetic imagery; we have to consider how an image is used and what effects it has in its context.[21] But since the analyses of imagery in the previous pages have implied critical evaluation, it does not seem necessary to make any value judgments more explicitly.

When we turn to symbolism, once more it may be desirable to make clear what is meant by the term, in view of the many different senses in which the words "symbol" and "symbolism" are used. Roughly speaking, I use the word "symbol" in two senses. In a general sense, every poem is a verbal symbol of the world it embodies. In a more specific sense, symbols refer to those verbal expressions that represent the abstract by the concrete or the universal by the particular.[22] It is with symbols in the latter sense that I shall be concerned in the ensuing discussions.

The terms "symbolism" (use of "symbols" in the second sense) and "imagery" overlap but are by no means coextensive in meaning. In so far as symbols are concrete and represent one thing by another, they are also compound images, but not all images, simple or compound, are necessarily symbolic. For example, in the lines

> On the steep bridge the piebald horse gallops;
> Over the long river the white birds soar

> [Poem 46, lines 1–2]

although it is true to say that the images describe an external scene in consonance with the inner mood, it would be going too far, I think, to say that they symbolize anything specifically. Or when the poet compares tiny leaves of pine trees to fox fur, a child's hair and a lady's eyebrows (Poem 48, lines 14–16), it would be absurd to take these images as symbols. Indeed, it seems to me that the tendency among certain modern Western critics to see "symbols," "myths," and "archetypes" everywhere in poetry is only a more sophisticated kind of pedantry than the tendency among traditional Chinese scholars to see moral allegory in every poem.

The distinctions between symbolism and imagery may be described

---

[21] Cf. Liu, *The Art of Chinese Poetry*, pp. 114–23.
[22] Cf. Wimsatt, *Hateful Contraries*, pp. 51–71.

as follows. In the first place, whereas a symbol represents the abstract and universal by the concrete and particular, an image may involve only two physical and particular objects. For instance, if a woman is compared to a flower, this constitutes a compound image, but if we think of the flower as representing all feminine beauty, it then becomes a symbol. Therefore, symbols have (or at least are meant to have) universal significance, but images have only local significance. Second, in symbolism, especially in private symbolism, the tenor (what is represented) cannot always be identified with ease, but the vehicle (that which represents) is always named. For instance, we may never reach general agreement on what the zither in Poem 1 symbolizes, but few, I imagine, will be content to take it literally and fail to recognize it as a symbol of some sort. With imagery, on the other hand, we can always identify the tenor, even if it is not mentioned (as in the case of images of substitution), but we may have difficulty in identifying the vehicle (as in the case of images of transference). Finally, imagery works on the sensuous and emotional levels, whereas symbolism functions mainly on the intellectual level. When we feel the sensuous effect of words and respond emotionally, we are responding to them as images, but when we come to perceive their deeper meaning, we are comprehending them as symbols. This is not to deny that symbols can have strong sensuous appeal and powerful emotional impact, but only to suggest that the act of recognizing the symbolic significance of an object, or of the words that refer to it, is an intellectual one, and that without such recognition no emotional impact can be felt. The sight of the cross, or even of the word "cross," may arouse powerful emotions in a Westerner, but to a Chinese who has never heard of Christianity it will obviously not create such an effect.

Symbolism plays an important part in Li Shang-yin's poetry, in which we find both conventional and private symbols.[23] Naturally, the two kinds of symbols cannot be rigidly and arbitrarily separated. We can, however, draw a rough distinction between, on the one hand, purely conventional symbols, and, on the other, conventional symbols used in an individual manner and private symbols.

Purely conventional symbols used by Li Shang-yin include mandarin ducks for conjugal happiness (in Poem 64, line 4), damaged wings for frustrated ambition (in Poem 88, line 1), "Huge Furnace" for heaven (in Poem 89, line 16), and thorns for a ruined country (in Poem 96, line 2). Such symbols are poetically of minor importance. Numerically, they form only a small proportion of Li's symbols.

Far more symbols are used in a personal way, even when they are derived from common usage or earlier literature. In Poem 1, for example, the butterfly as a symbol of the transciency and dreamlike nature of life, and the cuckoo as a symbol of unhappy, illicit love, are both conventional symbols, yet each may have additional private significance

---

[23] Cf. Liu, *The Art of Chinese Poetry*, pp. 125-30.

as well. Or take the silkworm and the candle in Poem 6: although both are derived from earlier poetry, they are given fresh force, because one is said to spin silk *till death comes* and the other to shed tears *till it turns to ashes*. They are therefore not merely conventional symbols of love and sorrow respectively, but new, personal symbols of these particular kinds of love and sorrow, felt in a particular way. Again, the wild goose is a common symbol for distant exile, but in Poem 47 it becomes a personal symbol of uncertain destiny, and in Poem 53 it symbolizes unheeded protest.

As for private symbols, we may mention the zither, the pearls, and the jade in Poem 1, the peonies in Poems 2–3, the iron net and corals in Poem 7, the moth in Poem 12, the stars in Poem 21, the lotus leaves in Poem 49, and the setting sun in Poem 80. Being private symbols, they are naturally liable to different interpretations, as we have seen before in the discussions on these poems. Although we can never prove what the poet consciously intended these symbols to signify, we may justi-fiably interpret them in several ways, so long as our interpretations do not contradict the general tone and mood of the poem concerned, or historical possibility. It would be patently absurd to say, for instance, that the moth symbolizes space flight, but we may see it as a symbol of universal human aspirations for the ideal, even though the poet may not consciously have intended it as such. Taken in this way, the symbols in Li's poetry add considerably to its intellectual richness, without losing any of their own concrete character or emotional force.

Some historical and legendary figures alluded to in Li Shang-yin's poetry may also be considered symbolic. As a matter of convenience, these will be discussed below, as allusions.

ALLUSIONS

Li Shang-yin has been both admired and condemned for the highly allusive character of much of his poetry. Actually we should neither admire his allusions simply because of the erudition they display nor condemn them simply because they make his poems difficult to under-stand. Instead, we should ask what poetic purposes they serve, what effects they produce. As for possible extraneous reasons for using allu-sions, such as the necessity not to refer to contemporary political figures by name, these may partly account for but do not necessarily justify the presence of allusions. Poetic effectiveness, therefore, remains our main criterion for judging allusions.

As I indicated elsewhere, allusions are of two kinds: general and specific.[24] General allusions (i.e. those to common knowledge, beliefs and assumptions) tend to be less effective than specific ones, since, like fossilized images and purely conventional symbols, they are virtually common idioms. Even originally specific allusions can, through long and repeated usage, lose much of their force and become no more

[24] Cf. Liu, *The Art of Chinese Poetry*, pp. 131–36.

effective than general ones, such as "cassia" and "toad" for the moon in Chinese, and "Cupid" for love in English. Such allusions are not frequently used in Li Shang-yin's poetry. A few examples are: "Yellow Springs" for the nether world in Poem 8, line 3; the spirit of *yang* in Poem 90, line 8; "Blue Bird" for a messenger in Poem 6, line 8; "cassia" and "toad" in Poem 8, line 9, Poem 9, line 2, and Poem 10, line 7. Sometimes, even when he uses general allusions, our poet endows them with specific significance. For instance, when he alludes to the goddess of the moon or to the story about the Weaving Maid and the Cowherd, these common allusions often appear to have special references and are not merely substitutes for "a beautiful woman" and "a pair of lovers" respectively. Or when he alludes to the common knowledge that the Chi river is clear and the Yellow river is muddy, in Poem 8, line 14, this allusion acquires a special significance in the poetic context, being used to represent the insuperable barrier between the lovers.

Specific allusions are used by Li Shang-yin in different ways. Sometimes they resemble symbols, in that they also represent the general by the particular or the abstract by the concrete. For example, in Poems 94–95, the Emperor Hsüan-tsung becomes a symbol of all infatuated rulers, and his favorite, Yang, represents all *femmes fatales*. The same is true of the ruler of Northern Ch'i and his favorite in Poems 96–97. In such cases, the persons and events alluded to assume universal significance. This is a concise and effective means of expression, just as, in English, to say "Micawber" is both more concise and more effective than saying "a man who cherishes ungrounded hopes that something good will turn up."

Sometimes allusions implicitly compare present persons or events with historical or legendary ones. Used in this way, allusions are like compound images of substitution, and the only difference is that human beings are now compared to other human beings instead of to non-human objects. This again is a concise and effective way of describing a person and introducing complimentary or derogatory implications. Obvious examples are the allusions in Poems 89–90, in which historical personages stand for the poet's contemporaries, and our knowledge of the relative merits of the former influences our attitude toward the latter. The effectiveness of this kind of allusion depends on how much the two persons or events compared have in common. For instance, when Li Shang-yin compares himself to Chia Yi (Poem 50), the allusion, though a common one in Chinese poetry, is appropriate enough, since both are young men with literary talents and frustrated political ambitions away from the Court, but when he alludes to Liu Chen and Yü Chi (Poem 65) simply because, like the former, he too is sick, and like the latter, he wishes to retire from office, the allusions seem to have less point and to be little more than substitutes for "a sick poet" and "a high-minded scholar."

Occasionally, allusions point to a contrast between the present situation of the poem and the story alluded to, instead of drawing an analogy. In Poem 95, the allusion to the Weaving Maid and the Cowherd ironically contrasts this mythical couple's annual reunion with the Emperor's eternal separation from his favorite. In Poem 45, the allusion to the holy monk Hui-shih forms a humorous contrast to the poet himself and his fellow guests ogling the attractive Taoist nuns at the party. Such allusions are comparable to Eliot's allusions to *Antony and Cleopatra* in *Burbank with a Baedeker: Bleistein with a Cigar*.

Some correlation may be discerned between the sources of allusions and the kind of world explored in a poem. It goes without saying that in poems ostensibly concerned with the supernatural (for example, Poems 21–26, 28–34, 38–41), allusions are made to mythology, and in poems on historical themes (Poems 93–98), allusions are made to history. Less obviously, in poems exploring the world of love (for example, Poems 4–6, 7–10, 17–18) we find allusions to legends and myths, as well as to earlier literature; in poems concerned with political and social conditions (Poems 89–90, 91, 100) there are no allusions to mythology or legends but only to the Confucian Classics and official history. Poems that explore complex worlds involving several levels of reality (Poems 1, 2–3, 48) use allusions to legends and myths, as well as to history and philosophy, but poems embodying simpler worlds, such as those of nostalgia, or of quiet enjoyment of nature, either use few allusions or none at all (Poems 55, 56, 57, 67, 68, 70, 73, 74, 75, 77, 80, 81, 84, 85, 86, 87, 88). This shows that Li Shang-yin does not pile up allusions simply to show off his learning but uses them with discrimination to achieve poetic ends.

The above discussions on various aspects of poetic language do not contradict the holistic conception of poetry, for the awareness that each poem is an integral whole should not prevent us from discussing common features of poems or comparing one poem with another. After all, one can hardly evaluate a poem without reference to other poems, or a poet without reference to other poets. As for the terms I have used—diction, syntax, imagery, and so forth—they are signposts that help us reach our destination: a better understanding and evaluation of Li Shang-yin's poetry. Once we arrive at this destination, we may forget about them, but without them we could hardly find our way there.

4

Li Shang-yin and the Modern Western Reader

Having examined Li Shang-yin's poetry from various points of view, logically I should proceed to place him in a historical context, but to do so adequately I would almost have to write a whole history of Chinese poetry, which is of course out of the question. Moreover, it would be difficult to show his indebtedness to earlier poets and his influence on later ones, because stylistic similarities and differences would inevitably be blurred in translation. In any case, questions of "sources" and "influences," which properly concern the literary historian, are of much less interest to the general reader than are the intrinsic qualities of a poet's works.[1] Nevertheless, the reader may wish to know, and has a right to be told, how Li Shang-yin's reputation has stood with Chinese critics and readers throughout the ages, and how the present writer rates him in relation to other Chinese poets. These questions I shall attempt to answer briefly, at the risk of appearing dogmatic. Finally, it may be interesting to see why, and in what ways, Li Shang-yin's poetry should have a special appeal to modern Western readers, more so than the works of many other Chinese poets.

In his own lifetime, Li Shang-yin already enjoyed a high literary reputation, although, as I suggested before, he seems to have been admired even more for his Parallel Prose than for his poetry. His posthumous fame reached its zenith at the beginning of the eleventh century, when a group of poets including Yang Yi, Ch'ien Wei-yen and Liu Yün made Li Shang-yin the special object of their imitation and went so far as to say that, beside him, Tu Fu appeared like a village schoolmaster! These poets came to be known as the Hsi-k'un School, because of the title of an anthology of their poems, *Hsi-k'un Ch'ou-ch'ang Chi*, or "Collection of Poems and Replies on Mount K'un-lun in the West," which alludes to the tradition that ancient kings kept treasures of books on this mountain, and the name "Hsi-k'un Style" has often been anachronistically applied to Li Shang-yin's own poetry. The Hsi-k'un poets have in fact rendered a disservice to Li Shang-yin by their imitation and their excessive adulation. On the one hand, since they succeeded merely in achieving a superficial resemblance to some of his stylistic idiosyncrasies but not in capturing the complexity and

---

[1] Specialists in Chinese literature may wish to consult the Chinese works mentioned in the list of references.

depth of his poetry, their mannerisms and affectations are sometimes blamed on him. On the other hand, their overzealous praise of him led other poets to reject Li's exuberant style and to cultivate a highly intellectual kind of poetry and an austere style during the late eleventh and early twelfth centuries, exemplified by the so-called Chiang-hsi (Kiangsi) School. Nevertheless, Li Shang-yin has continued to attract admirers and imitators, including such eminent poets as Wang An-shih (1021–86), Yüan Hao-wen (1186–1214), Wu Wei-yeh (1609–71), and Wang Shih-chen (1634–1711). Some critics have condemned his poetry, usually on the grounds of its allusiveness and ambiguity, or because of the sharp sarcasm of some of his political poems. On the whole, his admirers have outnumbered his detractors, and a handful of his poems (for example, those given as Poems 1, 4, 5, 6, 7, 18, 19, 28, 80, and 95 in this volume) have remained popular among Chinese readers to the present day. Twentieth-century Chinese critics are generally favorable in their estimation of Li Shang-yin, though some-times for moral or ideological rather than literary reasons, such as his concern for social conditions or his supposed "rebellion against feudal morality." It seems safe to predict that as long as there are people who can read Chinese in the traditional script, Li Shang-yin's poetry will continue to be read and enjoyed.

As for my own evaluation of Li Shang-yin's total achievement in comparison with other Chinese poets, let me say first of all that I am not interested in placing poets in a strict order of merit, as if they were examination candidates or beauty queen contestants, but rather in assessing the relative range, depth, intensity, and complexity of the worlds they explore and the extent to which each poet has modified and enriched the language as a poetic medium. On both counts Li Shang-yin should be considered a major poet. (I once referred to him as a "minor poet" in relation to Tu Fu;[2] I now wish to make clear that he is "minor" only in comparison with Tu Fu, but certainly "major" compared with most other Chinese poets.) Apart from Tu Fu, who is supreme in his universality and versatility, I cannot think of more than half a dozen Chinese poets who may, with any justification, be called greater than Li Shang-yin, and not many more who can be called equally great.[3] On the whole, the strength of his poetry does not lie in self-effacing contemplation of nature but in passionate involvement with life. Like Tu Fu, but unlike T'ao Ch'ien, Wang Wei, and Li Po, Li Shang-yin is a poet *engagé*. Whether writing of love or of politics, he commits himself with characteristic intensity. Consequently, his poetry lacks the feeling of submergence of the self in nature that we find in T'ao Ch'ien and Wang Wei, or the inspired loftiness of Li Po. Nor

[2] Liu, *The Art of Chinese Poetry*, p. 100.

[3] I have in mind chiefly poets who write in the *shih* genre, and not those who work in other genres such as dramatic poetry (*ch'ü*). To ask whether Li Shang-yin is a greater poet than Wang Shih-fu would be as meaningless as to ask, say, whether John Webster is a greater poet than Robert Browning.

does it show the all-embracing sympathy and great sense of humor we
see in Tu Fu. On the other hand, Li Shang-yin explores strange and
fascinating worlds of passion and fantasy that none of the other poets
has explored. Stylistically, his most distinctive contributions to Chinese
poetry lie in complex and subtle modes of expression, rich in imagery,
symbolism, and allusions and condensed in structure, usually in the
form of Regulated Verse, although, as we have seen, he is capable of
writing in a simple and straightforward style and in Ancient Verse. His
poetry shows more conscious artistry than spontaneity, unlike the
effortlessness of Li Po or the art that conceals art in the apparent simplicity of Wang Wei. He seems to have taken to heart Tu Fu's dictum:
"If your words do not astonish others, do not cease (trying) even if you
die." As an explorer of language, Li Shang-yin is a worthy successor of
Tu Fu. In his passionate commitment to life and his exploration of the
supernatural and fantastic, he may be called a spiritual heir of Ch'ü
Yüan, although Ch'ü Yüan's interest in mythology was rooted in an
actual religious cult, whereas Li Shang-yin's seems to have been more
literary than religious.

Turning to the question why Li Shang-yin should have a special
appeal to twentieth-century Western readers, we may observe that
both his sophisticated attitude toward life and his no less sophisticated
manner of expression are remarkably attuned to the modern temper.
His commitment to life should make his worlds more accessible than
the remote other-worldliness of T'ao Ch'ien and Wang Wei, and his
ability to probe into experiences and see them in a dramatic or ironic
light will perhaps make his poetry more congenial than the egocentric
outpourings of Li Po or the pedestrian moralizings of Po Chü-yi. His
exploration of the mysterious and the fantastic may strike a responsive
chord among readers interested in the nonrational and the "absurd."
At the same time, the worlds explored in some of his poems, with their
languorous beauties, exotic perfumes, strange drugs, embroideries and
precious stones, music and dance, are reminiscent of Baudelaire, and,
on a different level, reveal a life of material luxury, sensual indulgence,
and moral laxity, which might be called "La Dolce Vita" of ninth-
century China.

In his manner of expression, Li Shang-yin is generally subtle,
oblique, and ambiguous. I have referred many times to his ambiguity,
and it may be worthwhile to pause for a moment and consider what
kinds of ambiguity are present in his poetry and whether they contri-
bute to or detract from the total effect. Since the very word "ambiguity" may remind some readers of Professor William Empson's
famous book Seven Types of Ambiguity, perhaps I ought to make clear
in what sense I am using the term and how far I am following Professor
Empson. Generally speaking, I use the word "ambiguous" to describe
a word, a line, an image, or a whole poem, which allows for more than
one interpretation. This is largely similar to Empson's revised definition
of ambiguity as "any verbal nuance, however slight, which gives room

for alternative reactions to the same piece of language."[4] However, I do not propose to follow his scheme for the analysis of ambiguity, for it would obviously be unwise to expect to find exactly the same types of ambiguity in a language as different from English as Chinese. Moreover, Empson's classification of ambiguity, according to himself, is based on degrees of logical disorder, conscious apprehension, and psychological complexity,[5] all of which seem to me rather tricky and intractable, so that the distinctions between any two of the seven types are by no means always easy to see.[6] I shall therefore deal with ambiguities simply according to the sources from which they may arise.

First of all, ambiguities may arise from uncertainty of what a poem is about. This kind of ambiguity may be dubbed "ambiguity in reference." We have seen many examples of this kind of ambiguity in the preceding pages, and what attitude we should adopt toward such ambiguity has also been suggested in Part I, 3.

Then there is ambiguity in attitude, when the referent of a poem is not in doubt, but we are not sure what the poet's attitude toward his subject is and how we are meant to take it. For example, in the *Green Jade City* poems, is the poet expressing his own love for the nuns or satirizing other men's infatuation? In *Self-congratulation*, is he really congratulating himself on his leisurely way of life or ironically voicing discontent? Again, I have suggested how this ambiguity in attitude, which may seem confusing at first sight, perhaps reflects a conflicting state of mind.[7]

Other kinds of ambiguity arise from the nature of Chinese grammar, and from the use of imagery, symbolism, and allusions. The first kind has been discussed in connection with problems of translation;[8] I need only add one or two comments. The fluidity of Chinese grammar, which often leads to impersonality and universality, is a doubtful blessing for the writing of intimate personal poetry, although it has obvious advantages for certain other kinds of poetry, notably the kind of poetry that seeks to convey a sense of nature as it is and not as seen by man. It is a measure of Li Shang-yin's achievement that he managed to express intense, complex, and often conflicting emotions in his poetry, generally without using pronouns or identifying the subject of a verb. Such a feat would scarcely have been possible in English: one has only to imagine what Shakespeare's sonnets would have been like, had he been obliged to write them without using pronouns!

As for ambiguity in imagery and symbolism, this generally occurs in their application. In other words, there is usually no difficulty in identifying the vehicle (except in images of transference, but then the need will not arise), though we may have difficulty in identifying the tenor.

[4] *Seven Types of Ambiguity* (2d edition), p. 1.
[5] *Ibid.*, p. 48.
[6] Cf. Elder Olson, "William Empson, Contemporary Criticism, and Poetic Diction" in *Critics and Criticism*, ed. R. S. Crane, pp. 45–82, esp. p. 52.
[7] See Poems 76 and 77.
[8] See Part I, 4.

Similarly, in the use of allusions, except for a few cases, it is their applications rather than origins that are in doubt. We generally know the stories alluded to, but cannot always be sure of their significance. How such ambiguous images, symbols, and allusions affect the whole poem has been shown in the commentaries accompanying various poems.

In short, the various kinds of ambiguity, whether they occur separately or together, are not mere affectations or mannerisms but are inextricable from complexity of verbal structure and multiplicity of meaning.

Apart from ambiguity, Li Shang-yin's poetry shows a number of traits—conflict rather than serenity, tension between sensuality and spirituality, pursuit of the extraordinary or even bizarre, striving after heightened effect, tendency toward ornateness and elaboration—that would probably have been called "baroque" had he been a Western poet. I am aware of the numerous meanings of this term and their attendant controversies,[9] but I think it would be less misleading to apply the word "baroque" to Li Shang-yin than to use some other terms of Western origin like "romanticism" or "aestheticism," not only because of the above-mentioned traits, which are commonly considered typical of the baroque, but also because chronologically "baroque" refers to European art and literature of the seventeenth century, of the period between the Renaissance and the neo-classicism of the eighteenth century, and this period seems to bear some resemblance to the age in which Li Shang-yin lived. The ninth century in China, like the seventeenth in Europe, was an age of intellectual uncertainty. Compared with some other periods of Chinese history, it is not marked by great intellectual vigor like the "age of the philosophers" (fifth to third centuries B.C.), when various original schools of thought emerged, or by strong religious faith like the fifth and sixth centuries A.D., when the influence of Buddhism was at its height, or by rigid orthodoxy like the seventeenth and eighteenth centuries, when most scholars conformed to Chu Hsi's brand of Neo-Confucianism. In the ninth century, the final synthesis among Confucianism, Taoism, and Buddhism known as Neo-Confucianism had not yet taken place, and intellectuals might well have experienced unresolved mental conflicts. Such conflicts are perceptible in Li Shang-yin's poetry. We may note the conflict between Confucian puritanism and Buddhist asceticism on the one hand, and sybaritic hedonism, associated with the popular Taoist search for physical immortality, on the other—a conflict that can be seen in the *Green Jade City* and *Holy Lady's Temple* poems; or between the Confucian ideal of public service, mingled with personal ambitions for worldly fame, and the wish to withdraw from society, prompted by both Taoism and Buddhism, a conflict revealed in Poems 76 and 77, and especially in this couplet from Poem 50:

[9] See Wellek, *Concepts of Criticism*, pp. 69–127.

> For ever remembering the rivers and lakes to which I would
> return, white-haired,
> I yet wish to turn round heaven and earth before entering a
> tiny boat.

In cultural history, too, the ninth century in China is comparable to the seventeenth in Europe. Chinese literary historians customarily divide T'ang poetry into four periods, dubbed "early," "high," "middle," and "late" T'ang. This division, based mainly on the rise and fall of dynastic power, is somewhat artificial and not entirely satisfactory. It would be better to describe the development of T'ang poetry in terms of three successive phases: a formative phase (*ca.* 618–710) marked by experimentation and relative naïvety, a phase of full maturity (*ca.* 710–70) characterized by great creative vitality and technical perfection, and a phase of sophistication (*ca.* 770–900) typified by tendencies toward the exuberant or the grotesque.[10] It is not too fanciful to see a parallel between these three phases of T'ang poetry and the quatrocento, cinquecento, and baroque periods of Italian art. Or we may draw a parallel between these periods of T'ang poetry and three successive periods of English poetry: the T'ang poets of the formative phase are comparable to English poets of the early sixteenth century like Wyatt and Surrey, those of the mature phase to the great Elizabethans, and those of the sophisticated phase to the seventeenth-century poets traditionally called "metaphysical" and more recently labeled "baroque," such as Donne, Marvell, and Crashaw.

In brief, the ninth century in China came after an age of expansion and creativity and preceded one (the Sung period, 960–1279) that might be called "neo-classical" in its conservatism, its emphasis on reason rather than emotion in poetry and art, and its advocacy of imitation of earlier poets rather than spontaneous expression. To compare the ninth century in China to the baroque period in Europe is therefore not as farfetched as it may seem.

Of course, such parallels should not be pushed too far, and they are offered here merely as speculations that might serve as points of departure for future studies. My purpose in drawing them is mainly to suggest that it is not pure accident that Li Shang-yin's poetry should show "baroque" characteristics, and that the same qualities in baroque art and literature that appeal to current Western taste should also make Li's poetry appear interesting. However, I do not wish to imply any kind of historical determinism, for I do not believe that socioeconomic factors, or the "intellectual climate," or a mysterious entity called the *Zeitgeist*, can predetermine what kind of poetry shall be produced in a given age and how good it shall be. Historical environment may help explain the way in which a poet responded to life and the manner in which he expressed his response, but it can never explain why he was

---

[10] I have discussed this in greater detail in an article entitled "On the Periodization of T'ang Poetry" (in Chinese). See Bibliography.

able to do so. In the last analysis, it is not the historical environment but his individual genius that made Li Shang-yin the poet he is. Although poetry, as a product of finite human minds, cannot help being confined by its age in its consciously expressed ideas and its terms of expression, it can achieve a kind of timelessness, as we have seen. Thus poetry can reach readers across gulfs of space and time and transcend formidable linguistic and cultural barriers. Were it not so, any attempt to translate poetry or interpret it to speakers of a different language would be sheer madness. It only remains for me to say that if the translations and critical discussions in this book have succeeded in evoking a few faint echoes of the polyphonic music of Li Shang-yin's zither and some pale reflections of the jeweled splendor of his imagery, my labors have not been in vain.

Additional Notes

(For works referred to and abbreviations used, see Bibliography.)

1. Chief minister. Strictly speaking, there was no such official in T'ang times, though the term *tsai-hsiang* (**宰 相**), which in previous dynasties had meant "prime minister," was used informally for those holding the highest offices. The central government, as set up at the beginning of the T'ang, was divided into three branches: The Grand Secretariat (*Shang-shu-sheng*), the Central Secretariat (*Chung-shu-sheng*), and the Chancellery (*Men-hsia-sheng*); and theoretically the heads of these—the Grand Secretary (*shang-shu-ling*), the two chief secretaries (*chung-shu-ling*) and the two chancellors (*shih-chung*)—were the highest officers of the land. But in fact these posts were not always filled. In particular, the post of Grand Secretary was left vacant out of deference to Emperor T'ai-tsung, who occupied it at the beginning of the dynasty, and the senior and junior secretaries of state (*tso yu p'u-yeh* **左右僕射**) were the actual heads of the Grand Secretariat. After the An Lu-shan rebellion, the Grand Secretariat lost much of its power, and the real chief ministers came to be designated by a variety of titles, and as a rule held concurrent posts. In late T'ang times, the *de facto* chief ministers generally held the cumbersome title of "judging affairs, equal with the chief secretaries and the chancellors" (*t'ung shung-shu men-hsia p'ing-chang-shih*). There were usually several chief ministers at the same time. Cf. TT,[1] 21–22, CTS, 42; HTS, 46 (Des Rotours, II, pp. 4–15); THY, 82.

2. The number of Mu-tsung's sons. Mu-tsung is said to have had five sons (CTS, 175; HTS, 82), yet Prince Jung is described as his eighth son. We can only assume that there were three other sons who died at birth or in their infancy.

3. The Divine Strategy Armies. The name Divine Strategy Army (*Shen-ts'e-chün*) first came into being in 749, when Ch'eng Ju-ch'iu was appointed commander of the army stationed at Mo-huan-ch'uan, newly taken from the Tibetans by Ko-shu Han. When the An Lu-shan rebellion broke out, Ch'eng sent Wei Po-yü with a thousand men to go and fight the rebels, whereupon Emperor Su-tsung gave the title "Divine Strategy Army" to the troops under Wei's command, and appointed the eunuch Yü Ch'ao-en as its Observer. Later Yü took over control of this army and it became the main force of the palace guards. After 765 the army was divided into two wings (*hsiang*), called Left and

---

[1] See list of abbreviations

Right Wings. In 786 these were renamed the Left and Right Divine Strategy Armies. See Lü Ssu-mien, pp. 1222–25; Des Rotours, II, p. lviii.

4. The Niu and Li factions. Chao Yi (*chüan* 20, pp. 383–84) thinks that "Niu-Li" does not refer to Niu Seng-ju and Li Te-yü respectively as leaders of two rival factions, but to Niu Seng-ju and his friend Li Tsung-min. Ts'en Chung-mien (II, pp. 142–45) argues that Niu certainly had a faction but Li Te-yü did not, and points out the unreliable nature of historical accounts written by pro-Niu men. Nevertheless, even if Li Te-yü did not consciously form a faction, the fact remains that he and his friends acted against Niu and *his* friends, and the latter no doubt regarded the former as a rival clique. We might as well use the convenient labels "Niu faction" and "Li faction" in referring to the two cliques.

5. Li Shang-yin's brothers and sisters. Li Shang-yin had no elder brothers, but three elder sisters. Of the eldest, nothing is known except that she died before 844. The second elder sister married P'ei Yun-chung, a grandson of former chancellor P'ei Yao-ch'ing (681–743), in her eighteenth year, and died a year later in her father's home, soon after Shang-yin's birth in 813. She seems to have been divorced, for she died in her father's home and was reburied in 844 in the Li family burial ground instead of the P'eis'. The third elder sister married a man named Hsü, and died in 827. As for Shang-yin's younger brothers, we know the name of one, Sheng-p'u (courtesy name Hsi-sou), who was probably only a year or so younger than Shang-yin, since at the time of the second elder sister's death the two brothers were both infants, and there could not have been much difference in age between them. Sheng-p'u passed the Literary Examination in 847, and like his elder brother became a collator in the Imperial Library but was soon transferred to a provincial post. He married a daughter of Minister Lu Chün (776–862), apparently before Shang-yin married in 838 (cf. Additional Note 7). Shang-yin also mentions "three unmarried younger brothers and an unmarried younger sister" at the time of his mother's death in 842. Since Sheng-p'u had probably already married by then, the three unmarried younger brothers should not include him. Thus, Li Shang-yin had altogether three elder sisters, who all married and died before 844, four younger brothers, and one younger sister. When he married in 837, he had three younger brothers and a younger sister to support in addition to his mother. (See Chang Ts'ai-t'ien, I, pp. 12–13, 20, 88–89, 122, 157.)

6. Li Shang-yin's letter to Presented Scholar T'ao. Two points in this letter call for comment. First, Li refers to the examination he took at the Ministry of Civil Office (*Li-pu*) as the "Wide Learning and Grand Rhetoric" (*po-hsüeh hung-tz'u*). This should not be confused with the Imperial Examination of the same name held by special decree (*chih-chü*) at irregular intervals. In fact, the former is often called simply "Grand Rhetoric" (*hung-tz'u*). Des Rotours (I, pp. 220–21) is right in saying that the *po-hsüeh hung-tz'u* is nothing but the full name of the *hung-tz'u*, but may be mistaken in saying that the *po-hsüeh hung-tz'u* held in 731 was the beginning of the *hung-tz'u* held regularly by the Ministry of Civil Office, since according to the *T'ang Hui-yao* (76) this

was an Imperial Examination held by special decree (*chih-chü*). Secondly, according to the *T'ung Tien* (15) and the *Hsin T'ang Shu* (44–45), the list of successful candidates of the *hung-tz'u* examination was submitted to the Chancellery (*Men-hsia Sheng*) for confirmation, but Li's letter refers to the Central Secretariat (*Chung-shu Sheng*). Wang Ming-sheng (*chüan* 81) states that the Central Secretariat was responsible for the *hung-tz'u* examination and refers to Li's letter. Since this appears to be the sole evidence and contradicts the *T'ung Tien* and the *Hsin T'ang Shu*, we may doubt its truth, as Des Rotours does; on the other hand, it is unlikely that Li would make a mistake about something which meant so much to him. The question, therefore, remains open whether it was the Chancellery or the Central Secretariat that was ultimately responsible for passing candidates of the *hung-tz'u* examination.

7. Was Chi-chi Li Shang-yin's niece or daughter? Mr. Ku Yi-ch'ün (pp. 85–86) suspects that the little niece named Chi-chi, whom Li Shang-yin reburied in 844, was really his illegitimate daughter borne by the girl named Liu-chih ("Willow Branch"). The grounds for his suspicion are as follows. First, according to Shang-yin's funeral address to Chi-chi's spirit, written in the first month of 844, she died five years before (839). Further, the address contains the words, "It was not until four years after your birth that you first returned to your family, and a few months later you died." This means she was born in 834. Mr. Ku refers to Li's remark that at the time of his mother's death (842) he had three unmarried younger brothers (see Additional Note 5) as evidence that at that time his younger brother Hsi-sou (Sheng-p'u) was not yet married, and asks how the latter could have had a daughter. Mr. Ku further asks why the girl should have been boarded out for four years before returning to her own family. Mr. Ku is aware of the poem Li Shang-yin addressed to Lu Chün in 852, in which the poet refers to the fact that the latter had long ago (*tsao* 早) given his daughter in marriage to Sheng-p'u. However, Mr. Ku argues, from 833 (one year before Chi-chi's birth) to 852 was a period of 19 years, and in 833 Sheng-p'u was not yet grown up, so how could he have married then? Second, Mr. Ku quotes from Shang-yin's funeral address to Chi-chi the remark "Since I 'separately married' [*pieh ch'ü* 別娶], I have not yet had an heir," and wonders why Li used the expression *pieh-ch'ü*. He conjectures that Chi-chi was borne by Liu-chih and was reared outside the family for four years; then, after Shang-yin's marriage, she was adopted by Sheng-p'u.

Neither ground seems to me strong enough to justify the suspicion. Regarding the first one, Sheng-p'u was probably only one year younger than Shang-yin (see Additional Note 5). Assuming he was born in 814, he would be nineteen (twenty by Chinese reckoning) in 833, certainly old enough to be married. The expression that Lu Chün had "long ago" given his daughter in marriage to Sheng-p'u could be taken to mean that this took place before Shang-yin's own marriage in 838. (This is indeed how Chang Ts'ai-t'ien took it.) And the reference to "three unmarried younger brothers" at the time of Shang-yin's mother's death in 842 probably should not include Sheng-p'u. As for why Chi-chi was not reared in the family, of course we can only conjecture. Possibly this happened because her father, Sheng-p'u, was still studying. (He did not pass the examination till 857.) But in any case there is no strong evidence that Sheng-p'u could not have married in 833 and had a daughter in 834. With regard to the second reason for Mr. Ku's suspicion, the expression *pieh-ch'ü* could mean that Shang-yin had been married before and his marriage with Wang Mao-yüan's daughter was his second (see Chang Ts'ai-t'ien, I, p. 56; Chang Chen-p'ei, in *Hsüeh-feng*, III, 7, p. 43; however, the latter seems to have based his arguments on a misinterpretation of the phrase *fen-su* (墳素) used in Li's address to his father-in-law's spirit.) or perhaps he had been betrothed to a girl but his fiancée died before the marriage was consummated (I owe this suggestion to Professor Lien-sheng Yang), but it cannot imply a premarital illicit affair. Even if it were true that Chi-chi was Shang-yin's illegitimate daughter, he could hardly refer to his legal marriage as a "separate marriage." There is no good reason, then, to suppose that Chi-chi was the poet's daughter.

8. Lu Hung-chih. His name is often given as Lu Hung-cheng (盧弘正), but according to the *Lang-kuan chu t'i-ming* (list of principal secretaries of the Ministries inscribed on pillars) quoted by Ts'en Chung-mien (I, p. 237), the last character should be *chih* (止).

9. Textual note on Poem 2, lines 5–6. Some editions have 無蝶 ("no butterflies") instead of 舞蝶 ("dancing butterflies") and 有人 ("someone") instead of 佳人 ("beautiful lady"). If we adopt these readings, the lines would mean, "There are no butterflies to gather the scattered pollen, but there is someone to lament the fate of the flowers."

10. Note on Poem 11, line 8. The expression *hsüan-chih* (懸知) is rather puzzling. Some scholars (e.g. Takahashi, p. 68; Lien-sheng Yang, verbal communication) take it to mean "conjecture" or "imagine," but it is possible to take *hsüan* as "far," as in the compound *hsüan-shu* (懸殊), "far different" (cf. Juan Yüan, *chüan* 16, p. 4b), and *chih* as "hear" (*ibid.*, *chüan* 4, p. 3b), in which case the whole line would mean, "I heard from a distance that she was not yet married." I am indebted to Professor Chang Hsüan for suggesting the latter explanation.

11. Textual notes on Poem 42.

Title. I follow Chu Ho-ling's reading 聽雨夢後作 ("Written after a dream, while listening to the rain"), instead of the reading in several other editions including Feng Hao's, 聽雨後夢作 ("Written in a dream, after listening to the rain"), since the poem is clearly written after a dream and mentions listening to the rain after waking up.

Last line. I prefer the variant reading 獨 ("alone") to Feng's reading 未 ("not yet"), since it is hard to see how the poet can say he has "not yet slept" after having had a dream.

12. "His Excellency." The term thus translated in the title of Poem 45 is *ling-kung* (令公), which should only be used for a chief secretary (*chung-shu-ling*). Feng Hao tried to explain this by saying that the term is applied to Ling-hu Ch'u by courtesy, but Ts'en Chung-mien (II, p. 250) believes that *ling-kung* is a misprint for *hsiang-kung* (相公). The latter term was

used for chief ministers, and since Ling-hu had been a chief minister but not a chief secretary, this would be more appropriate.

It may further be pointed out that in the original title, 天平公座中呈令狐令公, we may either take the third and fourth characters to mean "official banquet" as I have done, or accept Wu Ch'iao's suggestion that the third character is superfluous (Wu Ch'iao, p. 7).

13. Textual notes on Poem 48.

Line 15. The line reads 鄒顙蕣髮軟, where the first character hardly makes sense. Yao P'ei-ch'ien (as recorded by Feng Hao) emended it to read 雛 ("chick," by extension, "child"), and the line then means, "[Like] thick soft hair on top of a child's head."

Line 20. The last two characters of this line in most editions read 敷峯 or 敷筆, which are hard to explain. Feng suggested 甹筆, which together mean "to pull."

Line 22. Feng changed the second character in 穹窿 (ch'iung-lung, "vault of heaven") to 籠 ("cage"), and conjectured that this meant the same as hsün-lung (熏籠), a kind of brazier filled with incense. He further suggested that this was meant to describe the scent of the pine trees. I find this hard to accept because there is no evidence that ch'iung-lung is the same as hsün-lung. Besides, ch'iung-lung or "vault of heaven" makes good sense: the foliage is compared to a green coverlet spread over the bed, like the overhanging vault of heaven. (Heaven of course was thought to be round.)

Line 29. Some editions have ch'ung-lan (重蘭) ("double orchid") instead of hsiang-lan (香蘭) ("fragrant orchid").

14. Note on Poem 73. In the title, whether we should read chi pei (寄北) ("to be sent to the north") or chi nei (寄內) ("to be sent to my wife") is hard to decide. Feng Hao and Chang Ts'ai-t'ien (I, p. 149) both date the poem 848, in which year they believe Li Shang-yin traveled to Szechwan, where the Pa Mountains lie. Ts'en Chung-mien (I, p. 235) questions this and thinks the poem was written after the poet had gone to Szechwan in 851 (see Part I, 2). If the latter date is the right one, the poem could not have been addressed to Li's wife, who was then already dead. Ts'en argues that it could have been addressed to a concubine, but there is no evidence that Li had one. In view of all these uncertainties, it seems best to leave open both questions—whether the poem was addressed to the poet's wife and when it was written.

15. Textual note on Poem 89, line 14. Feng suspects that 烽 ("beacons") is a misprint for 鋒 ("blades"), since there was no occasion to light beacons in a palace coup. But the poet could be using the expression as a conventional way of describing a battle.

16. Six armies (Poem 95). Strictly speaking, as Ch'en Yin-k'e (II, pp. 32–33) pointed out, the imperial guards at the time comprised only four armies: the Left and Right Lung-wu Armies and the Left and Right Yü-lin Armies. However, traditionally the emperor was entitled to "six armies," and Po Chü-yi had already used this expression in the famous Ch'ang-hen Ko to refer to Hsüan-tsung's guards.

References

Page	Topic	Reference
4	Hsien-tsung	CTS, 14–15; HTS, 7; Lü, pp. 337–38, 355, 358–59.
4	Mu-tsung	CTS, 16; HTS, 8; Lü, pp. 378–79.
4	Ching-tsung	CTS, 17; HTS, 8; Lü, pp. 378–79, 382–84.
4	Wen-tsung	CTS, 17; HTS, 8; Lü, pp. 384, 387, 399.
5	Wu-tsung	CTS, 18; HTS, 8; Lü, pp. 400–5, 1392.
5	Hsüan-tsung	CTS, 18; HTS, 8; Lü, pp. 405–10, 447–49.
6	eunuchs' control of army	CTS, 184; HTS, 207; TCTC, 263; Lü, pp. 226–27, 234, 340.
6	social origins of officials	Ch'en, I, pp. 36–37.
7	Yüan Chen	CTS, 166; HTS, 174; Lü, pp. 356, 375.
7	Liu Fen	CTS, 190; HTS, 103.
8	Niu and Li	CTS, 124 (Li Te-yü), 126 (Li Tsung-min), 172 (Niu Seng-ju); HTS, 174 (Niu, Li Tsung-min), 180 (Li Te-yü); Lü, pp. 374–75; Ts'en, II, pp. 142–43.
10	Li Te-yü's remark	CTS, 18; Lü, pp. 1129–30.
10	Cheng T'an	HTS, 44; Lü, p. 1126.
10	Wen-tsung's poem	CTS, 173; HTS, 165.
11	Wei-chou	CTS, 174; Lü, pp. 439–40.
11	civil administration	TT, 32; CTS, 44; HTS, 49 (Des Rotours, II, pp. 681–88); Lü, p. 1090.
12	military administration	HTS, 50 (Des Rotours, II, pp. 755–57); Lü, pp. 1207–9.
12	military governor	Lü, p. 1094.
12	Li Lin-fu	CTS, 106; Lü, p. 211.
14	Li Shang-yin's life	Chang, I, *passim;* Ts'en, I, *passim.*
15	letter to patron	Feng, II, 8, pp. 3b–4a.
15	preface	*Ibid.,* 7, p. 24a.
15	examinations	TT, 15; HTS, 44–45 (Des Rotours, I, *passim*); Lü, pp. 1107–10, 1112–14, 1124–25, 1139–41.
18	Li Hung's poem	*Ch'üan T'ang shih,* 542 (p. 6260).
18	Ling-hu's last memorial	Feng, II, 1, pp. 11a–16b.

Page	Topic	Reference
18	Wang Mao-yüan	CTS, 152; HTS, 170.
19	letter to T'ao	Feng, II, 8, pp. 5b–6a.
20	note on rank	CTS, 42; HTS, 46 (Des Rotours, II, pp. 35–37); THY, 82.
21	Liu Chen	HTS, 214; Lü, pp. 419–23.
21	letter to Liu	Feng, II, 8, pp. 7b–16a.
22	Li and Po	Ts'ai Ch'i (in Kuo Shao-yü, vol. II, p. 14).
22	Po's memorial inscription	Feng, II, 8, pp. 21b–27b; Ch'ien Chen-lun, 7, pp. 4b–6a.
24	preface	Feng, II, 7, pp. 25a–27a.
24	letter to Liu Chung-ying	*Ibid.*, 4, pp. 13b–15a.
28	poems to Ling-hu T'ao	Feng I, 1, pp. 23a–b; 2, pp. 11a–b; p. 19a; p. 30b; 3, pp. 5a–b; pp. 16b–17a; pp. 34a–b; pp. 46a–b; p. 52a.
29	poems to Sung sisters	*Ibid.*, 4, pp. 12b–13a; p. 24a.
29	zither	Ku, p. 80.
29	"palace purge"	Su, I, pp. 81–82.
30	Li as rebel against "feudal society"	Liu K'ai-yang, pp. 91–105, 121–25; Wang Meng-pai, pp. 342–47.
31	Yü Hsüan-chi's poems to Wen	Yü Hsüan-chi, pp. 41a, 6b, 8b.
31	Feng Pan's remark	Quoted in Sun Chen-t'ao, p. 229.
31	Liang's remark	Liang Ch'i-ch'ao, 71, p. 38.
32	"aestheticism"	Chang Chen-p'ei, HF, 8, p. 37; Chiang Shang-hsien, p. 156.
44	*chin se*	Chu Ho-ling, *shang*, p. 1a; Ying Hui-ch'ien, *hsia*, p. 45b.
44	*chu* (bridge)	Wang Kuang-ch'i, p. 72.
51	Poem 1	Text: Feng, I, 4, pp. 28a–b. Translations: Fletcher, II, p. 142; Bynner and Kiang, p. 78; Payne, p. 253; Takahashi, pp. 29–31; Ch'en Shih-hsiang, p. 804; Graham, p. 171; Liu, II, p. 129. Commentary: Cf. Liu Pin, p. 5b; Chi Yu-kung, 53, p. 11b; Hu Chen-heng, p. 205; Chi Yün (in Chou Ho-ling, *shang*, p. 1b); Su, I, pp. 110–18; Huang Ch'ao-ying (quoted in Hu Tzu, p. 147); Chu Ho-ling, *ut supra*; Chu Yi-tsun (*ibid*); Feng, *ut supra;* Meng Sen, pp. 157–64; Liu P'an-sui, pp. 75–78; Ho Cho (in Chu Ho-ling, *ut supra*); Chang, I, p. 195; II, p. 265; Hsü Yi, p. 14b; Chang Chen-p'ei, HF, III, 9, p. 28; Chu Hsieh, p. 826; Hsü Fu-kuan, pp. 69–72; Ku, pp. 103–5; Wang P'i-chiang, p. 185; Sung Hsiang-feng, 16, pp. 5b–6a; Ch'en Shih-hsiang, *ut supra*; Lao Kan, pp. 54–58; Liu, II, *ut supra*, pp. 129–38.

Page	Topic	Reference
57	Poems 2–3	Text: Feng, I, 1, pp. 45a–b. Commentary: Cf. Chang, I, p. 56; II, p. 510; Apollinaire, p. 162; Moore, p. 245.
62	Poems 4–5	Text: Feng, I, 3, pp. 42b–43a. Translations: Bynner and Kiang, p. 80; Payne, pp. 254–55; Takahashi, pp. 69–71, 44–46; Graham, pp. 145–46. Commentary: Cf. *Han Wu ku-shih*, p. 4.
66	Poem 6	Text: Feng, I, 3, p. 48a. Translations: Bynner and Kiang, p. 81; Payne, p. 253; Takahashi, pp. 49–50; Liu, IV, p. 137; Graham, p. 150. Commentary: Cf. Chang, I, p. 175; Chu Ho-ling, *shang*, p. 52b.
68	Poems 7–10	Text: Feng, I, 5, pp. 34a–37a. Commentary: Cf. Chu Ho-ling, *hsia*, pp. 21b–23a; Chang, II, pp. 466–71; Lao, pp. 46–47.
78	Poem 11	Text: Feng, I, 1, pp. 8a–b. Translation: Takahashi, pp. 67–68. Commentary: Cf. Chang, I, p. 20; Su, I, p. 114; Ch'ü Fu, p. 1b; Shen Te-ch'ien, 4, p. 1; 12, p. 9b; Keats, pp. 349–50.
80	Poem 12	Text: Feng, I, 1, pp. 4b–5a. Commentary: Cf. Chang, I, p. 199; Shelley, p. 571.
81	Poem 13	Text: Feng, I, 5, p. 18b. Commentary: Cf. Chang, II, p. 337.
82	Poem 14	Text: Feng, I, 5, p. 8a.
82	Poems 15–16	Text: *Ibid.*, 5, p. 15b.
83	Poems 17–18	Text: *Ibid.*, 4, pp. 15a–b. Translations: Bynner and Kiang, pp. 82–83; Takahashi, pp. 71–73; Liu, IV, p. 139; Graham, pp. 149, 152. Commentary: Cf. Chang, II, p. 408.
86	Poems 19–20	Text: Feng, I, 1, pp. 51a–b. Translations: Fletcher, II, p. 144; Bynner and Kiang, p. 79; Takahashi, pp. 47–48; Graham, p. 148. Commentary: Cf. Chang, I, p. 92; II, p. 310; Ku, p. 90.
89	Poems 21–23	Text: Feng, I, 5, pp. 11a–12a. Translations: Takahashi, pp. 56–64; Graham, pp. 167–68. Commentary: Cf. Chu Ho-ling, *shang*, pp. 52b–54a; Chang, II, p. 324; Li Tao-yüan, 1, p. 18.
93	Poem 24	Text: Feng, I, 6, pp. 10a–b. Commentary: Cf. Chu Ho-ling, *chung*, p. 2b; Sun Chen-t'ao, p. 206; Ku, p. 78.
94	Poem 25	Text: Feng, I, 3, pp. 36b–37a. Translation: Takahashi, pp. 41–42. Commentary: Cf. Chu Ho-ling, *shang*, pp. 2a–b; Chang, II, p. 266.
96	Poem 26	Text: Feng, I, 1, pp. 35b–36b. Commentary: Cf. Chu Ho-ling, *chung*, pp. 32a–b.
98	Poem 27	Text: Feng, I, 5, p. 8a.

Page	Topic	Reference
99	Poem 28	Text: *Ibid.*, 6, p. 20a. Translations: Bynner and Kiang, p. 75; Takahashi, pp. 55–56; Graham, p. 155. Commentary: Cf. Chu Ho-ling, *chung*, p. 33a; Chang, I, p. 206; Tu Fu, p. 507.
100	Poem 29	Text: Feng, I, 5, p. 23a. Commentary: Cf. Chu Ho-ling, *shang*, p. 71a; Wen Yi-to, vol. II, p. 328–29; Su, II, pp. 102–4.
100	Poem 30	Text: Feng, I, 5, pp. 1b–2a. Translations: Takahashi, p. 82; Graham, p. 155. Commentary: Cf. Chang, I, p. 202.
102	Poem 31	Text: Feng, I, 5, p. 6b.
103	Poem 32	Text: *Ibid.*, 6, p. 23a. Commentary: Cf. Chu Ho-ling, *chung*, p. 38b; Chang, I, p. 194.
104	Poem 33	Text: Feng, I, 5, p. 2b.
104	Poem 34	Text: *Ibid.*, 6, p. 32b.
105	Poem 35	Text: *Ibid.*, 6, p. 24b. Commentary: Cf. Su, I, pp. 15–30; T'ao Ch'ien, p. 29; *Shan hai ching*, p. 96.
107	Poem 36	Text: Feng, I, 3, pp. 51a–b. Commentary: Cf. Chang, II, p. 320.
108	Poem 37	Text: Feng, I, 6, pp. 11b–12a. Commentary: Cf. Ku, p. 78.
109	Poem 38	Text: Feng, I, 2, p. 36b.
110	Poem 39	Text: *Ibid.*, 4, pp. 9a–b. Translation: Takahashi, pp. 95–96.
112	Poem 40	Text: Feng, I, 4, p. 13b. Commentary: Cf. Chu Ho-ling, *shang*, p. 56b; Ho Cho, *Yi-men tu-shu chi*, p. 10a; Chang, I, p. 183.
113	Poem 41	Text: Feng, I, 4, p. 32b. Commentary: Cf. Tu Fu, p. 296.
114	Poem 42	Text: Feng, I, 2, pp. 17a–b. Commentary: Cf. Chang, I, p. 83; Su, I, p. 51.
116	Poem 43	Text: Feng, I, 2, pp. 15b–16b. Commentary: Cf. Chang, I, p. 289.
117	Poem 44	Text: Feng, I, 6, p. 11a.
118	Poem 45	Text: *Ibid.*, 1, pp. 9a–b. Commentary: Cf. Chang, I, p. 27; Su, I, pp. 9–10.
119	Poem 46	Text: Feng, I, 3, p. 3a. Commentary: Cf. Chang, I, p. 35.
120	Poem 47	Text: Feng, I, 1, p. 15b. Commentary: Cf. Chang, I, p. 42.
121	Poem 48	Text: Feng, I, 1, pp. 24b–27b.
128	Poem 49	Text: *Ibid.*, 1, pp. 14b–15a.
129	Poem 50	Text: *Ibid.*, 1, pp. 44a–b. Commentary: Cf. Chang, I, p. 56.
130	Poem 51	Text: Feng, I, 1, p. 54a.
132	Poem 52	Text: *Ibid.*, 2, p. 19b.
133	Poem 53	Text: *Ibid.*, 2, p. 20a. Translation: Takahashi, pp. 99–100.

Page	Topic	Reference
		hashi, p. 116; Graham, p. 156. Commentary: Cf. Chu Ho-ling, *chung*, p. 25b; Chang, II, p. 339; Ch'ien Chung-shu, p. 27.
166	Poem 87	Text: Feng, I, 4, p. 36a.
167	Poem 88	Text: *Ibid.*, 2, p. 27a. Translation: Takahashi, pp. 80–90. Commentary: Cf. Chu Ho-ling, *chung*, p. 68a. Chang, I, p. 199.
168	Poems 89–90	Text: Feng, I, 1, pp. 16a–18b. Commentary: Cf. CTS, 169; HTS, 179; Yen Keng-wang, p. 177.
172	Poem 91	Text: Feng, I, 1, pp. 37a–42b. Translation: Takahashi, pp. 154–88.
182	Poem 92	Text: Feng, I, 1, pp. 4a–b. Commentary: Cf. Su, I, pp. 68–77.
183	Poem 93	Text: Feng, I, 5, p. 21b. Commentary: Cf. Ch'en, II, pp. 17–20.
185	Poems 94–95	Text: Feng, I, 5, p. 24a. Translations (Poem 95): Fletcher, II, pp. 136–38; Payne, p. 254; Takahashi, pp. 140–43; Graham, pp. 163–64. Commentary: Cf. Ch'en, II, pp. 32–33; Ch'en Hung, *passim*; Po Chü-yi, 12.
187	Poems 96–97	Text: Feng, I, 6, pp. 16b–17a.
189	Poem 98	Text: *Ibid.*, 3, p. 15b. Translations: Bynner and Kiang, p. 75; Takahashi, pp. 123–24.
190	Poem 99	Text: Feng, I, 2, p. 1b. Commentary: Cf. Chang, I, p. 200.
191	Poem 100	Text: Feng, I, 1, pp. 1a–3b. Translations: Bynner and Kiang, pp. 83–85; Jenyns, pp. 50–53; Takahashi, pp. 188–201; Liu, I, pp. 13–19. Commentary: Cf. CTS, 15, 133, 145, 160, 170; HTS, 7, 154, 173, 176, 214; Han Yü, 30, pp. 10b–16b.
200	footnote	Liu, V, p. 333.
205	Eliot's remark	Eliot, II, p. 118.
223	Wang Li	Wang Li, pp. 182–252, 481–95.
239	Thomas	Thomas, pp. 102, 11.
240	Marvell	Marvell, p. 100.
249	Tu Fu derided	Yüan Hao-wen, *Chung-chou chi*, quoted in Feng, I, *ts'e* 1, *lei-pu*, p. 3b.
249	footnote	See Chang Chen-p'ei, HF, III, 7, pp. 38–41; Chu Hsieh, pp. 833–41; Sun Chen-t'ao pp. 237–39; Miao Yüeh, pp. 63–67; Hsiao Ai, pp. 329–40.
250	moral and ideological reasons	e.g. Ku, Sun, Chu Hsiu-hsia, Liu K'ai-yang, Wang Meng-pai.
254	footnote	Liu, III, p. 18–20.

Bibliography

Note. This bibliography consists of works referred to in the present book. It does not include every edition of Li Shang-yin's works or everything that has been written about him. Nor does it list all the works alluded to in Li's poems, for these would amount to a general bibliography of Chinese literature up to his time. Works listed below are referred to by author in the Additional Notes and the list of references. In the case of two or more works by the same author, a number is added after the author's name.

Abbreviations:

BIHP	*Bulletin of the Institute of History and Philology, Academia Sinica*
CTS	*Chiu T'ang Shu* (See Liu Hsü, Section D).
HJAS	*Harvard Journal of Asiatic Studies*
HTS	*Hsin T'ang Shu* (See Ou-yang Hsiu, Section D).
HYHP	*Hsin-ya Hsüeh-pao* [新亞學報]
HF	*Hsüeh Feng* [學風]
JAOS	*Journal of the American Oriental Society*
SPPY	*Ssu-pu Pei-yao* [四部備要]
SPTK	*Ssu-pu Ts'ung-k'an* [四部叢刊]
TCTC	*Tzu-chih T'ung-chien* (See Ssu-ma Kuang, Section D).
THY	*T'ang Hui-yao* (See Wang P'u, Section D).
TSCC	*Ts'ung-shu Chi-ch'eng* [叢書集成]
TT	*T'ung Tien* (See Tu Yu, Section D).
WYW K	*Wan-yu Wen-k'u* [萬有文庫]

SECTION A. LI SHANG-YIN'S WORKS

Poetry:

Chu Ho-ling [朱鶴齡] (1606–83), ed. *Li Yi-shan shih-chi* [李義山詩集] (1659, reprinted 1870 together with commentaries by Chu Yi-tsun [朱彝尊], Ho Cho [何焯] and Chi Yün [紀昀] under the title *Li Yi-shan Shih-chi chi-p'ing* [李義山詩集集評].

Feng Hao [馮浩] (1719–1801), ed. *Yü-hsi-sheng shih chien-chu* [玉溪生詩箋注]. 1780, reprinted in SPPY. Cited as Feng, I.

Prose:

Feng Hao, ed. *Fan-nan Wen-chi Hsiang-chu* [樊南文集詳注]. 1765, reprinted in SPPY. Cited as Feng, II.

Ch'ien Chen-lun [錢振倫] (1816–79), ed. *Fan-nan wen-chi pu-pien* [樊南文集補編]. 1864, reprinted in SPPY.

SECTION B. TRANSLATIONS

Bynner, Witter, and Kiang Kang-hu. *The Jade Mountain* (New York, 1920.) Contains 24 poems by Li Shang-yin.

Fletcher, W. J. B., *Gems of Chinese Verse*. Shanghai, 1919; reprinted New York, 1966. 1 poem. Cited as Fletcher, I.

———. *More Gems of Chinese Verse*. Reprinted with above. 6 poems. Cited as Fletcher, II.

Graham, A. C. *Poems of the Late T'ang*. Middlesex, England, 1965. 24 poems.

Jenyns, Soame. *A Further Selection from the Three Hundred Poems of the T'ang Dynasty*. London, 1944. 5 poems.

Payne, Robert, ed. *The White Pony*, 1947; Mentor Books, 1960. 7 poems.

Takahashi Kazumi [高橋和巳]. *Ri Shō-in* [李商隱]. Tokyo, 1958. 60 poems with notes in Japanese.

(For other isolated translations see Martha Davidson, *A List of Published Translations from Chinese*, part II, New Haven, Conn. 1957.)

SECTION C. BIOGRAPHICAL AND CRITICAL STUDIES

Chang Chen-p'ei [張振珮]. "Li Yi-shan p'ing-chuan" [李義山評傳], in HF, vol. III, nos. 7–9. Anching, 1933.

Chang Ts'ai-t'ien [張采田]. *Yü-hsi-sheng nien-p'u hui-chien* [玉溪生年譜會箋]]. Peking, 1917; reprinted Shanghai, 1963. Cited as Chang, I.

———. *Li Yi-shan shih pien-cheng* [李義山詩辨正] Comments written on a copy of the Chu edition, printed together with the above. Cited as Chang, II.

Ch'en Shih-hsiang [陳世驤]. "Shih-chien ho lü-tu tsai Chung-kuo shih chung chih shih-yi tso-yung" [時間和律度在中國詩中之示意作用], BIHP, vol. XXIX (Taipeh, 1958).

Chi Yu-kung [計有功] (*fl.* 1126–35) *T'ang-shih chi-shih* [唐詩紀事] (SPTK).

Chiang Shang-hsien [姜尚賢]. *Shih-ko hsin-shang* [詩歌欣賞]. Taipei, 1962.

Chu Ho-ling (See Section A).

Chu Hsieh [朱偰]. "Li Shang-yin shih hsin-ch'üan" [李商隱詩新詮] in *Wu-han Ta-hsüeh wen-che chi-k'an* [武漢大學文哲季刊], vol. VI, no. 3. Wuchang, 1937.

Chu Hsiu-hsia [祝秀俠]. "Li Shang-yin," in *Chung-kuo wen-hsüeh-shih lun-chi* [中國文學史論集]. Taipei, 1958.

Ch'ü Fu [屈復] (*fl.* 1736). *Yü-hsi-sheng shih yi* [玉溪生詩意] (1740).

Ho Cho [何焯] (1661–1722). *Yi-men tu-shu chi* [義門讀書記]. 1769.

Hsiao Ai [蕭艾]. "Shih-lun Li Shang-yi ti ch'i-yen lü-shih" [試論李商隱的七言律詩] in *T'ang-shih yen-chiu lun-wen chi* [唐詩研究論文集]. Peking, 1959.

Hsin-shih (See Meng Sen).

Hsü Fu-kuan [徐復觀]. *Huan-jao Li Yi-shan chin-se-shih ti chu wen-t'i* [環繞李義山錦瑟詩的諸問題]. Hong Kong, 1963.

Hsü Yi [許顗] (*fl.* 1111–23). *Yen-chou shih-hua* [彥周詩話] in *Li-tai shih-hua* [歷代詩話], *ts'e* 7.

Hu Chen-heng [胡震亨] (*fl.* 1573–1620). *T'ang-yin kuei-ch'ien* [唐音癸簽]. Reprinted Shanghai, 1959.

Hu Tzu [胡仔] (*fl.* 1147–67). *T'iao-hsi yü-yin ts'ung-hua* [苕溪漁隱叢話]. Reprinted Peking, 1962.

Ku Yi-ch'ün [顧翊羣]. *Li Shang-yin p'ing-lun* [李商隱評論]. Taipei, 1958.

Lao Kan [勞榦]. *Chung-kuo ti she-hui yü wen-hsüeh* [中國的社會與文學]. Taipei, 1964.

Liu, James J. Y. [劉若愚]. "Li Shang-yin's Poem 'The Memorial Inscription by Han Yü'," *East-West Center Review*, vol. I, no. 1. Honololu, 1964. Cited as Liu, I.

———. "Li Shang-yin's Poem 'The Ornamented Zither'," JAOS, vol. 85, no. 2. 1965. Cited as Liu, II.

Liu K'ai-yang [劉開揚]. *T'ang-shih lun-wen chi* [唐詩論文集]. Peking, 1961.

Liu P'an-sui [劉盼遂]. "Li Yi-shan chin-se-shih ting-ku" [李義山錦瑟詩定詁], *Wen-hsüeh nien-pao* [文學年報], no. 3, 1937.

Liu Pin [劉攽] (1025–89). *Chung-shan shih-hua* [中山詩話], in *Li-tai shih-hua, ts'e* 5.

Meng Sen [孟森]. "Li Yi-shan chin-se-shih k'ao-cheng" [李義山錦瑟詩考証], *Tung-fang tsa-chih* [東方雜志], vol. XXIII, no. 1. 1926.

Miao Yüeh [繆鉞]. *Shih tz'u san-lun* [詩詞散論]. Hong Kong, 1962.

Su Hsüeh-lin [蘇雪林]. *Li Yi-shan lüan-ai shih-chi k'ao* [李義山戀愛事蹟考]. Shanghai, 1927, reprinted as *Yü-hsi shih-mi* [玉溪詩謎]. Cited as Su, I.

Sun Chen-t'ao [孫甄陶] "Li Shang-yin shih t'an-wei" [李商隱詩探微], HYHP, vol. IV, no. 2. 1960.

Sung Hsiang-feng [宋翔鳳] (1776–1860). *Kuo-t'ing lu* [過庭錄] (1853, reprinted 1930).

Ts'ai Ch'i [蔡啓] (Sung dynasty). *Ts'ai K'uan-fu shih-hua* [蔡寬夫詩話], in Kuo Shao-yü, ed., *Sung shih-hua chi-yi* [宋詩話輯佚] (*Yenching Journal of Chinese Studies*, Monograph Series, no. 14, 1937).

Ts'en Chung-mien [岑仲勉]. "Yü-hsi-sheng Nien-p'u Hui-chien P'ing-chih" [玉溪生年譜會箋平質], BIHP, vol. XV, 1948; cited as Ts'en, I; reprinted together with Chang Ts'ai-t'ien, I, II.

Wang Meng-pai [王孟白]. "Kuan-yü Li Yi-shan ti shih" [關於李義山的詩], in *T'ang-shih yen-chiu lun-wen chi*.

Wang P'i-chiang [汪辟疆]. "Yü-hsi shih-chien chü-li" [玉溪詩箋舉例], in *Chung-hua wen-shih lun-ts'ung* [中華文史論叢], 4th series. Shanghai, 1965.

Wu Ch'iao [吳喬] (Ch'ing dynasty). *Hsi-k'un fa-wei* [西崑發微] (TSCC).

SECTION D. HISTORICAL WORKS

Chao Yi [趙翼] (1727–1814). *Kai-yü ts'ung-k'ao* [陔餘叢考], 1790, reprinted Shanghai, 1957.

Ch'en Yin-k'e [陳寅恪]. *T'ang-tai cheng-chih-shih shu-lun kao* [唐代政治史述論稿]. Chungking, 1943. Cited as Ch'en, I.

Des Rotours, Robert, tr. *Le Traité des Examens* (translation of HTS, 44–45. Paris, 1932. Cited as Des Rotours, I.

———. *Traité des fonctionnaires et traité de l'armée* (translation of HTS, 46–50). Leyden, 1947. Cited as Des Rotours, II.

Hiraoka Takeo [平岡武夫] (tr. Yang Li-san [楊勵三].) *Ch'ang-an yü Lo-yang* [長安與洛陽]. Hsi-an, 1957.

Liu Hsü [劉昫] (887–946). *Chiu T'ang shou* [舊唐書] CTS.

Lü Ssu-mien [呂思勉]. *Sui T'ang Wu-tai shih* [隋唐五代史]. Shanghai, 1959.

Ou-yang Hsiu [歐陽修] (1007–72) *et al. Hsin T'ang shu* [新唐書] HTS.

Pulleyblank, E. G. *Background of the Rebellion of An Lu-shan* (London, 1955.)

Ssu-ma Kuang [司馬光] (1019–86). *Tzu-chih t'ung-chien* [資治通鑑] TCTC.

Ts'en Chung-mien. *T'ang-shih yü-shen* [唐史餘瀋]. Shanghai, 1960. Cited as Ts'en, II.

Tu Yu [杜佑] (735–812). *T'ung tien* [通典]. TT.

Wang Ming-sheng [王鳴盛] (1722–97). *Shih-ch'i-shih shang-ch'üeh* [十七史商榷]. TSCC.

Wang P'u [王溥] (922–82). *T'ang hui-yao* [唐會要]. THY

Yen Keng-wang [嚴耕望]. *T'ang p'u shang ch'eng lang piao* [唐僕尚丞郎表]. Taipei, 1956.

SECTION E. OTHER WORKS

Anon. *Han Wu ku-shih* [漢武故事] in *Ku-chin yi-shih* [古今逸史]. *Yüan Ming shan-pen ts'ung-shu* [元明善本叢書].

Anon. *Shan hai ching* [山海經] ed. Wang Hsin-chan [王心湛]. Shanghai, 1936.

Apollinaire, Guillaume. *Œuvres Poétiques*, ed. M. Adéma et M. Décaudin. Paris, 1956.

Brontë, Emily. *Complete Poems*, ed. C. W. Hatfield. New York, 1941.

Ch'en Hung [陳鴻] (*fl.* 805–92). *Ch'ang-hen-ko chuan* [長恨歌傳], in *T'ai-p'ing kuang-chi* [太平廣記], 486.

Ch'en Yin-k'e. *Yüan Po shih chien-cheng kao* [元白詩箋証稿]. Rev. ed., 1955. Cited as Ch'en, II.

Ch'ien Chung-shu [錢鍾書], *T'an yi lu* [談藝錄]. Shanghai, 1937; reprinted Hong Kong, 1965.

Ch'üan T'ang shih. Complete T'ang Poetry. Shanghai, 1960 ed.

Coleridge, S. T. *Biographia Literaria*, ed. J. Shawcross. Oxford, 1907.

Collingwood, R. G. *The Principles of Art.* Oxford, 1938; reprinted 1950.

Crane, R. S. ed., *Critics and Criticism.* Chicago, 1952.

———. *The Languages of Criticism and the Structure of Poetry.* Toronto, 1953.

Donne, John. *Poems*, ed. Sir Herbert Grierson. Oxford, 1933.

Eliot, T. S. *Four Quartets*. London, 1944. Cited as Eliot, I.

———. *Notes Towards the Definition of Culture*. New York, 1949. Cited as Eliot, II.

Empson, William. *Seven Types of Ambiguity*, 2d ed., London, 1947.

Grove's Dictionary of Music and Musicians, 5th ed., London, 1954–61.

Han Yü [韓愈] (768–824). *Ch'ang-li hsien-sheng chi* [昌黎先生集]. SPPY.

Hawkes, David, tr. *Ch'u Tz'u, Songs of the South*. Oxford, 1959.

Juan Yuan [阮元] (1764–1849). *Ching-chi tsuan-ku* [經籍纂詁]. 1812.

Karlgren, B., tr. *The Book of Odes*. Stockholm, 1950.

Keats, John. *Poems and Verses*, ed. J. Middleton Murry. London, 1949.

Knight, G. Wilson. *The Starlit Dome*. London, 1941; new ed. 1959.

Legge, James, tr. *The Chinese Classics*. 1861–72; reprinted Hong Kong, 1960.

Li Tao-yuan [酈道元] (ob. 527). *Shui-ching chu* [水經注]. WYWK.

Liang Ch'i-ch'ao [梁啓超] (1873–1929). *Yin-ping-shih wen-chi* [飲冰室文集]. Shanghai, 1926.

Liu, James, J. Y. "Lun T'ang-shih chih fen-ch'i [論唐詩之分期], in *The Quill*. Hong Kong University, 1958/59. Cited as Liu, III.

———. *The Art of Chinese Poetry*. London and Chicago, 1962; Phoenix Books ed., Chicago, 1966. Cited as Liu, IV.

———. "Ch'ing-tai shih-shuo lun-yao" [清代詩説論要], in *Symposium on Chinese Studies*. Hong Kong University, 1964. Cited as Liu, V.

———. "Towards a Chinese Theory of Poetry," in *Yearbook of Comparative and General Literature*. Bloomington, Indiana, 1966. Cited as Liu, VI.

Marvell, Andrew. *Poems*. London, 1892.

Moore, Thomas. *Poetical Works*. New York, 1846.

Needham, Joseph. *Science and Civilization in China*, vol. IV, part 1. Cambridge, England, 1962.

New Oxford History of Music, vol. I. London, 1957.

Po Chü-yi [白居易] (772–846). *Po-shih Ch'ang-ch'ing chi* [白氏長慶集]. SPTK.

Poulet, Georges. "Timelessness and Romanticism," *Journal of the History of Ideas*, vol. XV, no. 1.

Richards, I. A. *The Screens and Other Poems*. New York, 1959.

Schafer, Edward H. *The Golden Peaches of Samarkand*. Berkeley and Los Angeles, 1963.

Shelley, P. B. *Poetical Works*, ed. Edward Dowden. New York, 1893.

Shen Te-ch'ien [沈德潛] (1673–1769). *Ku shih yüan* [古詩源]. SPPY.

Su Hsüeh-lin. "T'ien-wen hsüan-chieh" [天問懸解], HYHP, vol. IV, no. 2. Cited as Su, II.

T'ao Ch'ien [陶潛] (365–427). *T'ao Ching-chieh shih-chi* [陶靖節詩集]. TSCC.

Thomas, Dylan. *Collected Poems*. London, 1952.

Tu Fu [杜甫] (712–70). *Tu Fu Concordance*. Harvard-Yenching Index Series, 1940.

Waley, Arthur. *The Book of Songs*. London, 1937. Cited as Waley, I.

————. *The Life and Times of Po Chü-i*. London, 1949. Cited as Waley, II.

————. *The Poetry and Career of Li Po*. London, 1950. Cited as Waley, III.

Wang Kuang-ch'i [王光祈]. *Chung-kuo yin-yüeh shih* [中國音樂史], 2d ed., Taipei, 1956.

Wang Li [王力]. *Han-yü shih-lü hsüeh* [漢語詩律學]. Shanghai, 1958.

Wellek, René and Warren, Austin. *Theory of Literature*. New York, 1942.

Wellek, René. *Concepts of Criticism*. New Haven, 1963.

Wen Yi-to [聞一多]. *Wen Yi-to ch'üan-chi* [聞一多全集]. Shanghai, 1948.

Wilson, Edmund. "The Strange Case of Pushkin and Nabokov," *New York Review of Books*, vol. IV, no. 12 (July, 1965).

Wimsatt, W. K. Jr. *Hateful Contraries*. Kentucky, 1965.

Wimsatt, W. K. Jr., with Monroe Beardsley, *The Verbal Icon*. Kentucky, 1954.

Ying Hui-ch'ien [應撝謙] (1619–87). *Ku yüeh shu* [古樂書] *Ssu-k'u Ch'üan-shu chen-pen* [四庫全書珍本], Commercial Press facsimile reproduction, no date.

Yü Hsüan-chi [魚玄機] (9th century). *T'ang nü-lang Yü Hsüan-chi shih* [唐女郎魚玄機詩]. SPPY.

Glossary-Index